OTHER BOOKS BY ROBERT MAYER

Superfolks
The Execution
Midge & Decker
The Grace of Shortstops
Sweet Salt
The Search
The Dreams of Ada

ROBERT MAYER

E. P. DUTTON NEW YORK

Published in the United States by E. P. Dutton,
a division of NAL Penguin, Inc.,
2 Park Avenue, New York, N.Y. 10016.

Published simultaneously in Canada by Fitzhenry and Whiteside,
Limited, Toronto.

Mayer, Robert, 1939–
I, JFK / Robert Mayer.—1st ed.
p. cm.
ISBN 0-525-24776-9
1. Kennedy, John F. (John Fitzgerald), 1917–1963—Fiction.
2. United States—Politics and government—1961–1963—Fiction.
I. Title.
PS3563.A954I2 1989
813'.54—dc19   88-30483
                                                            CIP

Designed by Margo D. Barooshian

1   3   5   7   9   10   8   6   4   2

First Edition

Excerpt from "Mending the Wall," by Robert Frost. Copyright 1930,
1939, © 1969 by Holt, Rinehart and Winston. Copyright © 1958
by Robert Frost. Copyright © 1967 by Lesley Frost Ballantine.
Reprinted from The Poetry of Robert Frost edited by Edward
Connery Latham, by permission of Henry Holt and Company, Inc.

Excerpt from Markings by Dag Hammarskjöld, translated by Lief
Sjobert and W.H. Auden. Translation copyright © 1964 by Alfred
A. Knopf, Inc., and Faber and Faber, Ltd. Reprinted by permission
of Alfred A. Knopf, Inc.

For Amara—
who will grow into it—
with love

Tragedy is not always veiled in black.
—GENE FOWLER

The problem, at this late hour, is how to begin. What to offer, after all you have seen, heard, read, that will rivet your soul.

I am tempted to quote from the maps of ancient mariners as they sailed into uncharted waters: HERE BE DEMONS. Or to tell you the name of my favorite poem, which I read to my bride on our wedding night: "I Have a Rendezvous with Death." But all of us, heroes and fools, have demons. Each of us, knight and knave, has his own private rendezvous with death.

In a world without shadows, the shadows lengthen none-theless. Before all is darkness, or all is light, I must get on with it. So I shall simply choose a time, a place. And begin . . .

November morn slipped in through the windows. In the Rose Garden, a songbird trilled. Signing state papers, I checked my calendar of sailing ships: the twenty-first. My wife entered the office without knocking.

"Which suit would you like me to wear?" she asked. She

was holding a draped hanger in each hand. "The navy or the pink?"

It was a curious question; she rarely consulted me about her clothing; her sense of style, if not her sense of humor, was notorious.

"The pink," I said.

She seemed surprised, as if I had chosen wrong. "Why the pink?"

"Texas," I said. "All those tired cowgirls raising their brat kids to be Miss America. They adore pink in Texas."

Jackie eyed the pink at arm's length. I would like to conjure the image of her standing naked in the Oval Office, but she was too remote by then for such indulgences. She was wrapped in a bright kimono, a medley of dragons and birds of paradise, the gift of some insightful potentate.

"But the hat," I said. "Could you do without the hat? I hate those things."

"I'll need the hat. Without the bubble top on, my hair would be a mess."

I wanted to stand, come out from behind the desk, hold her shoulders gently as I spoke. But, like most married couples, we were long past that. Instead I leaned back, raised my legs, crossed my ankles on the desk. (Bobby once bought me argyles that bore the presidential seal.)

"Remember the times," I teased, "when we would drift down the Potomac, standing by the rail, the wind blowing wildly through your hair, and there on the river in the middle of the city you would sink sexily to your knees . . ."

"Drop dead, Jack," she said.

There was a hollowness in my laugh that I hoped would escape her. I don't think she cared enough to notice.

I swung my legs down from the desk. My loafers needed a shine. I wondered if Raymond was at his post yet.

"I must insist," I said, "on being addressed with respect. At least here in the office."

"Very well," Jackie said. "Drop dead, Mr. President."

2

This time my laugh was genuine; searching her face, I found no humor there.

"Bobby says we shouldn't go," she said.

"Bobby sees demons everywhere."

He'd also seen the FBI reports. Everybody covering their ass. Just in case.

"Yes," she said.

She looked at me in silence. The dark skirt slipped from the hanger to the rug. She seemed not to notice. She turned and left the office, carrying the pink. Someone would be along to pick up after her. The élan of the Bouviers.

I picked up the skirt, tossed it onto a chair. I rang for Raymond.

Perhaps I should have chosen the dark blue. My blood would not have photographed on the blue.

Perhaps I should have listened.

The road not taken. Even the poet couldn't tell us where it leads.

Hey, hey, JFK . . .

There are, of course, many fates worse than death.

Hey, hey, JFK,
How many kids did you kill today?

The monstrous words left unspoken.

Lyndon twists in torment in the quiet of the night, dentures gnashing to the rhythm. Prowls purgatory in a flannel gown, a flannel cap, Dickensian.

"Something will turn up," he growls.

It never does.

"The book is a patent fraud," the critic at *The Times* will write. "It doesn't ring with Kennedy's rhythms, Kennedy's cadences."

Ask not . . .
Let the word go forth . . .
The torch has been passed . . .

Understand, those were Sorensen's. I was not just the mouthpiece, I was the heart and soul to which he grafted himself, but the perfection of the words, the marching syllables, were his.

Here, among ghosts, there are no ghostwriters.

The point is that, perfect stylist or not, *Ich bin ein Geschreiber*.

That line, in fact, was mine, not Ted's. Only later did I realize that, had I fought in Europe instead of the Pacific, had I been among the liberators of the concentration camps, I might never have said such a thing. And only recently, when the old actor went to Bitburg, did I realize the enormity of the blunder it could have been. *Ich bin ein Berliner?* The Jews could have raised holy hell!

Grace and cadence cover a multitude of posturing.

That, and the Kennedy luck.

And having Dick Nixon as your shadow.

I know. You want to hear about Marilyn. Hoffa. Khrushchev. Sinatra. Oswald.

Patience. Patience. I shall illuminate all. But for the moment, a telling glimpse of Dick. It's three o'clock in the morning. He can't sleep. He's sitting on the side of his bed, wearing striped pajamas, haggard as a convict already. Pat is asleep in another room. (They always are.) The room is murky, the bedclothes twisted. He appears, if you will, ramrod gnarled.

He asks me what to do with the tapes.

"Destroy them," I say.

(In time, you learn compassion.)

He clears his throat, about to orate in the dark. He doesn't, but that throaty aspiration is in his voice. I'd been afraid that he would whine.

"I can't," he says. "They're history. We *must* honor history."

"Screw history," I say. "History will honor itself. It always does."

He didn't listen, of course. His fatal Quaker flaw. He thought he knew everything.

I, a good Catholic sinner, knew I knew nothing. My superiority lay in the unshakable belief that nobody else knew anything, either.

Such is the fine distinction between legend and disgrace.

(I can hear the militant chorus: *That, and a bullet in the brain.* Not so. Not so. Dick Nixon, a bullet in his brain, would be every bit as messy.)

But let the living bury the living.

"You wanted me, Mr. President?"

My first day in office, the evening of the inaugural balls, he'd come up to my bedroom wearing a brown suit, a white shirt, a yellow tie.

"You always shine shoes in a suit and tie?" I'd asked him.

"I do when it's the president's shoes," Raymond said.

"That's nonsense, Raymond," I said. "If overalls and flannel shirts are good enough for Harvard Yard, they're damn well good enough for Pennsylvania Avenue."

His dark brow furrowed, battling with three hundred years of the submission of his race. "With all respect, Mr. President, I don't think that's right."

"You don't? What about humility, Raymond? I shouldn't lose my humility, should I, just because I am now the most powerful man in the world? Given the arsenal of secret weapons I've been reading about, the most powerful man since Adam. You don't want that to go to my head, do you?"

"No, sir."

"It didn't go to Mr. Lincoln's head, did it?"

"I didn't know the man, sir."

"Come, come, Raymond, you've read all about President Lincoln. Do you think Abe Lincoln would want a man to shine his shoes wearing a suit and a silk tie?"

"I reckon Mr. Lincoln shined his own shoes," Raymond said.

I looked at the gilt clock on the mantelpiece. "It's getting late, Raymond," I said. "Shine the shoes."

"Yes, sir, Mr. President."

Then we both guffawed. I moved forward and embraced him, he in the only suit he owned, me in my pale blue boxer shorts. We passed several seconds that way, our hearts musing against each other's chests.

"I'm glad you agreed to come," I said when we separated.

"From Boston? I wouldn't miss it for the world. The next four years are gonna be fun!"

"Eight, Raymond. Eight."

"Yessir, Mr. President. Eight."

For some reason, perhaps of precognition, that scene flashed through my mind as he answered my summons—this man whose grandchildren had inspired my tardy civil rights speech. Now he was wearing overalls and plaid, as he had since the second day.

"I need a shine, Raymond. I'm going down to Texas to kick some ass. A gracious gentleman always gets a shine before he kicks ass."

He came around the desk with his box and his folding stool, and he began to do his work. His brown hands flitted across my shoes like the wings of a large hummingbird, as always, never hesitating, never faltering, never soiling a sock. Say this for the shoeshine man: he never had a Bay of Pigs.

"I hear they don't like you in Texas," Raymond said, shifting feet.

"Have you been reading FBI reports again?"

"Just a few, Mr. President. Just a few."

"That Bobby. Can't learn to keep his mouth shut."

"Seriously, sir. That's what I hear."

"They don't like anybody in Texas, Raymond. Most of all they don't like each other. It's the Hatfields and the McCoys down there. Got to go straighten things out before it costs us the next election."

"Can't Mr. Lyndon do that?"

"You'd think so, wouldn't you? A man so desperate to run the country, you'd think he could keep his own house in order."

"That's what you'd think," Raymond said.

"Have you seen him lately? How's he doing?"

"I haven't seen him for several months, sir."

"You haven't? You're not telling me Lyndon has taken to shining his own shoes, I hope." I jotted a word on the blue pad on my desk. "I'll tell Bobby to find some work for him. Can't have the vice president going bananas on us. We'd lose the whole damn South."

"No sir, Mr. President. He's not shining his own shoes. He just don't call for Raymond anymore. He's installed his own personal shoeshine man, over at the Blair House."

"His own shoeshine man?"

"Well, shoeshine lady. A pretty little Oriental thing. From Vietnam, I think."

"You're not shitting me, Raymond?"

"Would I shit you, Mr. President?"

"Well, well, well. So Lyndon likes it crosswise. Is that what you're telling me?"

"I wouldn't know about that, Mr. President."

When he was through my loafers shone like a moonlit sea. I walked with him across the office. I had a strong, strange impulse to shake his hand, but it was greasy with polish.

"Have a good trip, Mr. President," he said.

"I will. I will. 'Kicking Ass in Texas.' Make a good country song, don't you think?"

"Make a *very* good country song," Raymond said.

As you've already surmised, my intent here is not to write linear autobiography; all that David Copperfield kind of crap, as Salinger (not Pierre) said. You can find that in the encyclopedias. In the libraries, under BIOGRAPHY—K. See also, in the library card files: Presidents—U.S.; Senators—U.S.; Legislators—Mass.; Kennedy, Joseph Patrick; Kennedy, Rose Fitzgerald; Atomic Weapons and Disarmament; Catholics—U.S.; Humphrey, Hubert Horatio; Nixon, Richard Milhous; Assassination—U.S. Et cetera. That is the torment, it turns out, of fame, of power: your memory lives on, but in the words of others. Dry as proverbial dust. It doesn't matter if they loved you or hated you, it's all brittle stuff. And it's *them*, of course, not *you*. The Bible, I dare say, got it backward: in the *end* there is the word.

Unless, of course, what we call the end is only the beginning. They haven't told me that—yet.

What we are permitted, in this brief afterlife, is twenty-five years of memory. A quarter century in which to look back, reflect, consider (repenting is optional). Then all memory vanishes, like a blackboard erased. Consciousness disappears, or moves on to the next step. (They haven't told me that yet, either.) I am using my last allotment of time before it vanishes entirely to set down some reflections, some scenes. Private scenes. Private views of public scenes. Anything that will lift the dust. My friends, my family, my women thought they were serving me well by keeping secrets. Now, on the edge of nothingness, I choose to have no secrets. Naked before mine enemies. Naked before my God.

If others find shame in this, let them deal with their own gods.

They will, in any case.

In time, they will.

A word about accuracy. What I shall set down is the truth. Otherwise, why bother? But, unlike Bobby, I have always been a sucker for subtlety. So pay attention.

In the opening scene, for instance: my brutal reference to Jackie slipping to her knees before me on the yacht on the Potomac. Doesn't sound like Jackie?

Marilyn, yes. Judy, yes. Jackie, no. But I didn't say it happened. I merely quoted my actual remark to her. A reference to the unthinkable. A sore spot, a thorn in her bougainvillea facade. That's why she answered as she did.

You got it the first time? Let us continue.

(Or not, as the case may be. It's up to you.)

The structure, then, is scattershot. Emotional mosaic. Hopefully, it will resonate to its own internal beat.

Call it the rhythm method.

The slim, dark, boyish body of Madame Nhu, the soft, gentle flesh of Marilyn, in bed together, undulating, entwined.

My wife.

(The wife of my dreams.)

I would not have sent in troops.

Advisers, yes. But green boys to die in jungles, no. You do not defend freedom by the light of burning Buddhists.

Fifty-eight thousand boys still alive. A hundred thousand children never born.

You cut your losses.

I would not, I think, have sent in troops.

On the other hand, there was McNamara. Rusk. Bundy. Bobby. The best and the brightest. My own dear hawks might have convinced me.

On the other hand, there was George Ball. And Adlai.

I used to dream in the symbols of *Animal Farm.* The horses were the West, I think. But the head pig was always Khrushchev. (You noticed, perhaps, the resemblance.)

So I might have sent in troops.

I think not. After the Cuban crisis, there was no further need to prove my macho, to show my balls.

Unlike Lyndon, I wasn't getting my Tom McAns rubbed by a distant niece of the Dragon Lady.

I had no need for a Kiwi war.

The house in Brookline, in which I was born, was yellow clapboard. It had two stories, and gabled windows peering from an attic. Later, I had a retarded sister.

My father sympathized with the Nazis. That was, I believe, the ultimate sin of the twentieth century: for a rich man to sympathize with the Nazis.

God, the sea was cold. We were not torpedoed. A Jap destroyer simply sliced us in half, at midnight, and continued on its way. We clung to the hull of the boat. The Japs did not bother to finish us off. Nor did they bother to rescue us, to take us as prisoners. The captain, I have convinced myself, died a thousand deaths in the afterburns of Nagasaki.

Two of my men were killed on impact. One was the officer of the deck. I do not know why we got no warning from the officer of the deck.

My back felt broken. Ten of us survived. We clung to the broken boat till dawn. Then I ordered them to swim to an island visible in the distance. The more we swam, the more the island receded. A junior officer was hurt too badly to swim. I lugged him along with me through the salt. It was four hours later that we washed up, at last, on the beach.

I do not know why we got no warning from the officer of the deck.

I do know that Oswald didn't act alone.

In the spring of '58 I spoke at a Democratic fund-raiser in Los Angeles, raising money for the midterm elections, also collecting IOUs for 1960. After my speech, Billy Wilder approached. I'd met him years before. Hollywood was good Democratic money in those days, and I'd always been interested in show biz: of which politics is the historical, the archival, branch. Wilder said he was in the middle of shooting a film with some stars it might be useful for me to meet. He invited me to visit the set the next morning.

The film was *Some Like It Hot.*

In a studio on the United Artists lot, the interior of a railroad coach had been created. Technicians and lighting men were bustling about. A few minutes after I arrived, Wilder escorted the three stars onto the set. They all were wearing lovely dresses.

"I don't think you folks have met," Wilder said. "Senator Kennedy, of Massachusetts, meet . . ."

"The Andrews Sisters?"

Tony Curtis guffawed. Jack Lemmon smiled. Marilyn Monroe's expression didn't change.

Wilder completed the introductions.

"Nice to meet you," Lemmon said, shaking hands.

"Delighted," Curtis said, doing the same.

"Charmed, I'm sure," Monroe said. And she did a deep curtsy. She was wearing the spangled dress that the film would make famous. She was all there.

"If I may ask," I said to them, "without giving away trade secrets, why are you in drag?"

"I'm not," Monroe said, straight-faced. Her lips had that pouty, deadpan innocence she used so effectively on the screen. I wasn't sure if she was in character, or if that was the real her.

"We're musicians," Lemmon said. "Witnesses to a gangland rubout."

"We're in disguise," Curtis elucidated. "The gang boss of Chicago wants to rub us out."

"Momo?" I said.

"Momo? Who's Momo?" Jack Lemmon asked.

"Sam Giancana," Marilyn said. "The Mafia boss of Chicago." She hadn't moved her eyes from mine while speaking. "This is a period piece," she continued. "Prohibition days."

"Oh."

Her voice crawled over me. It was Jackie's voice, exactly. I wondered, for the first but not the last time, if Jackie, somewhere, somehow, had copied it with some precise intent.

In the railroad car, the lights went on. "Ready on the set," someone called.

"I need the boys first," Wilder said. "Let's go, girls."

The "Nice to have met you, Senators" took only a moment. Lemmon and Curtis followed Wilder to the set. I was left alone with Marilyn Monroe, and for the first time in my life I could think of nothing to say. (If you don't count all the times with Pop. Or all the times with Rosemary.) In the awkward silence I sputtered as usual onto Bobby as a fall guy.

"My brother Bobby wanted me to ask you something," I said. "He wants to know what Arthur Miller has that he doesn't have."

Marilyn Monroe smiled. "While your brother was working for Joe McCarthy," she said, "my husband was writing *The Crucible*."

11

I tried not to wince. But I felt as if she'd slugged me; and Bobby, and Pop, and even great-grandfather Patrick Kennedy, who sailed for America when the potatoes in Ireland turned black. I decided at that moment that I would take her to bed one day.

What I said was "I didn't know you were interested in politics."

"You don't have to hit in fifty-six straight," she said, "to know which team you're on."

I couldn't believe what I was hearing. As if I was out of my league with this dumb blonde.

"Bobby was young then," I said.

"Yes," she replied. "And you were sick."

The bitch was amazing.

"I take it, then," I said, "that I'll have your full support in nineteen sixty?"

Her eyes danced lightly. I'd scored a point at last.

"I'm for Adlai," she said.

"Adlai's wonderful," I said. "But he's a two-time loser."

"So am I," Marilyn Monroe said.

Again our eyes didn't waver. We were staring into windows of the sea. I was sailing alone into perilous waters, and I felt exhilarated. It was she who broke the silence.

"Do you think a pretty face is enough?"

"Obviously," I said, "you've got a lot more going for you than a pretty face."

Marilyn frowned. "I was referring to you," she said.

I wanted to smile. But I was much too angry. Or frustrated. I couldn't tell if she was serious or was putting me on. About everything.

"Perhaps," I said, "we need to get to know each other better sometime."

She looked at me coolly, levelly. "Perhaps."

Then she was needed on the set. We shook hands; no more deep curtsies. (And what had *that* been about?) She turned and walked away in that almost-dress, her buttocks grinding; the mills of the gods.

12

Yes, I thought. Yes. And ambled after her. And watched her sing "Runnin' Wild."

Another take was ordered. I watched her sing it a second time. Then I left, to catch a plane; a true believer.

I knew we would meet again.

When the potatoes turned black, Patrick Kennedy of Dunganstown booked passage on a ship to America. The year was 1848, the ship was a sailing schooner; the trip took forty days, during which Patrick was crammed with hundreds of other emigrants deep in the narrow hold of steerage. The only sport in the dark and fetid hold was rat catching.

"There's one!" he'd cry, and he'd dive among the stained and foul boards that passed for sleeping spots.

"Gotcha!" he cried one day, but the rat squirmed from his grasp, squirmed deeper into the planking.

"Tricky Dicky, aren't you!" he said, and with hardly a hesitation he dove into the darkness after it, skinning his knees, grabbing, fumbling. Finally he emerged, squeezing the flea-bitten rat in his large hands.

"Got you this time, Tricky Dicky," he said, as the watching men cheered.

Among the watching men there was only one woman with the stomach for it. Her name was Bridget Murphy. She watched as Patrick held the rat by the tail and slammed its head against a board.

"Where are you from?" Patrick Kennedy asked.

"County Wexford," Bridget Murphy replied.

"You don't say," Patrick said. "Well so am I, so am I. And where would you be heading?"

Bridget looked at the floorboards, shyly. "I do believe the entire ship be headed for Boston," she said.

And so it was. Before long there would be more Irish in Boston than in Dublin.

The ship left them on Nobbles Island, part of East Boston, and that was where most of them stayed. Bridget found work as a clerk in a notions shop. Patrick, experienced with his hands, got a job as a cooper, a maker of wine barrels. His son would become a saloon keeper, and his grandson—my pop—would get rich importing booze during Prohibition. The Kennedys never had trouble with alcohol; their vice was making money.

The marriage of Bridget Murphy and Patrick Kennedy was blessed with three daughters and two sons, one of whom died in infancy. After ten years, an epidemic of cholera struck East Boston. Patrick Kennedy's face turned green, then as black as the potatoes he'd left behind. The local priest performed the last rites in their small apartment near the harbor. The authorities came for the body, tossed it into a mass grave stinking with the corpses of other victims.

"Rue the day!" Bridget Kennedy said, shaking her fist at the ceiling. "Rue the day the Good Lord made the twenty-second of November!"

It's God's honest truth. You could look it up.

Poor Patrick, of course, got no eternal flame.

Inga Binga. Inga Binga. Ingabinga.

Some people scar your soul.

Later, in the worst of times—during the Bay of Pigs, or during the Cuban blockade, when we were risking the end of human history, and no sane man could sleep—I would lie awake in Abe Lincoln's bed, restless, mind searing out of control, and then, to relax, I would say the words, over and over, a litany, a catechism, an om.

Inga Binga. Inga Binga. Ingabinga.

And drift to sleep on the gentle waves of her.

Ingabinga . . .

She was a former Miss Denmark; I will let you imagine her beauty, her roundnesses, the texture of her fair skin. She was working, that war-torn summer of '42, as a reporter for the *Washington Times-Herald*. I was an ensign junior grade in the navy, assigned to a desk in naval intelligence, eager for sea duty but unable to get it. I hoped to be a journalist myself, after the war.

Her real name was only Inga. Naked, she was Inga Binga. We played games in hotel rooms. We played games in an apartment we shared. We talked; we fucked; we talked.

J. Edgar Hoover taped all of it: the talking and the fucking both.

What Inga neglected to tell me, between mouthfuls—this bright young officer in naval intelligence—was that she had once attended the wedding of Hermann Goering, whose best man was Adolf Hitler; that she had spoken with *der Führer* afterward. That the FBI believed she was a Nazi sympathizer. That the FBI suspected that she might be a Nazi spy.

Some in the navy wanted to kick me out. Pop had connections; Pop pulled strings. I was reassigned—to the sea duty I wanted so desperately.

The sea, it's been said, engulfs you, like a woman.

The destroyer split us asunder. For four hours I swam, clenching between my teeth a strap of the life jacket of Pat McMahon, my wounded chief engineer. For this they wrote me up as a hero. The commander of *PT-109*.

"Let me go," McMahon kept gurgling, vomiting seawater. "You'll never make it, Jack! Let me die."

It was a small step, in 1946, from hero to congressman.

Ask not what your country can do for you, Inga Binga.

I don't know what happened to her when I went to sea.

I do know what happened to the tapes.

J. Edgar kept them in his private files.

Fucking.

Talking.

They colored all that happened afterward.

Hoover is sitting behind the desk in his spacious office, beside a large American flag. It is not true that he uses the flag as a hand towel. His friend is on the sofa. J. Edgar punches the PLAY button with his pudgy fingers.

15

"Mmmmmm."

"You like that, Jack?"

"Inga . . . Inga . . ."

"Who is it?" his friend asks.

"Joseph P. Kennedy's son. Naval intelligence."

"What about this, Jack? You like this too, Jack?"

"Oh, Inga. Inga Binga. Oh, God!"

When his friend leaves, J. Edgar rewinds the tape. He punches the button again, leans back in his leather swivel chair. On his desk, he opens a large magazine centerfold of John Dillinger.

"Oh, Inga. Inga Binga. Oh, God!"

. . . as the director plays with himself.

"What are you doing?" Lyndon asks.

"Writing," I reply.

"Why?"

That's what I was supposed to do when I left office. An ex-president at fifty-one. Jewish ladies in the Bronx used to worry about it. "Such a young man, what will he do afterward?"

"I hope he don't become a bum."

"He'll teach, he'll write. You'll see."

So I'm writing.

"Will you tell them it wasn't me?"

"Of course."

"Some people think it was me," Lyndon says. "Happening right there in Dallas. Why did they do it in Texas? Probably to make people think it was me."

He paces about in the flannel nightshirt, the flannel cap.

"You promise you'll tell them it wasn't?"

"Yes. I'll tell them the blood on your hands came later, Lyndon."

He stops pacing; he pulls at his ear. "You're a bastard, Jack, you know that?"

"So I've been told."

"You needed me," Lyndon says. "If I hadn't carried Texas

16

for you, the weasel would have won the election. You used me and tossed me aside, like a whore."

"You didn't carry Texas," I remind him. "You had to get the Board of Elections to disqualify eighty thousand Nixon votes in order to carry Texas."

"Exactly! And did you ever show any gratitude?"

I don't answer. He's right, of course. But he's not exactly the kind of person you invite to dinner. (That's what Jackie used to say.)

"Think about it," Lyndon says. "How can you be so god-damn sure it wasn't me?"

"Lyndon, Lyndon . . . ," I say, wearily.

My older brother, Joe Jr., was a bully. Ask Bobby. Ask Teddy. Ask Eunice. He was big and strong, and since I was the next boy in line, I was the one he always beat up.

"Win! Win! Win!" my father screams in the sound track of my youth.

At Hyannis Port, we all had to be on the beach at eight o'clock every morning for calisthenics. (Everyone except poor Rosemary.) A hired gym teacher grunted us through our ex-ercises while Father watched from the porch. Then there would be races: swimming races, sailing races, bicycle races.

"Win, win, win," my father screamed.

Joe held my head under the water, and won. Joe sank my boat, and won. Joe rammed into my bike—I needed twenty-two stitches to get the bleeding stopped—and he won.

Joe was going to be president someday.

I was the sickly one. Thin. Frail. Most likely I would write books, like the ones I spread across the beds of my youth.

Then came the medal for bravery. *PT-109*. Joe couldn't stand it. Jack was a hero, and Joe hadn't even seen combat yet.

He'd show me, he would. He volunteered for a dangerous assignment. German V-I rockets were devastating London. The launch sites in France had to be destroyed, and saturation bombing hadn't taken them out. What the Allies were going to do was pack airplanes full of explosives. A pilot would get

17

them into the air, set them on course for precise impact on a launching site. A mother plane would arm the payload electronically. Then the pilot would parachute out; the plane would cross the channel and explode into the target.

Simple.

The morning in southern England is gray with fog. Navy pilot Joe Kennedy, Jr., strides across the strip toward his plane, which is packed to the gills with explosives. An engineer approaches him.

"I checked out the plane, Joe," the engineer says. "The electronic system isn't wired right. You can't fly that plane today. It could blow at any time."

"I'm flying," Joe said.

"You don't have to, Joe. Scrub the mission. Make them check the wiring."

"I'm flying," Joe insists. Thinking: my rat-brother Jack has got a medal!

Joe swings himself into the cockpit. He ignites the engine; the propellers turn.

"Don't do it!" I scream at him. "Don't go!"

He taxies down the runway as the fog begins to lift.

"Don't, Joe, don't!" I cry out through the years.

Even though I hated him.

High over farm country, a fellow navy man in the mother plane flipped a switch, to arm the payload. The explosion that followed, it is said, was the biggest blast of the war in British skies.

They did not find enough of Joe for even Pop to nominate for Congress.

"Don't go, Joe!" I scream. "I'm not a hero, Joe!"

He scrambles into the plane, every time. He doesn't wait; he doesn't listen.

"My boat got cut in half, Goddamnit! The only PT boat that happened to in the whole fucking war! I was the commanding officer! You can see the wake of a destroyer from nearly two thousand yards! Why the hell didn't we see it? Why the hell didn't we take evasive action? When we survived we were ashamed. We had fucked up royally. I never said I was a hero, Joe!"

He scrambles into the plane. He doesn't listen.

Pop ran me for Congress in his place.

"Win!" he screamed. "Win!"

Thank you, Joe Jr.

Thank you, Inga Binga.

Ah, well. Most likely, I couldn't have written *Moby-Dick*.

Why England Slept made some best-seller lists. But Arthur Krock wrote much of that for me. *Profiles in Courage* won the Pulitzer Prize. But Sorensen did much of that for me.

What the fuck, I say. How many times did Melville get laid?

"Don't!"

"Don't go!"

"Don't go to Dallas!" Bobby screams.

P.J.'s Saloon, a throbbing establishment of beer and sawdust, stood smack in Haymarket Square. Laborers stopped in after work before going home to the missus and the ton of kids. P.J. served them himself, had an ear for everyman's trouble. He was my grandfather, P. J. Kennedy, son of poor Patrick Kennedy, who died of the cholera. I would inherit his ability to listen.

"But it's not enough," P.J. said one day while still in his twenties.

"What's not enough?" Corky McGonagle said.

"Serving up the whiskey," P.J. said. "Lending an ear. I want to be able to help folks with their troubles."

"Sure and begorra," Corky said. "P.J.'s getting an eye for power."

"You're not listening to what I'm sayin'," P.J. said.

"But I'm hearing what you be meaning," Corky said.

P.J. twisted the end of his handlebar mustache. He ran his

hand through his shock of reddish brown hair. He wiped his hands on the apron around his waist before shaking hands with a customer whose wife had just had a baby.

"A drink for the little one," P.J. bellowed. "A round of drinks on the house!"

There were eighteen customers in the saloon at the time; he'd just bought himself eighteen votes.

He was only twenty-seven when he was elected East Boston representative to the Massachusetts legislature. The year was 1885. He would serve five terms.

He married a girl named Mary, and they had their first son in 1888. Joseph Patrick Kennedy. Pop.

"So what's next?" Corky McGonagle said.

"Why, the state senate, of course," P.J. said.

He had a wholesale and retail liquor business as well as the saloon. Was there a wedding that needed whiskey? Or a wake? P. J. Kennedy supplied it all. In truth, there were only two Kennedys that made any money. P.J. made his tens of thousands. Pop made his hundreds of millions.

P.J. soon could deliver the votes of East Boston. He was named to the Democratic Board of Strategy, becoming one of Boston's four "mayor makers." In the saloons and back rooms he wielded Irish power fairly and honestly and with respect. Never stuff a ballot box, he said, unless you have to.

It became the family motto.

"So now you've got power," Corky McGonagle said. "So now what is it you be wanting?"

"Respect," P.J. said. "Respect."

The saloon was crowded. They almost had to shout over the noise. "Respect?" Corky said. "That's the one thing they'll never give you. The Yankees hate us, P.J., you know that. The Cabots and the Lodges with their *Mayflower* airs. Power you can take from them, P.J., but not their respect, and that's what they'll never give."

"I can darn well try," P.J. said.

"That why you're sending the boy to Boston Latin," Corky asked, "instead of a good Catholic school?"

"That's the reason," P.J. said. "He'll stick it in the ear of those Protestant boys."

"Maybe," Corky said, finishing his beer. "Maybe he just will do that. But that don't mean he'll get their respect. Mean-spirited, those Yankees are. As soon respect a nigger as a mick."

Pop played baseball at Boston Latin for four years. One year he batted .667, the best in the city school league. They elected him president of the senior class.

This Pop told me years later, and he showed me the mayor's cup he won as proof.

He never said if he had any friends.

(Hold your sympathy; Joe Kennedy never needed it.)

He was, as you know, a world-class s.o.b.

And proud of it.

To Pop, the "world-class" was the only part that mattered.

"That's it!" Lyndon says.

"What?"

"It was your father! Your own goddamn father had you killed!"

"Lyndon . . ."

"I wouldn't put it past him. He was known to stop at nothing. He spent half his fortune to get you elected. To buy the election for you. Ass-kissed Hoover to keep him quiet. And you turn liberal on him. The Peace Corps. Encouraging King and them other Nigras. It probably turned his stomach."

"Lyndon . . ."

"You weren't worthy to follow brother Joe. That's what your old man was thinking. But he had other sons. Bobby. Bobby worked for McCarthy. Bobby was tougher than you, a chip off the old block. The sooner you were gone, the sooner Bobby would come to bat. Perhaps in the old man's lifetime. That's it! Just like that Condon fella wrote in that weird book!"

"Lyndon . . ."

"Jesus. Your old man had you killed! This is getting interesting. Downright Shakespearean."

"Lyndon . . ."

"What?"

"Go to bed."

At Harvard, my father was snubbed by every club. The Brahmins still would have nothing to do with the immigrant-class Irish. To annoy them, he went out, after graduation, and amassed three different fortunes.

His first millions he made in the stock market. Money matters are boring. Suffice it to say that he indulged in any number of practices which he, upon being named the first head of the Securities and Exchange Commission in 1934, would immediately declare illegal.

"You set a thief to catch a thief," President Roosevelt declared to a stunned nation in announcing my father's appointment.

Pop, seeing the big crash coming, had sold short, had gotten out of the stock market in the spring of '29. His first fortune intact, he actively supported Roosevelt for president in 1932, unlike most businessmen. The difference was that Pop was not a businessman, he was a gambler; he was gambling that FDR had the better chance of saving the nation—and, not incidentally, Pop's millions.

As a reward for his support, Pop hoped to be named Secretary of the Treasury. But Roosevelt decided you don't set a thief *there*. Accepting the SEC as consolation, Pop began putting businessmen out of business. "A traitor to his class," he was called—by those who'd never allowed him any class.

His second fortune he made in Hollywood. He went to the coast, bought up ailing film companies, streamlined them, merged them, turned them into money machines. He produced more than a hundred movies, few of which had any artistic merit, and most of which made a great deal of money.

During this time he lived in a glittering mansion with Gloria Swanson, the brightest of Hollywood's stars. It did not appear to trouble him that, back east, our mother was raising the nine of us children, albeit with paid help. Periodically we would hear reports of sparkling poolside parties, the champagne rolling in like the sea itself.

I would lie awake at night and envision my father in the bed of the world's most glamorous movie star.

I was a good learner.

When he tired of movie money and movie twat, Pop came home and began his third fortune. He decided one night to show me what he was doing. The year was 1930: Prohibition. I was thirteen years old. We walked, after dinner at Hyannis, down to the beach. Pop was wearing one of the white suits he favored in summertime. I was wearing white ducks, a white pullover. A half-moon poured snowy light onto the deserted beach as, out on the horizon, we saw a ship's lights twinkling.

Slowly the ship drew closer. Then, to my father's consternation, the lights of a second ship appeared.

"Better not be the blasted Coast Guard," Pop muttered.

We walked farther up the beach, to the spot where the ship my father was expecting was due to put in. The moon was hidden for a time behind dark gray clouds. When the light broke through again, we were confronted by another man walking toward us on the beach, not a hundred yards away. My father stopped, apparently startled. The other man did the same. Each placed his right hand inside his jacket as they resumed moving toward each other.

At a distance of ten feet, the two men stopped.

"Costello!" my father said, icily.

"Joseph P. Kennedy!" Frank Costello spat. "What the shit are you doing here?"

"That's my ship coming in," Pop said.

"Oh yeah? Well, the other one is mine. I suggest you disappear. This is mob territory."

"Is that so?" Pop said. "Well, I suggest you scram. This is my beach."

"You're a troublemaker, Kennedy," the mobster said.

"Get off my beach," Pop ordered.

Frank Costello didn't move. We were near the water's

edge. Pop bent down, picked up a handful of wet sand. He threw it at Costello, splattering the mobster's pale blue jacket.

"Is that so?" Costello said. "You want to play rough, eh?"

He hesitated. I was transfixed, frightened. Frank Costello bent over. He picked up a handful of muddy sand. He threw it at my father.

I was horrified. My father's favorite white suit was dripping with mud. It looked, in the moonlight, like blood.

Pop leaned over, scooped up a double handful. He stepped forward, shoveled it into Costello's chest. The gangster bellowed. He grabbed two fistfuls of his own, hurled them at my father, first his right hand, then his left, soiling my father's pants.

I didn't know what to do. I wanted to join in, help my father. But that would be two against one.

They kept throwing mud at each other until all of their clothing was covered. Then they stopped, panting. Out at sea the ships were coming closer.

"Who's that?" Frank Costello said, short of breath, noticing me for the first time.

"My son," my father said, gasping. "John."

Costello looked at me. He seemed uncertain whether to shake my hand or to throw some mud at me. In the end, he did neither.

"The ships!" I said, pointing out to sea. "They're gone!"

"Dumb kid," Costello said.

"They're out there," my father told me. "They're coming in without their lights."

"Why?" I asked.

"Dumb kid," Costello said again.

I glared at him. I wanted to reach down for some mud. My father's touch on my shoulder stopped me.

"Leave him be," Costello said. "Don't you believe in baptism, Joseph P.?" And he kicked wet sand onto my pants.

"You're a gangster!" My father spat.

"And what are you?" Costello asked.

24

"I'm in the import business," Pop said.

Frank Costello laughed. He was still laughing his evil gangster's laugh as we left him behind and walked on up the beach, to watch my father's ship unload.

Pop never understood why people thought he had no class.

He was determined to change their opinion, however. He contributed a huge sum to FDR's reelection campaign and was rewarded, two years later, with the ambassadorship to the Court of St. James.

He was ecstatic. "Rose, Rose!" he said to my mother. "I've done it! Ambassador to England. The filthy British have Ireland underfoot. They practically forced my grandfather out of the country, to America. Now I'm going back across the ocean, as the American ambassador! That ought to stick it to 'em!"

"Yes, Joe," my mother said.

"Yes, *Ambassador*," my pop corrected.

He made her call him "Ambassador" ever after.

He made everyone call him "Ambassador" ever after.

The year was 1938. Hitler was beginning to stir in Europe. Pop was sworn in as ambassador in the Oval Office, by a judge, while FDR looked on, seated.

"One thing," the president said, as Pop was about to leave.

"What's that, Mr. President?"

"Don't throw mud at the queen."

My father's face flushed. "Of course not," he said.

Then he added, "The queen is a pretty cute trick."

Franklin Delano Roosevelt, a true patrician, groaned with foreboding.

Of the preceding sequence, there is one remark that even I do not understand: Roosevelt's comment about the mud.

The moonlit scene on the beach, between my father and Frank Costello, really happened: but not as I have described it. What really happened was that, when they unexpectedly confronted each other on the beach, my father pulled a pistol from his pocket, and pointed it at the chest of Frank Costello. Simultaneously, Costello whipped a gun from his jacket, and aimed it at my father's head.

They stood that way, motionless, arms extended, deadly weapons aimed, for what seemed to me an hour, though of course it was only seconds, or minutes. I was terrified, frozen, unable to move, while they exchanged threats, bitter vows; till they reached some temporary peace. Only when the dark ships drew near did they pocket their guns, unused.

I never knew, till then, that my father carried a gun. Or knew the likes of mobsters.

"You will," he ordered, as we watched the crates of booze unloaded, "never speak of what you have seen here tonight. Not to anyone."

"Of course not, Pop," I swore.

But it had happened, it would not go away. And so in my schoolboy brain I transformed the scene. I metamorphosed Evil into the Three Stooges. That way it was tolerable.

For a moment I could not reveal the truth, even here. Such was the power my father had over me. Such is the power of our own internal lies.

It was a lesson I learned early: the truth can be transformed; reality can be made to disappear, and myth to take its place. And the myth will be more powerful.

For even now that I have spoken the truth, what I see in my mind's eye, on the moonlit beach, are two men in pale suits, cavorting, hurling dark mud at one another.

Somehow, that's what Roosevelt saw as well.

Was his warning about the queen a figure of speech?

Or was FDR, as some people believed, really God?

Air Force One stood proudly on the tarmac, America's manhood, gleaming in the rising sun.

The phallic notion triggers free associations—the Washington Monument, then the Lincoln Memorial, then the statue of Lincoln as it would appear in Bill Mauldin's cartoon a few days later, the great stone figure of Abe slumped over in his thronelike chair, his head in his hands, weeping. Weeping for me.

The overwhelming power of myth.

That's what Nixon the Narrow never could grasp: that history *is* myth.

"Where's Lyndon?" I asked Pierre, as we mounted the portable stairs.

"Lyndon's in Texas," Pierre said, puffing.

"Already?"

"He's been there for three weeks, vacationing at his ranch."

"I didn't know that," I said.

Lyndon sweeps the flannel nightcap from his head,

squeezes it in his hand. His remaining hair is mussed, like a little boy's. Like John-John's.

"You see!" Lyndon says. "You didn't even know where I was. Goddamnit, Jack. The most powerful, the best majority leader the Senate ever had. And you castrated me like a Texas bull. You and your runty brother."

"It wasn't me, Lyndon. I appreciated you. We were both men of the world. (By the way, how is your Texas lady? What's her name, Madeline?) It's the job, that's all. Vice president is the worst job in the world. Raymond the shoeshine man serves a more useful purpose."

"Of course, Raymond never became president," Lyndon interjects.

"Yes, there's that."

"But I wouldn't have either, if they hadn't nailed you. You wanted to dump me from the ticket in '64. Who would you have replaced me with? Bobby? *Kennedy and Kennedy in '64?* Even you boys couldn't have made the country stand for that."

"The country will stand for anything, as long as their cars gleam and their TVs work. But I wouldn't have dumped you, Lyndon. Bobby and some of the others were urging it, but I had already said no."

"Because you knew I would make the best president?" Lyndon asks, trying to swallow a smile of pleasure.

"Because the Republicans would be running Goldwater. Because I *had* to carry Texas."

Lyndon stuffs his nightcap back onto his head. "Thanks, Jack," he says.

"Any time," I say.

Pierre was puffing mightily as we reached the top of the stairs and entered the plane. "You ought to swim laps," I said. "That belly is bad for your health."

"It's the béarnaise sauce," Pierre said. "I love béarnaise sauce."

"You ought to give it up."

"When you give up pussy," Pierre said.

Evelyn Lincoln, my secretary, keeper of the White House logs, whose seat we were passing, flushed a bright Harvard crimson. A real trouper, Evelyn. She would protect my secrets forever.

Pierre peeked into Jackie's compartment, gave her a word of advice. "In the motorcade, never look to the side where Jack is. Always look to your own side. That way we don't waste two smiles on one voter."

"I still don't see why I have to go," Jackie said. She had a copy of *Vogue* on her lap.

"Because they love you," I said. "Because the whole damn country loves you. Because we have to carry Texas. Because Pop gave you a million bucks."

That last was a little joke. The old Kennedy irony. A deadpan reference to malicious rumor in the supermarket-counter press.

Jackie was not amused.

We moved farther back, settled into our comfortable seats. On my lap were the morning's intelligence briefings on South America, on Vietnam. I gazed through the small window at the skyline of the capital.

"I have a rendezvous . . . ," I said.

"What?"

"If something happened to me," I said, "what kind of president would Lyndon make?"

"The same as you," Pierre said.

"Great?"

"Horny."

"You're a goddamn liar!" Lyndon says, slamming down the first chapter.

"Where?"

"Right here. Vietnam. Where you say you wouldn't have sent in troops. You already had. You wouldn't have pulled out. You couldn't have cut and run. No more than I could."

"Shall I take that as a compliment?"

"Take it any damn way you please," Lyndon says.

"All those dead," I tell him. "All those crippled. The land mines. The napalm. The Agent Orange. The bombs. It was your war, Lyndon. Yours and Nixon's. So it says in the history books. So it shall remain."

"And you? Your hands are clean?"

"What can I tell you, Lyndon? I was just a pretty face."

A word about Pop. In life, I called him Dad. We all did. But does he remind you of your own daddy? In retrospect, he was a madman, a megalomaniac, a grasping, comic terror of a millionaire. In retrospect, he is Pop.

For example: two weeks before he was named ambassador to the Court of St. James, when he was lobbying mightily for the position, FDR summoned him to the Oval Office. The president was in his wheelchair; my father was standing near the fireplace.

"Drop your trousers," FDR said.

"What?" my father asked.

"You heard me," the greatest president of the twentieth century said. "Drop your pants."

My father wanted the job. He unhooked his belt buckle, zipped down his fly, let his pants slide down to his ankles. He stood there in his jacket and tie and shirt and shorts in front of the president.

Would your dad have done that, for any job in the world, except at gunpoint?

Pop did.

"Look at your bony legs," Franklin Roosevelt said. "Look how bowlegged you are. To be sworn in as ambassador at the Court, you would have to wear knee britches and silk stockings. You'd be a laughingstock. In the photographs, America would be a laughingstock. I can't let that happen, Joe. I can't give you the appointment."

"I'll get permission," my father begged. "I'll get permission to wear striped pants and a cutaway coat."

In two weeks he got permission. In two weeks he got the

job. He hoisted his pants and sailed for England, where the rest of us would join him later.

Pop.

"I wonder," FDR said to Eleanor, "what Gloria Swanson ever saw in him."

"I wonder," Eleanor harrumphed, descending into a coal mine, "what Missy LeHand sees in you."

Lyndon keeps calling Bobby a runt. It's true that he was small and slight, smaller even than the girls. But a more important difficulty, I think, was his uncertain position in the middle of the family. Joe Jr. and I were the big boys. Teddy was the baby, and acted accordingly. Bobby didn't know where he fit in, and so he always craved action, always craved excitement, as if action would define his role, and therefore his character.

One day the three of us went sailing in the bay. Bobby was clearly upset.

"What's wrong?" Joe asked.

"I can't swim," Bobby moaned. "It's taking me too darn long to learn how to swim."

Suddenly, with no warning, he jumped off the boat into the sea. He was going to learn how to swim, or drown trying.

I stood on the deck, watching him flounder, watching his head go under, watching him gulp for air. I was thinking; I was pondering the existential quality of what he had done. Was it very brave? Or very foolish?

While I pondered deeper truths, and the sea beat against the boat, Joe jumped into the water and saved him. Dragged him back to the boat, limp and turning blue.

Joe's hero was Tarzan. Mine was Hamlet. Joe swung from vines and treetops till he crashed. I listened to my father's rattling chains. Joe should have soared to the presidency. I should have drowned at sea.

Joe would not have had a Bay of Pigs.

"On the other hand," Bobby says, "during the Cuban missile thing, Joe would have blown up the world."

Perhaps, I concede. Perhaps.

31

The dining hall at the London embassy was a magnificent room of chandeliers, of red velvet curtains, of gilt. (Easy pun intended.) Across the oval mahogany table, over the genteel clatter of sterling on Wedgwood, my father did his gentile best to ignore the destruction of the Jews.

His best-known aide-de-concentration-camp was the Lone Eagle, Lucky Lindy, the most adored American hero till me. The colonel, a bitter man since the kidnap-slaying of his son in New Jersey, had taken up temporary residence in Paris. But he made frequent trips to Germany, was a great admirer of the Nazi war machine. Hearing this and glad of heart, Pop invited Colonel Lindbergh to dinner.

We kids, at one end of the table, were served up fish and chips. Pop and the colonel dined with pleasure on Jewish hearts and Jewish lungs, in a borscht of Jewish blood.

"The German army is magnificent to behold," Lindbergh told my father. "The Panzer divisions roll unstoppable across the fields, like Roman chariots. No country in Europe has the strength or the guts to resist." He sipped from a crystal glass of Polish tears, broke a piece of Austrian bread.

"And the air force?" my father asked. "Tell me about the Luftwaffe."

I gazed from one to the other. I was struck by how alike they looked: both tall and slim, with soft blue eyes that camouflaged bayonets. Their careers had parallels, too. Both had flown on the wings of their own moxie from obscurity to the pinnacles of fame, of wealth.

In the course of which, they both had become pricks.

(There is a time to live and a time to die, Mom. After which comes a time to tell the truth.)

"Ah, the Luftwaffe!" the colonel said. His eyes widened in an ecstasy that seemed almost spiritual. "A hundred, a thousand Lone Eagles, flying in formation, strafing and bombing the villages below."

"Can they cross the channel?" my father asked, hopefully. "Can they defeat the British?"

"In a week," Lindy said. "Two at the most."

"Oh, rapture," my father said. "Then Chamberlain will have to surrender. There will be no war. America will not get involved. That's just what I've been cabling the president. All this unpleasantness is none of our affair."

"The shipping lanes will be safe from attack," Joe Jr. put in, excited.

"The Haig & Haig will get through," I said.

Pop looked at me askance, not sure if I was being sarcastic. He had the exclusive license to import Haig & Haig Scotch from the British Isles to America, a flow of booze that kept his millions rolling in. An America at war would interrupt that flow. Booze ships would become troopships. What would democracy in America be if the corner saloon closed down? If Pop's fortune didn't grow at its normal pace?

Pop raised a glass of Hebrew tears. His eyes glittered brilliantly. "Heil Hitler!" he said.

Lindy echoed his toast. We kids remained silent. Pop looked sternly from one of us to the next, that look that always made us cower. Bobby was the only one who broke, but he hadn't heard the toast quite right. (Or perhaps he had, and was only pretending.) He raised his glass and looked at Lindy.

"Hi ya, Hitler!" he said.

I looked at my plate to hide my joy. Under the table with its white lace cloth I pinched Bobby's knee. It was then that I made him attorney general.

"Tell me something, Lindy," I said. (I felt I had a right to speak; he was only a colonel; I was already a freshman at Harvard.) "How can you be so friendly with the Germans, when it was a German who kidnapped your baby and killed him?"

"Hauptmann? Bruno Richard Hauptmann? That immigrant carpenter?" Lindbergh frowned. "Hauptmann didn't kill my baby."

"But he was convicted," I said. "He was executed."

"Hauptmann was innocent," the colonel said.

I was mystified, uncertain, innocent myself.

"But he was convicted on *your* testimony. All the evidence

was phony, contradictory: the ladder, the ransom notes the cops made him write. He might have gotten off if it wasn't for you. You said he was the man you saw one night who came for the ransom money. You said his was the voice you heard!"

"It was dark, that night in the Bronx," Charles Lindbergh said. "I couldn't tell Hauptmann from Superman."

"You testified it was him," I said. "You testified you recognized his voice."

"He said one word. In the dark. Two years before the trial. How should I know if that was his voice?"

"You swore under oath! That's why the jury convicted. Because Colonel Lindbergh, the national hero, the poor, bereaved father of the child, swore that this was the killer. How could you do that, if it wasn't him? You sent an innocent man to his death?"

"My baby was dead," Lindy said. "Someone had to pay for it."

"Even someone innocent?"

"It didn't matter," Lindbergh said. He looked toward my father. "I'm disappointed, Joe," he said. "Haven't you taught these boys anything?" He turned to me again. "I was a national hero. The killing of my baby was an affront to the national honor. Someone had to pay, someone had to die, to salve the national psyche. It didn't matter who it was. Hauptmann was framed, Hauptmann was executed, the nation could relax again. The Lindbergh baby's killer was no longer at large; justice had been done. The FBI was back in heaven, and all was right with the world."

"The FBI?" I asked. "It was a local police matter. What did the FBI have to do with it?"

"Hoover's boys knew the truth," the colonel said. "They knew enough to keep out of it. You don't unravel justice once it's been done."

The fish and chips were sticking in my chest. I thought I was going to vomit. "And truth?" I asked, weakly. "What about truth?"

"Truth is what the masses believe," Lucky Lindy said.

"And they believe what those with authority, those with power, tell them."

I looked at my father for some contradiction, as did we all. None was forthcoming.

"Kids, kids," Pop said, sipping from his foul glass. "Didn't you know that already? What do you think your trust funds are for? So you can all get fat on vichyssoise? Is that what I made my millions for? Of course not, of course not. It's so that you, my children, could have the education, and the power, to become the *creators* of the truth."

"And that's why they killed him," I murmured. "An innocent carpenter. Just so the ignorant masses would believe."

"What?" Pop said. "What?"

"Nothing," I said. "Nothing."

(Aside to Theodore White: I like you, Teddy Bear, but you blew it. That was the real Making of the President: 1938.)

That prewar summer, between freshman and sophomore years, my friend Wayne and I toured Europe. The trip was more portentous and self-revealing than I could ever have imagined at the time. In Spain we were fascinated by our first bullfights— the grace and sparkle and courage of the matadors, the fatal ignorance of the bulls. We had a grand evening of drinking tequila with an American named Jake, who'd been out fighting Fascists in the boondocks. Wayne and I ended the evening merrily in a Spanish brothel; we asked Jake to join us, but, sadly and earnestly, he declined.

"You think he's queer?" Wayne asked.

"Perhaps he just isn't in the mood," I allowed.

From Spain we went to Hamburg, to take in the garish sights of the Reeperbahn. Much to our dismay, we just missed Hitler himself. Each evening at five o'clock, when he finished being *der Führer*, my father's Aryan idol had been moonlighting: doing a strip act at the Boom Boom Room. Unfortunately, his act had closed the night before we arrived; but we did catch Eva Braun in a nude tableau of Marie Antoinette. Wayne and I agreed that she was nothing to go bunkers about.

"That's *bonkers*," Lyndon corrects, looking over my shoulder.

"That's *bunkers*," I reply. "You fight your war and I'll fight mine."

From Hamburg we went to Copenhagen. Nothing much happened there, and yet, if the act of creating, of writing, reveals your inner self, then Denmark drew me out the most. I was keeping a half-assed diary of the trip. I would like to quote briefly two of the Danish entries. They reveal to me now, as they did not then (consciously), the gap between the boy called Jack and the man called JFK.

(Of all the things to apologize for in this book—indeed, in my life, which are one and the same—I apologize only for the boyish enthusiasm of this early prose, which I shall quote verbatim. If Sorensen's word processor blows a microchip, so be it.)

Both entries are from early August. The first is dated Sunday, two days after our arrival in Copenhagen:

"Denmark at a glance: an inviting mélange of beautiful blondes, creamy chocolates, succulent sandwiches. Happy, healthy, handsome, helpful people everywhere. Grapes and bananas at streetside stands. Attractive statues appear unexpected, and ancient castles, and proffered hands.

"Blondes, brunettes, blondes. Pretty, pert, pleasant. What do they do with their ugly babies? It bears investigation.

"Where are your acned, your knock-kneed? Are all the ones at home like you? It's a schoolgirl-complexion people in an Easter Bunny world.

"In England they wear high heels all the time and in France they are chic or sophisticated, but girlwise there is nothing like a Dane. In England their noses are pointed and in France their remarks, but in Denmark so many are appealing it's appalling.

"Some are redheads and some are brunettes but most are natural blondes. Unless they're dressing up, their heels are flat, but their bodies never are.

"And they are everywhere. Walking the streets with their dates, mainly, but also working in camera stores and restaurants and bakeries, and fixing window displays, and selling hot dogs, and riding bikes. And gradually they blend into one ideal blonde vision of a girl, who is ubiquitous—demure but not coquettish, quiet but not shy—a wholesome bundle of dynamite, a luscious chocolate éclair."

So what? you ask.

So this: for me there is portent, Joycean, in almost every line. But focus, for now, on only one aspect: the infatuated blondeness. I'd been a sickly child, a sickly teenager, racked with the Addison's disease my family kept hushed. (Malaria, they called it, jaundice, any mad lie they could invent.) What did this deep, genetic, glandular infatuation with Danish blondes represent, beyond the obvious horny yearnings? A turning away from my father's dark past, perhaps; a yearning for the golden sun.

So what? you ask again.

So this: four years later I met Inga. I was as preprogrammed to fall in love with her by this visit to Denmark as Condon's Manchurian assassin was preprogrammed to kill. Inga Binga. Miss Denmark. Blonde. Blonde all over. I buried myself headfirst in the sun, a cunning Icarus: while fat J. Edgar taped it all, fat Hoover, who squatted like a dark shadow over the American century, keeping his filthy files, binding my ankles and wrists with his sadistic tapes.

Claiming Inga Binga was a spy!

Inga in bed with Hitler? I'd sooner envision bullets splattering brains.

"Inga Banga! Inga Banga! Inga Banga!"

"Shut up, Lyndon."

"Go ahead, Jack, show us. I dare you. Show us Inga in bed: with Adolf and Eva both!"

What shall I tell him? "I never promised you a Berchtesgaden."

I think of Rosemary. Sweet, round-faced sister. The other family secret: the needle they stuck in her brain.

Perhaps Shirley is wrong; perhaps there is no reincarnation at all. Perhaps, after these twenty-five years to remember and reflect, death is only this: a prefrontal lobotomy.

All those new-age pulp best-sellers, all those forests destroyed! It offends the *Geschreiber* in me.

I'll let you know. (If they allow it.)

Lyndon made me digress. I was going to quote a second entry from my Danish diary. This one more dark than blonde:

"Guarded by three red ramparts and two moats on one side, overlooking the turbulent sound toward Sweden on the other, its pale green towers spiraling into a gray El Greco sky, stands Kronborg Castle at Elsinore—grand home of the Danish kings, made great by the pen of the Avon tanner's son. The Bard may never have been there in life, but he is there now, in stone—at the entrance to the dungeon. A strange place of honor for the man who gave the castle immortality. But perhaps not. For there in the dungeon is the place to see the ghosts—and to hear the chains and to smell the mildewed earth, and to imagine the past come alive, much as it does in immortal iambic pentameter. Crouch through the low stone passageways and be Bernardo come from the watch. Hear your footsteps echo on the rocky floor and be Horatio shouting 'What, ho!' Back into a triangular stone cell not wide enough for your shoulder blades, and swear fealty to Claudius in return for sitting room. Climb the uneven winding stairs in darkness and be the prince himself, seeking the fateful apparition that, once seen, can never be erased, can never be forgot. Smell the musty smells and be Rosencrantz and Guildenstern, looking for Polonius, who is dinner for worms. Cross the cobblestone courtyard and be Gertrude, awaiting her son's return.

"Upstairs, in the light, is the chapel, but Claudius is not praying there. That was only Shakespeare's fantasy. Upstairs, too, is the queen's room, but it is just a room. There is not an arras there, much less a rat.

"But go, go downstairs. Somewhere, somehow, they have found an ugly old lady in Denmark. They have dressed her in black; they have given her a candle. Follow her to the darkness of the dungeons. She will light the way to history."

So what? you ask yet again.

So this: I wrote those entries in 1938. Twenty-five years before the bullets. Fifty years ago as I set this down. I swear it! (Perhaps, from the boyish prose, you believe.) Yet look what a little editing could do:

"Hear footsteps on a jungle trail and be Allen Dulles crying 'What, ho!'

"Back yourself into a corner and swear fealty to Giancana, in return for Illinois!

"Smell the musty smells and be the Warren Commission, looking for Oswald, who is dinner for worms.

"Go to Hyannis and be Rose Kennedy, awaiting her son's return. (And her son's.) (And her son's.)"

So did I cast my lot, my life. I stood on the glowing ramparts in the bright light of conjured myth, beside my lady dressed in pink. But in secret I followed the ugly old lady with the candle, through the hidden dungeons, to history; to death. Which are the same.

"Tell me something, Jack."

"What, Lyndon?"

"If you were a bull in a whorehouse for blondes, why did you marry Jackie?"

"The Bouvier French ancestry. The Auchincloss respect. Jackie was the head of the class."

"And Judy Campbell? You were pissing your pants for blondes, why a dark mistress?"

"She was a friend of Sinatra. Of Giancana. Of Roselli. For business and pleasure both. She was—"

"Don't say it, Jack."

"—the class of the head."

"You had to say it, didn't you? You were the grace of the White House, they say, and I was a boorish clod!"

"A myth is as good as a mile, Lyndon Baines."

39

"And all this Hamlet stuff. A strange identification for a pol, if you ask me. The knock they used to put in Adlai, as I recall. Hamlet vacillated, couldn't make decisions, couldn't take action. Feared his father's words might really be those of the devil. Whatever happened to Prince Hal, Jack? I thought you were Prince Hal."

"That's what you were supposed to think. That's what everyone was supposed to think."

Lyndon is quiet for a time, pondering.

"You know what was the weirdest thing Nixon ever told me?" I say.

"What?"

"We were talking about images once. Identifications. It was backstage, before the first debate. I asked him what character in all of literature he most identified with, most wanted to be. And you know what he replied?"

"What?"

"Uriah Heep. Uriah goddamn Heep."

"No shit."

"That's what he said. Uriah Heep."

"You've got to give the weasel credit," Lyndon says.

"Credit? For what?"

"He made it."

I suppose he did.

Which reminds me. It is a little-known, but historic, fact that among those people in Dallas on November 22, 1963, was Richard Milhous Nixon.

"Jack," Lyndon says, "nobody's gonna believe *that*. Nixon couldn't shoot the side of a barn."

"Not shooting. Talking. He'd lost his race for governor of California in nineteen sixty-two. The press wasn't going to have him to kick around anymore."

"Of course not. They'd have me."

"So he was working as a lawyer—"

"A contradiction in terms," Lyndon says.

"—for the Pepsi-Cola Company. He was addressing a convention of *bottlers*."

Lyndon raises both his arms, awkwardly, in a passing-good imitation. "I am not disposable!" he says.

"He took off from Love Field less than three hours before Air Force One arrived."

"Pepsi-Cola?"

"So?"

"—hits the spot!"

"Don't be gory, Lyndon."

"How do you know? How can you be sure that he left Dallas before you arrived? The Book Depository. Always sounded to me like something Nixon would take for constipation. How do you know he was on that plane? He could have doubled back. Gone to the grassy knoll. He—"

"Lyndon . . ."

"I'm serious, Jack. You know how people like to wear those funny Nixon masks? Suppose that was him in the window. Tricky Dick Nixon wearing a Lee Oswald mask!"

"Lyndon . . ."

"I like it, Jack, I like it. Put it in."

The funny thing is, I like it, too.

It didn't happen that way, of course. But I do enjoy the conceit.

Nineteen sixty-three was also the year they marketed Valium.

As the old radio serials used to intone, we're getting ahead of our story. In 1938, I was dividing my time between Harvard and England, Lyndon was a skinny young congressman, Nixon was learning how to shave (something which, thank God, he never did quite get the hang of), and Adolf Hitler was inventing his own form of antidepressants. In the absence of little yellow pills, he swallowed Austria, then Czechoslovakia, then Poland. From across the channel, Neville Chamberlain, the prime minister, and my father, the American ambassador, looked on and

41

thought it was rather cute: like watching an adolescent boy gorge down another steak.

My father was more concerned about his own publicity than about the fate of Europe, employing a personal PR man to spread the Kennedy name throughout the British Isles, cajoling his good friend Henry Luce to spread the Kennedy name across the States in two different cover stories in *Time*. This attitude did not go unnoticed by the British ruling class. One described Pop as "a tycoon who seemed to me when I met him to combine all the disagreeable traits of all the very rich men I had ever met with hardly any of their virtues." Another said: "His chief merit seems to be that he has nine children." A third called him "a great publicity seeker who is apparently ambitious to be the first Catholic president of the United States."

Who am I to argue with the British ruling class?

As each new country disappeared into Hitler's belly, my father reaffirmed his opinion that "none of these moves has any significance for the United States." As the president's man in London, he followed a simple, unswerving rule: see no evil, hear no evil, and always sneak your girlfriends out through the back door.

Are you paying attention, Jack?

Yes, Dad.

My mother lived by a not dissimilar rule: see no girlfriends, hear no girlfriends, but fumigate the bedroom every day.

His anti-Semitism he did not attempt to hide. For someone who spent his life railing against anti-Irish, anti-Catholic bias, this was a sacrament my friend Arthur Goldberg would describe as Extreme Chutzpah. It did not go unnoticed, even by the German ambassador. One day this gentleman cabled home to his *Führer*: "Today, too, as during former conversations, Kennedy mentioned that very strong anti-Semitic tendencies existed in the United States and that a large portion of the population had an understanding of the German attitude toward the Jews . . . from his whole personality I believe he would get on well with the *Führer*."

(When Pop arrived at the Pearly Gates, he included that endorsement on his résumé. The response of St. Peter is, alas, lost to history.)

(I can't ask Pop; there is no communication between here and there.)

Neville Chamberlain went to Munich. He sold out the Czechs for "peace in our time." My father, elated, went out and bought an umbrella. Then came the *Kristallnacht*, the night when Nazi mobs rampaged through Germany, destroying synagogues, smashing the windows of Jewish shops, rounding up 30,000 men, women, and children for deportation to the concentration camps. My father was not hurt by the flying glass; he had his umbrella for protection. But he did exhibit a rare sensitivity, telling the German ambassador, "We don't care what you do to the Jews, but we'd rather you weren't so awfully noisy about it."

My brother Joe, I regret to say, shared my father's views. During a visit to Germany, he wrote home: "They are really a marvelous people, and it is going to be an awful tough thing to keep them from getting what they want."

In Washington, Franklin Delano Roosevelt did not share the views of his bowlegged ambassador. Each new, reassuring cable from Pop infuriated him further. The president was beginning to agree with the leader of Britain's loyal opposition, Winston Churchill, that Hitler would have to be stopped, with force if necessary. The president opened up a secret line of communication to Churchill. My father was relegated to messenger, personally carrying sealed letters from the diplomatic pouch to Churchill's residence, without knowing what they contained. When the Nazis invaded Poland, the British declared war. Pop the Ambassador gracefully opined that the British would be "thrashed."

Winston Churchill, first lord of the Admiralty, said in a speech to the House of Commons: "This is a war, viewed in its inherent quality, to establish, on impregnable rocks, the rights of the individual, and it is a war to revive the stature of man."

My father, listening, groaned. "There goes the Haig & Haig," he echoed.

He continued to urge Roosevelt to keep America out of the war. One member of the British foreign office called Pop "a very foul specimen of double-crosser and defeatist." Another called him "malevolent and pigeon-livered."

"You see," my father told us kids, "the old anti-Irish prejudice continues to rear its head."

In May of 1940, when Germany invaded Belgium and Holland, and the Chamberlain government fell, Winston Churchill became prime minister. He offered his country "blood, toil, tears and sweat."

"Low class," Pop muttered.

"You ask, what is our policy?" Churchill intoned. "I will say: it is to wage war, by sea, land, and air, with all our might and with all the strength that God can give us: to wage war against a monstrous tyranny, never surpassed in the dark, lamentable catalog of human crime."

"A very excitable chap," my father said.

The Germans began the bombing of Britain. Pop sent us kids home. And he began to spend his nights at his country place, far from burning London. All the while still telling the president that the war was not our business.

The British rulers were gracious about this. One declared: "Whilst we do not regard Mr. Kennedy as anti-British, we consider that he is undoubtedly a coward." Another called him "a defeatist and a crook."

"Defend yourself, Dad!" little Teddy wailed into the transatlantic telephone one night.

"I am not a crook!" Pop said.

Teddy drank some Scotch and went to bed.

With the bombs falling all around him, my father came up with a brilliant plan. He would go home. He would go home and warn the American people: "Roosevelt and the kikes are taking us into war."

With the support of his good friends Henry Luce and William Randolph Hearst, he might even run for president himself.

"Say what?" Martin Luther King, Jr., asks. "Run for president himself? Your anti-Jew, anti-Negro pop?"

"Roosevelt took it as a real threat," I reply. "He knew there would be plenty of sentiment against America's entering the war. He knew there would be opposition to his seeking a third term; no one had ever done that before."

"So what did the old fox do?" the reverend asks.

"He cabled Pop to call the White House the minute he got home. He told Pop over the phone, sounding as friendly as could be: 'Joe, old friend, please come to the White House tonight for a little family dinner. I'm dying to talk to you.'"

"The president said that?"

"What Pop didn't know," I say, "is that while FDR was talking into the phone, he was drawing his finger across his throat."

"And then what happened? This is a good story. This is a real cliff-hanger."

"What happened," I say, "is that before the dinner was over, Pop agreed to support FDR for reelection. Not only support him, but make a nominating speech at the convention."

"You don't say," Martin says. "Now how did Roosevelt pull off a thing like that?"

"I guess the man was a sweet talker."

"Dig!" the reverend says. "I dig. Indeed I do."

"I thought you would," I say.

"I have a dream!" the reverend says.

"Yes, Martin, I know."

"No, not that dream. Another one."

"Another one?"

"In my dream, me, you, and Bobby get together. We form a group."

"A group?"

"You know. A singing group. Like the Will Mastin trio. Or the Supremes."

"I don't know, Reverend."

"The Supremes! That would have been the perfect name. Too bad it's been used."

The reverend has been a little spacey ever since he got here. I think perhaps it was not quite what he expected, what he'd been led to believe. I try to humor him.

"You mean like a gospel group or something?"

"There's no money in gospel, Jack. I'm talking pop. The charts. Headlining at Caesars Palace: King and the Kennedys. Get Jackie Mason to open for us. Or Robin Williams. We'd pack the joint."

"Las Vegas?"

"That's where the money is, Jack. And the girls."

"King and the Kennedys?"

"First thing that came to mind, Jack. I don't need top billing; don't really care. Kennedy, King, and Kennedy. Whatever."

"KKK?"

"Jack! You're a wordsmith from way back. Short and snappy. Big letters on the marquee: KKK. I like it. I like it."

"I don't know, Reverend. I just don't know."

Thus far in these recollections I appear to be slighting my mother; I suspect that slight will continue. She was gracious and lovely and kind, and outlived us all; I intend no disrespect. But she was much less of an emotional presence than my father. While Pop's whims and outrages blew across our lives like mad typhoons, Mom saw to the needs of our daily existence yet somehow blended into the wallpaper, just one more Rose in the garden of our lives. Try as I might to conjure images, I see only one: she is frozen in time, seated ladylike on a sofa. It is the pope's sofa. The sofa and my mother are protected by velvet ropes.

Her father was John F. Fitzgerald. He was the mayor of Boston in an era when knights-errant, not bureaucrats, ruled the cities of the land, dispensing patronage like feudal scalawags, asking in return only fidelity on election day, and a silver lining for the family mattress. He was the power on the Boston throne at the same time P. J. Kennedy was the sage of the saloon, the mayor maker, the boilerplate of East Boston. When Honey Fitz, as her father was called—so smooth was he—consented to the marriage of his daughter Rose to Joseph P. Kennedy, banker—my father's camouflage during his stock-raiding days—it was rather like an Irish recombination of the Austro-Hungarian Empire. There would be the devil to pay.

Their firstborn was my father's boy: Joseph Patrick, Jr. Their second was christened by my mother: John Fitzgerald. Me. I was saved from being a mama's boy, I suppose, by all the babies that followed in quick succession. (It may be instructive, in that respect, that while Joe Jr. blew up over England, and I took a bullet in the head, and Bobby took a bullet in the heart, Teddy, the baby, would hitch his star to the soiled diaper of Chappaquiddick.)

Throughout our childhood Mom was physically present: feeding, nurturing, directing the hired help. And yet in an equally real sense she wasn't there at all. I will cite just one example, the only one I recollect. For three years, as I have mentioned, my father lived in Hollywood with Gloria Swanson, the most glamorous actress of the day. Half the marquees in America billed the flick Illicit Interlude, starring Gloria Swanson as the actress and Joseph P. Kennedy, Sr., as the rich movie mogul. When the passion had waned and Pop returned home, he invited Miss Swanson for a visit. He introduced her at Hyannis as his business associate. Mom didn't blink. She shook hands graciously; she entertained Pop's mistress with perfect class.

Then, in the next few years, Mom made seventeen different pleasure trips to Europe.

I think that I would rather she had blinked. She might be more vivid now in my memory.

(I know, I know. I invited Angie Dickinson to my inauguration. And Jackie didn't blink. What can I tell you? Pop was a powerful teacher.)

So I see Mom now in only this one snapshot, seated,

ladylike, on the spotless couch. It is not just any couch, not to my mother. In 1936, while we were living in a large house in the Riverdale section of New York, Cardinal Pacelli came from Italy to visit the States. He stayed for a time as our houseguest. He sat, at times, on a sofa. When the cardinal left, Mom bought red velvet ropes, and roped off the sofa on which the prelate had rested his rear. No one else would sit on it, ever.

Two years later, when Pope Pius XI died, Eugenio Cardinal Pacelli became pope. Pop was the ambassador by then. We went from London to Rome for the coronation. The next day, we Kennedys had a private audience with the family's new pope. He gave me communion, personally. Then Mom took the first boat home, and installed a second line of ropes around the sofa.

There, in my memory, she sits: beside, but not on, the very spot where Cardinal Pacelli sat. The lingering hint of papal incense, and the red velvet ropes, protect her from the dirt, from the dark profanities of life.

There are, however, four stains on the sofa that the ropes could not deflect: the blood of Joe Jr.; the blood of Kathleen; the blood of Bobby; the blood of Jack.

I can only assume that sometimes, in private, seated on the sofa, Mother cries.

But she never blinks.

(In 1960, at the height of the campaign, I appeared before a conference of ministers in Houston, to allay their fears—and much of the nation's—about the prospect of a Catholic president, about where my loyalty would lie. The ministers didn't know, didn't ask, about Mother's velvet ropes, about Cardinal Pacelli's ass. If they had, it would have been Nixon in a landslide, and history dancing a different dance.)

"I don't suppose," Lyndon says, "it was a Castro Convertible."

I ignore the remark. Sometimes that's all you can do with Lyndon.

□ □ □

When the president won a third term, defeating Wendell Willkie by a surprisingly slim margin, with the aid of my father's reluctant endorsement, Pop went down to his mansion in Palm Beach to await a further call to serve his country.

It didn't come. Pearl Harbor came instead. America was at war, and my father was in the nation's largest doghouse.

He wrote letters, sent telegrams, to the White House, offering to help in any way he could in the war effort. He received no replies.

My senior thesis was published, with an introduction by Henry Luce, with some quiet rewriting by Arthur Krock, the Washington bureau chief of *The New York Times*. The book explored why Britain had been unprepared for the war in Europe. It was called *Why England Slept*. It sold a lot of copies, earned a lot of attention.

Some said it should have been called *Why Daddy Slept*.

His own ambitions finally thwarted, Pop turned his attention to the future of Joe Jr. With Joe as president, Pop figured, his telegrams would be more likely to be read.

When we were kids, two lessons were drummed into us incessantly. The first was: win, win, win. The second was that Kennedys never cry. But when Joe exploded over Britain, my father—my daddy—cried. He cried for a very long time.

Then he turned his ambition to me.

His ambition wasn't *Moby-Dick*.

Vegas. Ever since Dr. King mentioned it, I can't get it out of my mind. Not a singing group; I never could sing worth a damn. But memory. Nineteen sixty. The seventh of February.

"A date which will live in infamy," Lyndon says.

His tone shocks me. I have never heard him so serious. Moral outrage? From LBJ? I dare not question him. I do not know how much he knows.

The seventh of February. I'd been on the coast for a fundraiser, getting ready for the primaries. Teddy was with me. We

49

hopped over to Vegas to have a meal with Frank. A new family friend, Sinatra was raising money among the stars.

Or so I thought.

We met in the lounge of the Sands. Frank showed up with a girl on his arm. This was not unusual; Frank alone would have been a cause for concern. But something about the way he made the introductions—some indefinable excitement in his eyes, something vaguely businesslike in his tone—suggested that the girl wasn't his. Or that if she was, he now was through with her.

Her name was Judith Campbell.

(The one lesson Pop had omitted: beware of Italians bearing gifts.)

Perhaps I should have suspected something. But with Frank it never seemed like pimping, only generosity.

Or maybe that's just what I wanted to believe.

Frank showed an inordinate interest in conversing with young Ted that night, which left Judy and me making eye contact as we talked. She was dark, she was pretty, she was smart. Before we finished our lobsters, I knew I had enchanted her.

And she knew she'd enchanted me.

We went to the main ballroom, then, to watch Frank's show. I'd never, in person, seen him sing before. But from the moment the spotlight picked him out on the dark stage, I found myself riveted. There were a thousand people in that huge room, seated on rising tiers, many behind tables, midway through their meals. But the instant he started to sing, all noise ceased. Silverware stopped clicking. People stopped talking. Meals went uneaten as the audience, with its eyes, devoured Frank Sinatra. I'd never seen that happen before—such total rapture—in any nightclub, with any performer.

He had a quality, a glow, when he sang in person, that was hard to define. I'd seen it only once before, somewhere; not, I knew, in a club. In an odd way it seemed political.

Then I knew. Eisenhower. Ike. Hero. The mastermind of D day. The president of the United States. Eisenhower, at his press conferences, and on television, was a pathetic rambler, running his sentences together like a walk in the woods, leaving his listeners lost. The man, in those forums, could not communicate. But Eisenhower in person, on a public stage, his smooth, reddish face glowing like a baby's, was a sight to behold. The North Star when it is the only star in the sky. A gold coin, spinning, in the hands of a hypnotist. The blood of the onlooker, the listener, turned to love.

That's what poor Adlai had been up against.

And that's what Sinatra had going for him now—an adoration somehow induced.

There have been singers with better voices, singers with better tunes. I knew that night that there was only one Frank.

I studied him as we watched, looking for his method, his secret. He somehow conveyed to every person in the audience, male and female both, that he was alone with them in that vast, crowded hall, that he was singing only to them. This was the only aspect I could define. How he did it I did not know.

A year passed, I was already president, before I got around to asking him how he did it.

"I don't know," Sinatra replied. "How do *you* do it?"

His question elated me.

It still does.

Perhaps Sinatra's singing that night enhanced the sudden passion between Judith Campbell and me. Perhaps it was even planned that way. But it was Teddy who asked her out after the show.

I called her the next morning. We made a date to have lunch on Sinatra's patio. She told me, over lunch, about showing Teddy the sights of Vegas. And how, at the end, he had made a pass at her.

"That little rascal!" I said. Confident. Amused.

Ted and I flew east that night, to campaign in New Hampshire. For the next thirty days I telephoned Judy incessantly. We arranged, breathless, to meet at the Plaza Hotel in New York on the seventh of March—the day before the New Hampshire primary.

51

Sinatra had done the first half of his job.

The night we made the date, I dreamed again of *Animal Farm*. I assumed again that the horses were the West, horses who, if I won the election, would gallop at my command.

Now, looking back, I think of an anachronism: the severed head of a horse, in a singer's bed.

As World War II wound down—if that is the proper word for Hiroshima—the saga of *PT-109* was the subject of a long article by John Hersey in *The New Yorker*. The author kindly focused on our struggle for survival, not on the prior screwup that ditched us in the water. My father was elated—and also frustrated. The circulation of *The New Yorker* wasn't large. He arranged with his friends at *Reader's Digest* for a condensation of the article, which in time went out to millions of subscribers in every city and town in America. In the condensed version, I appeared even more heroic than in the original.

Learning that a congressional seat in Boston would be opening up in the 1946 election, Pop ordered a hundred thousand reprints of the *Reader's Digest* article. Then he telephoned me from Palm Beach.

"How would you like to be a congressman?" he asked. "A member of the House of Representatives?"

I held the receiver quietly for a moment.

"A congressman?" I asked.

"For openers," Daddy said.

The great engines shuddered, rumbled, roared. Air Force One taxied down the runway, gathering speed, like some great beast reaching deep within itself to find its true purpose. As it lifted off the ground, flaunting its silver nose at gravity like some disdainful debutante, I was thrilled, as always, in a little-boy way, at the reality of flight. It symbolized to me, I suppose, man at his most courageous, breaking earthly chains, reaching for the highest in his nature. That was why I promised we'd put a man on the moon before the decade was done.

I only wish I'd lived to see it.

(In a manner of speaking, of course, I did.)

You're mixing metaphors, I can hear Sorensen saying. Air Force One can't be a beast and a debutante in the same paragraph.

The hell it can't, I say. It can if you're Beyond Editing.

Beast and debutante. Passion and poise. Coiled strength and arch posturing. The fusion that comprises us all.

That compromises us all, as well.

I was a hero, you see.

In addition to all that has come after.

I was a hero to you yourself, perhaps. Or to your neighbors. Certainly to tens of millions of Americans. To hundreds of millions around the world—the hopeless, the desperate, the simply adoring.

"Keh-neh-dee, Keh-neh-dee!"

It was a universal chant, if you'll recall.

Nothing in this memoir disclaims that. Here be demons, perhaps. Here be women. Here be mobsters. But here also is the Peace Corps. The Alliance for Progress. A higher minimum wage. The integration of Ole Miss. The federalization of the National Guard to integrate the schools in Alabama. The test-ban treaty. The removal of Khrushchev's missiles from Cuba. Yes, and that man on the moon.

Never forget it.

I urged you, implored you, exalted you to a higher purpose.

And you responded.

At least, the 49.7 percent of you who voted for me responded.

A landslide of the spirit, it was.

Curious thing. In June of 1963, they took a poll. Nearly 59 percent of Americans remembered voting for me. After I was killed, they took another poll. Now it was 65 percent who remembered voting for me.

Easy line coming: I must have been doing *something* right.

Besides dying.

Then there were those who hated me.

Never mind them; they've all long since been sent to hell.

(It's the thing that concerns me about Pop: all those unfriendly faces.)

The truth is, great beast or not, there *was* no Air Force One. There were four different planes. Whichever one I happened to be on became Air Force One.

Illusion.

Like so much of what we were doing.

Like so much of what *you* do, every day.

The identity of this bristling machine changed in direct relation to my position with regard to it. An injection of fuel to the ego. Kennedy $= mc^2$.

And the man in uniform, carrying the black box, never far from where I went. A specter to quake one's soul.

As the plane reached its cruising altitude, I opened the briefing book on Vietnam. There had been a meeting about the 'Nam situation in Hawaii the day before: Rusk, McNamara, Bundy, and General Taylor had flown over to get an update from Ambassador Lodge and General Harkins. President Diem had recently been overthrown. According to the briefing book, Lodge and Harkins felt the new military government was doing a good job. They were optimistic about the way the war was going. I took the yellow marker attached to the book and under-lined one worrisome sentence, and drew a question mark in the margin—a reminder to ask for more details on this. The sentence said the Vietcong had made some important gains in the period of confusion that followed Diem's overthrow.

I set the book aside, got up to stroll the cabin, to ease the pressure on my back. I put my reading glasses in my pocket—another dark secret!—and looked around for someone to tease. Pierre wasn't there, I remember now. The exchange about the béarnaise sauce must have been on another trip. Pierre was off in Hawaii with half the cabinet. Goofing off. Then they'd be going on to Japan for an economic conference. Pierre, quietly, would be scouting the turf; I was thinking of visiting Japan in '64.

For a moment I am upset that he wasn't there. Not every-one's death is the biggest story of his life; mine would be. You'd think your press secretary would want to be there.

(Perhaps, privately, for the individual, death *is* everyone's biggest story. It's a thought that you find, I imagine, mostly terrifying, and only slightly hopeful.)

I can hear Pierre now: "The president has asked me to inform you that he will not be attending the Harvard-Yale game next week, since he is no longer with us."

QUESTION FROM MERRIMAN SMITH: Is that on the record, or for background?

MR. SALINGER: Since President Johnson has already moved into the Oval Office, I suppose we might as well go on the record with it.

Poor Pierre. The contortions I put him through. I remember one time we were flying from Washington to Syracuse, New York, for a political speech. I was on Air Force One, Pierre was on the press plane trailing us. I had him announce that the president would be stopping briefly in New York for a private conference, but that no news would come out of it, so the press plane would fly straight through to Syracuse. You should have heard the shit hit the fan, as Pierre told me later. The reporters were all over him. "We're the White House press corps! We go wherever the president goes! If the president's plane is touching down in New York, then the press plane is touching down in New York. We don't care if he's just going to pee! Suppose someone shoots him on the way to the men's room!"

Pierre caved in; he had no choice. The entire White House press corps camped out in the lobby of the Carlyle Hotel while I spent three hours upstairs.

Luckily, Marilyn had arrived before we did.

When we were through, I called Pierre upstairs. We pondered what to do. We didn't *have* to explain anything, but there would be a lot of questions.

It was Marilyn herself, listening as she emerged from the shower, wrapped in a blue terry-cloth robe, drying her hair with a towel, who had the inspiration.

"I know!" she said. "What about Adlai?"

"What *about* Adlai?" I said. I knew she still had a crush on him; her and her egghead types. I thought her bringing it up, after the delights of the past few hours, was not very sensitive.

"He's your ambassador to the United Nations, isn't he?"

"The last time I looked," I replied.

"He lives in New York, doesn't he?"

"Of course," Pierre said, impatient. "So what?"

"The U.N. is in session isn't it?" Marilyn with that little-girl voice, that little-girl sexiness. One bright pink areola visible where her robe was coming open.

"Yes," Pierre said. "No. Today is Saturday."

"Precisely," Marilyn said. "But they'll be meeting again Monday. Some important questions will be coming up. Questions about which the president and the ambassador need to have a private discussion. If you get my meaning."

A broad grin split my face. Her brain, too, was a constant source of delight.

"Do you think we can get him over here?" Pierre said to me. "On such short notice? We've got to get on to Syracuse."

"If he won't come to see the president," Marilyn said, smiling sweetly, "I'm sure he'd come to see me."

I'd heard enough. "Find him," I barked to Pierre. "Get him over here. On the double."

So it was that the White House press corps, not ten minutes later, saw Adlai Stevenson emerge from a taxi in front of the Carlyle and cross the lobby to the elevators. He was wearing blue denim overalls and a plaid wool shirt. As the reporters gawked at the sight—something they had never seen before—the ambassador waited for the elevator, ignoring all questions, and rode it up to my suite.

I made Marilyn wait in the bedroom while Adlai and I talked. He'd been working in his rooftop garden when Pierre called. He seemed, throughout, as puzzled at the sudden summons as was the press below.

I let a modest ten minutes pass. Then I stood abruptly and shook his hand. "Thank you for coming on such short notice, ambassador. You will, of course, keep the nature of our discussions top secret. A matter of national security. Tell the press you are not at liberty to reveal what we discussed."

"Of course," Adlai said, shaking his head.

What we had discussed, mostly, were his rutabagas.

He was mobbed as he recrossed the lobby in his overalls, ignoring all questions, and slipped wordlessly into a waiting cab. I was not the least embarrassed at having used him that way. If the state of the president's cock is not national security, what is?

Ten minutes later we headed for the airport.

Marilyn, of course, would linger till we all were gone.

Marilyn. Inga Binga minus Hitler.

But not exactly. I was never hopelessly infatuated with Marilyn, the way I was with Inga.

That would be Bobby's problem, a year later. Bobby's and Marilyn's both.

And assorted agencies'.

The plane began to dip through some sudden turbulence. I slipped into the nearest seat. Raymond was in the seat adjacent, reading the *National Review*.

"What are you, Raymond?" I asked. "A closet fascist?"

I'd asked him, at the last minute, to make the trip with us. We'd be spending the final night at Lyndon's ranch. Have you ever seen what cow chips can do to Guccis?

"Bullshit!" Lyndon interrupts.

"Bullshit what? You don't have cow chips in Texas?"

" 'Course we got cow chips in Texas. We got cow chips bigger'n Bobby. Heck, we got cow chips bigger'n Teddy, and that's going some. But cow chips are dry, they ain't gonna hurt your loafers. It's the bullshit that you needed Raymond for. Didn't they teach you anything at Hahvid?"

You hear that, Raymond? It's the bullshit we needed you for.

"The way I figure," Raymond said, closing the *National Review*, "it's a good idea to find out what the other guy is calling you."

"So you can prepare an answer?"

"So that you can think about if maybe he's right."

"And what is it that Mr. Buckley is calling me?"

"Can't rightly tell, amid all the verbiage," Raymond said. "Lordy, does that man need an editor. For the next election, however, he does seem to favor Mr. Goldwater. That much slithers through without a dictionary. Seems to think Goldwater would do a better job of getting rid of Castro."

With effort, I kept my mouth shut; I didn't tell Raymond that it was sour grapes; that Bill Buckley had wanted to be in on the Castro kill; but that it had gone to Johnny Roselli instead.

(Buckley, it turns out, might have done a better job of it. But that's hindsight.)

Lyndon interrupts: "What was it Nixon used to say? 'We can't stand Pat!' "

Don't be nasty, Lyndon.

"Now you take Jackie over there," I said to Raymond. "She's reading *Vogue*. Polishing up her charge cards for Neiman-Marcus. That *National Review* is downright subversive, with no advertising. Downright un-American. How are we going to keep the American economy strong, with no advertisements?"

"Rifles," Raymond said.

"Rifles?"

He flipped to the rear pages. "See. They do have advertisements. For mail-order rifles."

"And a good thing, too," I said, glancing at the magazine. "We have to keep America strong."

"Yes, sir."

"It's every citizen's constitutional right: the right to keep and bear arms."

"Yes, sir."

"In case the British come back."

"My thought exactly, Mr. President."

The congressional elections of 1946, more than any other, would set the stage for the second half of the American century. In Massachusetts, I would win a landslide victory; in California, young Dick Nixon—he *was* young once, chronologically— would upset liberal congressman Jerry Voorhis; and the good people of Wisconsin would boost into the Senate—and onto a national platform—a phony war hero who called himself "Tail

Gunner" Joe McCarthy. We were not, at the time, as dissimilar as it now appears. We were, unbeknownst to all, Atropos, Clotho, and Lachesis: the three Fates of the nation's postwar generation, whose intertwined machinations are, to this day, still not fully unraveled.

"Those are girls' names," Joe McCarthy says.

"So?"

"Whaddaya mean, *so*? What are you, some kind of homo queer? Some kind of gay faggot Commie queer?"

He's not here, I warn myself, and never was. It's just my imagination. He died in '57; Joe McCarthy's ghost was erased from hell in '82, when his twenty-five years were up. (Would you on earth were so lucky, eh?)

"Aw, Jack. Give the guy a break. He wasn't as bad as all that. The Trickster is all he was. The Barnum & Bailey of the American destiny. It was all a game."

"I told you, Bobby. I don't want to discuss him with you. We were wrong on that one, okay? After death, even *we* can admit we were wrong."

"Yeah, *The Crucible*, I know, I know. Marilyn sure had a hang-up about that one."

"What do you expect? Her husband was called before the House committee. He sat there and stared at them and refused to name names."

"So?" Bobby says. "It made him a hero among his friends. It gave him an idea for a play. What's wrong with that?"

HUAC as the Muse. I never looked at it that way before.

"Joe McCarthy made a lot of heroes," Bobby says.

"Not to mention some suicides."

The little-known fact is, McCarthy and I were social friends back in those early days. Eunice, who was sharing my house in Georgetown, even dated him a few times. We went to barbecues in his backyard, laughed at his dirty jokes. The odd thing is, he claimed to have known me long before that; claimed to have known me in the Solomon Islands, to have been aboard *PT-109*, to have been allowed once to fire its guns. I remember none of that; I suspect it was one of his fantasies, like the names of all those Communists he used to see on the blank sheet of paper he'd wave around. Never did know what his problem was. Indigestion, perhaps.

As for why I never actively opposed his witch-hunts, you should have guessed by now. McCarthy and Hoover were two withered peas in a pod; Hoover had the Inga tapes; Pop wanted me to be president someday.

It's ambition, not conscience, that makes cowards of us all.

Inga. I did see her again. In Hollywood.

My back problems forced me out of the navy in 1944. I went to sunny Phoenix to recuperate. Frequently, for nightlife, a friend and I would drive across the desert to Hollywood. Inga was there, trying to make it as an actress. One time, stopping at Schwab's Drugstore for some aspirin, I saw her, sitting at the counter, waiting. I swiveled onto the stool beside her.

"Hi, Jack," she said, nonchalantly.

I was tempted to say "Heil Hitler!" I resisted. Instead we made small talk. It was clear that there was nothing left between us.

This is the woman, I thought; this is the woman with whom I was so in love. My first true love. My sun goddess. My adoring Aryan beauty. My hardness, my wetness, my soul mate: the reason for my very existence. In one inspired day God had created the heavens and the earth and Inga. And Inga He had given to me. So I used to think. So I used to feel. So I used to tell her, alone—we thought—in our nakedness. So it was on Hoover's tapes.

And there, in the drugstore, a few years later, nothing. The first wonder of the world is love. The second is its absolute and total death. Chatting over coffee, I asked myself what I'd seen in her: this slightly pudgy, mostly silent blonde. It was hard to believe it had ever happened at all.

Except that it was preserved on tape.

Now there's a worthy function for the FBI. The eternal preservation of love.

"Disgusting!" mutters Hoover, passing by.

□ □ □

I couldn't bring myself to ask her about *der Führer*. I didn't want to know if it was true. Very soon we ran out of words.

Just in time, an attractive brunette entered the drugstore and sat beside Inga. Our eyes played games. Inga, salvaging some grace, asked if we two had met.

"Jack Kennedy," I said, extending my hand.

"Gene Tierney," my new flame said.

And so I began to commute across the desert.

On April 12, 1945, with victory in Europe at hand, with victory in the Pacific being perfected at Los Alamos, President Franklin Delano Roosevelt died.

In the Bronx, the Jewish ladies cried.

"It's a great thing for the country," my pop said.

It could be argued that I was elected to Congress because of the Boston Tea Party, Kennedy style. Instead of dumping tea in the harbor, we dumped sex appeal and dreams of Kennedy wealth down the demure décolletages of thousands of quivering young ladies and their jellied moms.

In the end it was a landslide, but my election was by no means certain at the beginning. The seat from the Eleventh Congressional District was being vacated by James Curley, who would make his last hurrah with another run for mayor. And the Eleventh, which included both East Boston and the North End, was Kennedy Country. But there were nine other candidates entered in the Democratic primary, and I was nothing but an underweight Harvard man whose scrawny neck couldn't fill his collar unless it was stuffed with reprints from *Reader's Digest*.

Pop spent months reestablishing his old contacts in the state for this race that Joe Jr. had been supposed to make. He spent a fortune to counter the comments that I was just a kid running for office on an old and bloated incident from the war— which, of course, is what I was. Pop, in his typical, self-effacing way, said it best himself: "With what I'm spending, I could elect my chauffeur." With my back nearly killing me, I went out and made puerile speeches for twelve hours a day, doing it because Pop wanted me to, running as the ghost of Young Joe.

As the primary neared, someone in the campaign had an idea: the Kennedys would throw a tea party for the candidate—and would invite every registered Democratic female in the district. The other candidates scoffed—but the night of the tea party at the Cambridge Hotel, more than two thousand women lined up—in the ballroom and down the carpeted stairs and out into the street—to shake hands with me and my folks. I grinned and touched their soft female flesh and thanked them for coming. They blushed and looked demure in their pastel evening dresses—many of them rented for the occasion, no doubt, from some sad tuxedo shop—and their breasts flared with the wild hope that I might notice them—or their daughters—more than all the others; that afterward I might look them up, take them out to dinner. That tea with the Kennedys might lead, through some rub-off of the American dream, to marriage with the Kennedys. And so they stood in line through the long spring evening, and waited.

"A tea party?" Lyndon scoffs. "Lordy, lordy, Massuh Jack."

On election day I got half the votes; the other nine candidates divided the other half.

"Your pa's money," Lyndon says. "That don't mean they all was dying to hop into bed with you."

"Consider this, Lyndon. Six years later I ran for the Senate. Against the incumbent Republican, Henry Cabot Lodge—and, you'll recall, the Lodges owned Massachusetts long before Patrick Kennedy arrived from Ireland in steerage. It was the year Ike was gonna sweep the country for the GOP. No way some skinny congressman from the Eleventh was gonna run statewide for the very first time and unseat Lodge. So how did we do it? Tea parties! We held tea parties in every fucking district in the state. The Cambridge ladies from all over came to press the flesh. I was still the dashing bachelor with the trust-fund teeth. Half of them wanted to mother me, it's true. But the other half wanted to marry me."

"So?"

"So, in the course of the campaign against Lodge, we had seventy thousand quivering ladies to tea."

"Don't tell me."

"And on election day, we won, statewide, in the face of the Eisenhower sweep, by seventy thousand votes."

"Jesus," Lyndon says. "Lord Almighty. Imagine what you could have done if you'da thrown in some barbecues!"

"We tried that," I remind him.

"You did?"

"In nineteen sixty."

"Oh."

"And we still had to steal fucking Texas."

"Now, Jack. You're not gonna tell them about that!"

"I already have."

"Jesus, Jack. And Illinois?"

Illinois I'm debating about.

"Jack?"

"What, Lyndon?"

"How many of those seventy thousand ladies did you actually get around to fucking?"

"Gimme a break, Lyndon. I had a bad back, remember?"

So it was that the first week in January, 1947, Joseph P. Kennedy, Jr., took his long-awaited seat in Congress.

I mean Jack.

Jack.

Definitely.

Jack.

The one it should have been was Eunice. After Joe got killed, Eunice became the leader among the kids. She was the strong one, the outgoing one, the natural politician. It was she who wanted desperately to run for Congress. But Pop wouldn't hear of it. He didn't exactly drown his girl babies, that was frowned upon, but . . .

It should have been Eunice sitting in Congress, but it wasn't, no sirree. It was Jack.

(When I wasn't too bored to show up.)

Harry Truman was living in the White House.

I was living—for the time being—in a house in Georgetown.

With Eunice. And a cook. And a valet.

I was a twenty-nine-year-old millionaire congressman. Mom and Pop came down frequently and stayed over. Pop came to spy on me, pumping information from the valet and the cook. About who I might be seeing.

Inga was back in town.

We had one last secret tryst, for old times' sake. (What the hell, I figured. Hitler was dead.) I don't know if J. Edgar taped that one.

Three months later, Inga got married. Six months after that, she had a baby boy. Many years later, she would tell her son his real father was me.

Was that true? I haven't the foggiest.

"Perhaps Hoover knows," Bobby says.

I can't ask Hoover, of course. He's down below, with Pop. I can't talk to them, but I can see them: sitting together in the fires, laughing hysterically.

As they listen to the tapes.

Pop, who made a point of knowing everybody worth knowing, was acquainted with Harry Truman. In 1944, when the candidate for vice president came to Massachusetts for some politicking, Pop took him aside. "Harry," he asked, "what are you doing campaigning for that crippled son of a bitch that killed my son Joe?"

He also was a good friend of Archbishop Cushing, of whom

he once shouted: "Who the hell does he think he is? If he wants that little red cardinal's hat he'd better shape up, because I've got a hell of a lot more friends in Rome than he does."

(My mother, sitting on the sofa behind the double line of velvet ropes, smiled.)

I wonder, sometimes, how history would have been different if Pop had been the one they'd lobotomized.

Somewhere in Africa, in the early sixties, a small boy in a remote mountain village was very sick. His large brown eyes had lost their luster. His empty stomach was bloated, because he couldn't keep any food down. The entire village was upset, because the boy was the eldest son of the tribal chief. The medicine man rubbed the boy with herbal salves, and chanted holy chants. The little boy continued to weaken.

In desperation, the boy's father decided on a last resort. He had heard, through the jungle drums, that a medicine man from far-off America had come to the distant city to help the people. The tribal chief did not really believe that there was an America, but, spear in hand, he set off down the mountain to find out. For three days he walked down the mountain like a goat, then through the dangerous jungle like a tiger, till he emerged at last at the distant city by the sea. He found his way to the little clinic that had been set up by the doctor from America.

He waited outside in the steaming sun till the doctor had finished seeing all of the brown people waiting on line. Then the chief approached the doctor. He did not know how he would talk; he could not speak American. He was amazed to discover that the American doctor could speak the tribal tongue.

The chief told the doctor about his son. The doctor listened with concern. He filled his black bag, climbed into his jeep, the chief beside him, and drove the three-day walk from the sea to the mountains in several hours. In the village he looked at the boy: peered deep into his eyes, deep into his throat, poked his belly. Then he took a needle from his bag, filled it with a liquid, and stuck it into the boy, who was, by then, almost dead.

Three days later, long after the doctor had returned to his clinic in the city, the little boy awoke. His eyes were as bright as they used to be before he had gotten sick. He told his mother he was hungry. His mother gave him food.

After several weeks, the boy was well again. The chief, the entire village, was overjoyed. And the chief never forgot the magic worked by the doctor from America. When the boy was old enough, the chief sent him to school in the city by the sea. His son would not be a mere mountain chieftain. His son's life had been spared so he could do more than that.

The little boy is in the prime of life today. He is the progressive minister of agriculture of his country, a position he has held for several years. As minister, he has started irrigation projects throughout the country, with machinery bought from distant America. There is much less famine, much less starvation, in his country than there used to be before he took over as minister. Hundreds, thousands, perhaps even tens of thousands of his people are alive today who would have starved to death, their bodies wracked by flies, if it weren't for him—and for the American doctor in the Peace Corps who had traveled across half the globe to save his life.

"Is that a true story?" Bobby asks.

"More or less. Here or there."

"Why are you telling it now? Here?"

"I have to spread the good stuff around. I was a lousy congressman."

"No you weren't. You stood up to Pop sometimes."

"I don't think that would make much of a campaign slogan."

"It was the hardest thing in our lives. For all of us," Bobby says. "He wanted to play Edgar Bergen in the House, to your Charlie McCarthy. He wanted to tell you how to vote on every bill. But you didn't listen to him."

"Some of the time."

"The important times. Pop was against the Marshall Plan, against aid to Greece and Turkey. You opposed Pop and supported Truman. You supported affordable housing for servicemen. Which the bankers and the realtors opposed. When even the dumb American Legion came out against the housing bill, you proclaimed: 'The leadership of the American Legion has not had a constructive thought for the benefit of this country since nineteen eighteen.' "

I remember. That felt good.

"There were other things. You . . ."

"Bobby?"

"What?"

"It's okay, it's okay. Calm down, you've got the job."

"I do?"

"You can be my campaign manager."

"I can?"

"I wouldn't want anybody else."

I wouldn't *trust* anybody else.

Bobby, dear heart, chooses not to remember some of the dumber things I said in those early days in the House: that a sick President Roosevelt had given away too much to the Russians at Yalta . . . that the State Department had given away China . . .

I can only plead youthful ignorance. I had just come out of my father's house, and those were the gospels I'd been taught.

During the 1960 campaign, when Dr. King was jailed in Atlanta for his civil rights work, I called his wife to express my support. Nixon didn't; I won 70 percent of the black vote, and the election.

(Give or take Illinois.)

Dr. King's father announced at the time that he had been against me until then, because I was a Catholic, but that now he supported me. I was highly amused. "Imagine," I told my friend William Manchester, "Martin Luther King's father being a bigot. But then," I added, "we all have fathers, don't we?"

"Amen," Martin says. "Amen."

"Hello, Martin. What gives?"

"You been thinking about our group? The KKK Singers?"

"I've been trying not to. Been thinking about something else, though. Coretta was such a beautiful woman. Why did you have to cheat on Coretta?"

"Hoover had all these blank tapes," the reverend says. "Couldn't leave a man like Hoover with a lot of blank tapes. Might get himself into mischief. Give him some motel rooms to bug; it kept him happy. Kept him from interfering with our work. *Civil rights* work."

I can't help smiling. The rev can talk, all right.

"That, Martin," I say, "is the neatest justification for adultery I have heard in all my life, or in all the years since."

"What about yourself?" the reverend says. "Jackie was a beautiful woman, too."

"Horses," I reply. "Jackie liked horses between her legs."

"Say what?"

"Riding. Riding. She loved horses more than anything. Got so she'd spend more time at our place in Virginia, riding, than she did at the White House. You know what they say: an empty bed is the devil's playground."

"Who is it exactly who says that?" the reverend asks.

"Me, Martin, me. Funny thing is—and this is the gospel—I was allergic to horses. Couldn't get anywhere near them. And Jackie spending her days straddling them. Even if we got stirred up, got excited, I couldn't go near . . ."

"Sounds like a marriage," Martin says. "Sounds like a marriage, all right."

"There's a glitch in your manuscript."

"Where?"

Lyndon is reading over my shoulder. "Hoover. A few pages ago you had him burning in hell with your father. But a few pages before that, you had him passing by up here."

"You're right. But look, down there. Can't you see him down there in the flames?"

"Yep."

"And yet—I swear he passed by a minute ago. Muttering."

"I think you're right, Jack. I thought I saw him, too."

"Can it be? What does it mean? There couldn't have been two Hoovers."

"Maybe he commutes. Some kind of trial passage. Maybe God can't make up His mind about J. Edgar."

"Not make up His mind? The man was pure evil."

"He caught John Dillinger. Public Enemy Number One."

"What was so terrible about Dillinger? All he did was rob banks."

"Maybe," Lyndon says, "God likes banks."

"No doubt He does," I agree, sounding a bit like Michael J. Fox. "But still, J. Edgar in heaven? It's impossible."

"Maybe he's got some tapes."

"On Him?"

"Could be."

"Who with?"

"Mary Magdalene. Greta Garbo. How the hell should I know who with?"

"You think?"

"Put it this way, Jack. I don't know anyone else who commutes."

It's true. Neither do I.

Getting reelected to the House in 1948 and again in 1950 was no problem. But serving among all those anonymous drones and clones was like a prison term. I couldn't wait to get away. My main interest, outside of women, was foreign relations, which was a good excuse for any number of trips abroad. One of the most memorable occurred in October of 1951. Pop insisted that my sister Pat and my brother Bobby accompany me. I was hesitant at first; I hardly knew Bobby. Growing up, he was lost in the younger group, skinny and pugnacious. Then I went off to college and law school, and then to war. I was afraid he would be a pain in the butt on the trip.

Instead, he was a revelation. We started in Israel, where

we met with Ben-Gurion. We moved from the Middle East to the Far East, to Saigon. And then on to Japan. In each capital, as we met with foreign leaders, Bobby asked insightful questions. He showed a deep desire to learn. Having grown up with the huge trust funds Pop had established, millionaires in our own right by the time we could vote, the poverty of the Third World was a revelation to both of us.

In Saigon, we stayed at the U.S. embassy residence. The Vietminh were locked in a battle with the French army, as France tried to hold on to its territorial possessions. An American consular official there warned us that there was a big difference between the Korean War then raging, in which the West was trying to stop Communist aggression, and Vietnam, where the French were trying to stop not Communism, he said, but nationalism. There was no way, he said, that nationalism could be stopped; in two decades, he said, there would be no more colonies.

We sat there and listened to his analysis, thoughtful, absorbed. It was a lesson we almost learned.

In Israel, Bobby already had a friend in Ben-Gurion. Bob had gone to Jerusalem in 1948, as the end of the British mandate approached, as the new state of Israel was about to be created. Perhaps in revolt against Pop's anti-Semitism, Bobby had been greatly impressed with the Jewish pioneers. In a series of articles he sent home to the *Boston Post*, he openly took the side of the Jews against the Arabs who would soon be displaced from their lands.

As Bobby wrote his dispatches from Jerusalem that spring, a little Arab boy looked down from a hillside village nearby. Mountain goats moved among the ramshackle huts. Veiled women brewed bitter coffee. The little boy . . .

"Please, Jack, not another apocryphal Peace Corps tale," Lyndon says.

The little boy was frightened. He had heard the talk of the hillside: that he and his family might have to leave their land.

A few months later, as Israel was created, war broke out. The Jews and the Arabs battled. The little Arab boy had an older brother, who was killed in the fighting. The boy cried when he learned his big brother had been killed. He cried again when his family moved from its hillside home into a refugee camp in the city.

He was four years old, the little boy with large brown eyes, when he stood on the hillside looking down, as Bobby sent his pro-Israeli dispatches back home.

His name was Sirhan Sirhan.

"Is that a true story?" Bobby asks, from where he is seated near my feet, looking up at me with clear blue eyes.

"Yes," I reply.

That same year, 1948, my sister Kathleen—we called her Kick— fell in love with a married man. It was a pure passion she could not resist. She came home and, with great trepidation, told the family about him. Her lover planned to be divorced; then he and Kick would marry. Mom warned Kick she would be disinherited; Kick didn't care about the money. Mom warned that she would be lost to the Catholic church if she married a divorced man; Kick didn't care. Mom said she would never see her or speak to her again. . . .

Kick returned to Europe, bitter.

She and her married lover were killed soon after, when his private plane smashed into a mountain during a storm.

Pop told the press Kick had merely hitched a plane ride with a casual acquaintance. Her fierce passion was stuffed into the family closet, alongside my recurring bouts of Addison's disease, alongside Rosemary.

"The plane crash was God's revenge on Kick," my mother said.

A gentle, passing cloud bellows: *"No!"*

Our Lady of the Velvet Ropes doesn't hear.

Joe gone. Kick gone. I was the next oldest.

I have a rendezvous with Addison's . . .

We told people it was a recurring bout of malaria that I

had picked up years before in the Solomon Islands. I tanned the skin that the disease was turning brown, and looked even healthier. But with Addison's, any slight infection can soon become fatal.

One doctor gave me six months to live. I pondered the best way to die: drowning, or hanging, or poison, or being shot.

I felt I would not live to be forty-five.

I determined then to live every day as if it would be my last day on earth.

"And every night," Martin adds, winking.

There is a brotherhood of martyrs . . .

In 1946, Pop sold all his liquor-importing interests, at an unbelievable profit over what he had paid for them long before. Behind him lay three decades of running booze—first legally, then during Prohibition, then legally again. But it was time to quit the business, he said, so it wouldn't tarnish my career.

He left behind a thirty-year war with the mob. The blossoming Mafia and dear old Dad had battled in every port, in every saloon, for the right to bring in the gin. We've all seen, in those great old B movies, the tactics of which the mob was capable. Since Pop more than held his own, I can only assume he employed the same tactics.

That he never talked about.

Two men in pale suits on a moonlit beach, hurling mud . . .

That same year, the man who almost single-handedly built the mob in America, Lucky Luciano, was released from prison, with the gratitude of his country, and allowed to return to his native Italy. Luciano controlled the dockworkers in New York and California, as well as in southern Italy, where the Allies had planned to invade. From his prison cell, during the war, he ordered the mob-controlled dockworkers in both countries to support with their muscles and sweat the U.S. effort, and not to side with Mussolini. The *soldati* on both sides of the ocean obeyed, as is their habit. When the war was over, Luciano's prison term was ended by a grateful nation.

It was the first known collusion between the government of the United States and Organized Crime. It would not be the last.

I leap out of the way of a spring of foul vomit. It's J. Edgar, clutching at his throat, looking ill.

"There is no organized crime," he croaks.

"No Mafia?" I ask.

"No Mafia." There are sweat beads on his flushed face.

"No Cosa Nostra?"

"No Cosa nothing."

"Then who is it that met at Apalachin? Who is it that's doing all the stuff out there?"

"Commies. They're all Commies. In a disguise thought up by the head Commie, Mario Cuomo."

"You mean Puzo?"

"Whatever," Hoover says. He's sitting now, catching his breath, wiping his face with a handkerchief.

I look at Lyndon. Lyndon looks at me. I shrug.

"Boy," Lyndon says to J. Edgar. "You must have *some* tapes."

"Tapes?" Hoover says. "What tapes? I never made any tapes." He pauses. "Oh, tapes! You want some tapes, cheap? Debbie Gibson? Madonna? Tiffany? The boys hijacked a truck this morning. Name your artist. Name your price. We got . . ."

Suddenly, in midsentence, Hoover isn't there anymore. Through the mists we can see him down below, among the flames.

"That's some kinda weird bargain He made with J. Edgar," Lyndon says.

"Didn't we all," I reply. "Didn't we all."

Adlai Stevenson has been standing in his wings, watching. Now he approaches. He's always been a bit naive about the mob himself, considering he's from Illinois.

"I couldn't help overhearing," he says, politely. "There's one question I would like to ask. Why was Hoover always so insistent that there was no organized crime? Right to the end?"

"Because," I explain, "it got organized during his thirty years as director."

"Proving," Lyndon adds, "if he were ever to admit it exists, that, contrary to popular myth, as FBI director he was a total fuck-up."

"But still, you kept him on, Jack. And so did you, Lyndon."

This time we reply in unison: "Grow up, Adlai. Please?"

Adlai blushes. He's never really comfortable with us. But he doesn't leave. "One other thing, Jack," he says. "I wish you'd have told me the truth at the time."

"About the Bay of Pigs?" I ask.

"About the rutabagas," Adlai says.

"Would you have come?"

"Yes."

"You were that loyal?"

"Yes."

"I'm sorry," I say. "I guess I underestimated you."

Adlai sighs a long, deep sigh. Then he says, "You were not alone."

There is a weary droop to his shoulders, his wings, as he walks away. We're both wondering, as we watch him, what kind of president he really would have made.

"Did you notice?" Lyndon says, finally.

"Notice what?"

"He still hasn't gone to a shoemaker."

Senator Henry Cabot Lodge, in 1952, had earned the applause and gratitude of much of America. It was he, personally, who had convinced General Eisenhower to be the Republican candidate for president. Without him, the GOP candidate would have been Robert Taft of Ohio.

"I will go to Korea!" Ike was able to proclaim, a war hero thrilling the nation with a promise to end yet another war, to bring the boys back home. Whereas the best the conservative

Taft's speech writers could come up with was "I will go to Cincinnati."

Lodge was Ike's boy. Lodge had a good, liberal Republican voting record. Lodge was also a Lodge, who, as everyone knew, talked only to Cabots. And he was also a Cabot, who, as everyone knew, talked only to God.

(I pause, awaiting confirmation from the passing white cloud. The passing white cloud says nothing.)

For a skinny, undistinguished congressman with no real credentials to attempt to oust Lodge from the Senate that year—the year of I LIKE IKE—was, in retrospect, an act of madness, an act to tempt the Fates.

Needless to add, the Fates were tempted.

"Win, win, win," Pop said. "If I can elect you senator, I can elect you president."

The day I announced for the office, Lodge called Pop on his private phone. "Save your money, Joe," he advised. Through Pop's mind flashed the election of 1916, when my grandpa, Honey Fitz, had run for this same Senate seat against Lodge's grandfather, and had been soundly beaten. "I've been saving my money," Pop replied to Lodge. "I've been saving my money for forty-five years. And this is what I've been saving it for."

Supremely confident, Lodge went off around the country to campaign for Ike. While I went up to Massachusetts to campaign for me. I vowed that before the campaign was over I would appear personally in every city and town and village in the state. And I did. We'd get up in a dingy hotel room at six in the morning to greet the workers at a factory gate. Then on to the breakfasts, the lunches, the dinners. By the middle of the day I would be walking with crutches because of my ailing back. But at each stop I would hand the crutches to an aide backstage, then stride briskly and confidently to the rostrum, the image of health.

At first, the campaign sputtered; my campaign manager quit when Pop, as always, insisted on pulling the strings from behind the scenes. Then Kenny O'Donnell had a brilliant idea:

get Bobby to run the campaign. Bobby, just out of Virginia Law School, in his first job with the Justice Department—which Pop, of course, had gotten him—was reluctant. But we insisted, and Bobby came—and took to it like a duck to orange sauce. Bobby the Tough, Bobby the Ruthless, Bobby the S.O.B. was born.

Allowing me to be Jack the Prince.

If my back got so bad I couldn't appear somewhere, there was always a Kennedy available to fill in. I got a hilarious report once of the very first campaign speech Bobby himself made for me. His hands and knees were shaking, as they would continue to do during public speeches all his life.

"My brother Jack couldn't be here," Bobby muttered, stuttering with fright, to the assembled crowd. "My mother couldn't be here. My sister Eunice couldn't be here. My sister Pat couldn't be here. My sister Jean couldn't be here. But if my brother Jack were here, he'd tell you Lodge has a very bad voting record. Thank you."

"What's so bad about that?" Bobby asks, looking up at me from his perch at my feet.

"Nothing," I reply, "if you discount the fact that Lodge and I had the exact same voting record."

It was true. No real issues divided us. The outcome would be determined by popularity alone. (It could be argued that we were trailblazers that year, pioneers of the politics to come.)

Lodge had the Eisenhower grin going for him.

I had the tea parties.

Election night stretched into the wee hours of the morning. We sweated. We groaned. We waited. In the end I won, by the width of a bag of Lipton.

Used.

Almost unbeknownst to us huddled at Hyannis, America also elected a president that night. Ike.

"It was beknownst," Adlai mutters. "Beknownst it was."

"Okay," I concede. "But almost unbeknownst, the country also elected that night its greatest embarrassment."

77

"You?" J. Edgar asks.

"Tricky Dicky," I reply.

Dwight Eisenhower and Richard Nixon were sworn in as president and vice president on the twentieth of January 1953. At the inaugural ball that night, the new senator from Massachusetts, looking dashing as always in his tuxedo, was escorted by three hundred nameless young secretaries and stewardesses, all of whom he had taken to bed for one-night stands during the preceding two years. None of them was wearing any clothing.

"Why did Jack bring all those bimbos?" Pop asked. "It's no good for his image."

"What's a bimbo?" Mom whispered.

"All those naked girls," Pop said.

"Hush, Joe!" Mom said. "I mean, Ambassador. What are you talking about? Jack has only one young lady with him. And she's wearing a pretty pink gown."

"She's new," Pop said, adjusting his spectacles. "I don't think we've taped—I mean met—her yet."

"Let's do!" Mom said.

When the band finished Richard Nixon's favorite song— "How Much Is That Doggie in the Window?"—Mom and Pop approached. I introduced them to my lovely date, Miss Jacqueline Bouvier.

"Pleased to meet you," Mom said.

"Are you rich?" Pop asked.

Jackie snuggled closer against my arm. Lovingly she looked into my eyes.

"Not yet, Ambassador," she said. "But soon."

I left them that way, chatting amiably. I went outside with my buddy Dave Powers, to toss a football around.

Our first stop in Texas would be San Antonio. I went to my dressing room on the plane to wash up. Taped to the mirror were some figures I had asked the staff to dig out—the vote totals showing how far Lyndon and I had run behind the rest of the state Democratic ticket in 1960. I planned to use them in my speeches, to fire up the party. If we couldn't carry Texas, we'd be dead in '64.

I called Kenny O'Donnell in to double-check the arrangements. I made sure he and Dave Powers would be in the Secret Service car, right behind my limousine. I wanted them there scrutinizing the crowds: checking the faces of the Texans, gauging their reactions to Jackie and me.

Jackie had made a trip to Europe that summer. In France she had spoken to the people in French; in Spain she'd talked in Spanish. She'd been adored everywhere she went. That's why I'd convinced her to come with me to Texas. It was a crucial state, and this was the start of my battle for reelection.

In return, I promised, she could run up and down the

aisles of Neiman-Marcus with a shopping basket for an hour, and keep everything she could stuff into it.

What the hell, I figured; it would be worth every cent.

"Thrift, I've always heard, was not Jackie's strong suit," Lyndon interjects.

"Thrift? The way she could spend used to drive me crazy. One day I complained to Bobby about it. He said the answer was simple: we'd just have to tell Pop to make another fortune."

Her spending did have a positive side, however. All that clothing, all that jewelry, all that perfume. Her spending kept the economy strong.

"Unfortunately," Lyndon notes, "it was the French economy."

Jackie. When I first met her, she was making $42.50 a week. She was the inquiring photographer for the *Washington Times-Herald*—the exact same job that Inga used to have. (How's that for coincidence? Or perversity?) Despite being born a Bouvier and—after her mother remarried—raised an Auchincloss, she did not have money of her own. But with her breeding and my trust fund, we were a perfect match.

Pop had sat me on his knee the morning after I beat Lodge for the Senate. "Joe," he said, "if you want to be president—"

"Jack," I interrupted. "I'm Jack."

"Of course. Jack, if you want me to elect you president, you have to give up the monkey business."

"Give up my boat? Why?"

"Not your boat. You can just change the name of your boat. But you have to give up what you do on it. And off it. And everyplace else. You have to stop screwing around. I've never met anyone as randy as you."

"I take after my pop," I said. "You even made a pass at Inga once."

"She told you that?"

"Yes."

"You gonna take the word of some Nazi?"

I didn't answer him.

"The point is this," Pop said. "America is not going to elect

80

a playboy president. You have to get married, have kids. You can walk down the aisle right into the White House."

So it was that Jackie was born. Or invented.

I can see them now, in a dimly lit laboratory. The doctor in a white smock, a white cap, a gauze mask. The female figure stretched out on the table. The doctor decides on brunette for the hair; for the face a mixture of American and French—pretty, but not excessively classic; modest but shapely breasts. The doctor studies the upper half of the body, and is pleased. Unfortunately, the lower part is in dimmer light; the feet come out a bit too big; the pelvis a bit too small for easy childbearing.

The doctor doesn't notice; goes to a tape deck, listens to possible voices for the Next First Lady, who is stretched out on the table, waiting for the breath of life. Katharine Hepburn? Too arch, too rat-a-tat. Lauren Bacall? Too deep, too sexy, too threatening. What about . . . does the doctor dare? . . . Marilyn Monroe? The doctor listens, studies the voice on the tape, again, again. A certain innocent quality, which will not be threatening to women voters; yet a girlish, sexy tone that will appeal to men. At first it seems like a lark, but it might work, it just might work! Carefully the doctor inserts into the larynx of the patient the voice of Marilyn Monroe.

All is in readiness. The doctor, perspiring lightly, moves to the wall, reaches out—and with a sudden, devil-may-care motion, throws a switch. Lightning crackles. Sparks leap through the basement room like fireflies. The doctor's hand seems riveted to the switch. Then it drops away. The lightning ceases. The fireflies go dark. On the stark table the naked female form stirs; its eyes open; it looks about. Slowly, carefully, the Next First Lady moves her legs off the table, bends them at the knees, rises to a sitting position. Her brown eyes peer around the dim room. When she sees the doctor standing near the wall, near the switch, she smiles with a luminous glow.

"Thank you ever-so," she says. "I needed that."

The doctor watches, appraisingly. The Next First Lady discovers her nakedness, much like the first first lady.

"But I don't have a thing to wear," she says.

The doctor nods. "Soon. Soon. But tell me: do you know your name?"

"Of course," the NFL says. "Ja-kleen. Ja-kleen Bouvier."

"Try again," the doctor says.

"I'm sure it's Ja-kleen. Ja-kleen . . . Bouvier . . . Kennedy. That's it. Ja-kleen Kennedy."

"She's got it," the doctor says. "By George, she's got it!"

The doctor approaches the patient. They hold hands. They dance in a circle, until the operating table disappears in the dervish of their joy; until the walls of the basement itself disappear—to reveal: a rose garden.

I sit in silence, savoring the image.

"That's it?" Lyndon asks.

"Who was the doctor?" Bobby wants to know.

"That's easy," Lyndon says. "It was Dr. Frankenstein."

"Wrong," I say.

"I know!" Bobby says. "It was Pop!"

"Wrong again," I reply.

I enjoy their consternation, though I'm somewhat surprised by it. Finally, I soften. "Look," I say, pointing.

Down in the Rose Garden, the doctor removes her mask. Like a springtime blossom, her laboratory gown deepens from white to pink. She steps closer to her creation, closer, closer still; until they merge, until they are one. Until Jackie is standing alone, in a pink evening gown. Smiling.

The dawn breaks upon them at last.

"Jackie invented herself!" Bobby says.

"Damn!" Lyndon says, visibly upset.

"What's the matter, Lyndon?" I ask.

"Why didn't Lady Bird know a trick like that!"

To propose to her in person was impossible. It would have been a humiliation, a submission of myself. That's not what women are *for*. I solved the dilemma by suggesting marriage in a telegram while she was traveling abroad.

We had to keep the engagement a secret until after June 13, because the *Saturday Evening Post* was coming out with an article called "Jack Kennedy: The Senate's Gay Young Bachelor." Later, when I invited her to go sailing, she was upset to discover that a *Life* magazine photographer would be coming with us; they'd be doing an article called "*Life* Goes Courting with a U.S. Senator." This, I explained, is how a president begins to invent *him*self.

We were married—united?—in St. Mary's Church in Newport on September 12, 1953. Jackie's mother and stepfather paid for the lavish wedding; my father browbeat his way into making all the arrangements anyway, right down to having Archbishop Cushing officiate, though neither of Jackie's parents was Catholic. Her real father, Jack Bouvier, drank too much that morning and was not permitted to attend his daughter's wedding, for fear he would create a scene before the national press.

Jack Bouvier's reputation as a philanderer was the equal of Pop's. If it's true, as Freud suggested, that women marry their fathers, then Jackie had come to the right place.

Who was I to disappoint her?

"Oh, Jack, Jack," Bobby says. "You know how devoted I was to you. Rarely have such brothers walked the earth. But I liked Jackie, too, and the way you treated her used to kill me. While you were engaged, even while you were newly married, you'd go to parties, and some other chick would catch your eye, and you'd just leave with her. You'd leave Jackie stranded, abandoned, having to make some excuse to get a ride home."

Bobby is the puritan of the family. He married Ethel in 1950 and believed in fidelity. Talk about a closet conservative . . .

"Jackie didn't know what was going on," I say, lamely.

"Of course she did!"

"Then it was what she wanted. It excited her. At Vassar, she used to tell her girlfriends about her father's conquests. Dirty dorm talk."

"And the group stuff?" Bobby says. "George Smathers told

me all about it. How you'd pick up two secretaries and disappear with them to a hotel room. Mere adultery wasn't good enough for you. You needed them two at a time!"

"It was Jackie's fault," I say.

"Jackie's fault? How was it Jackie's fault?"

"She should have invented two of herself."

Bobby pulls at his wispy hair, like some demented prophet. He shakes his head, speechless.

"Before you throw a fit," I say, "what about Marilyn?"

Bobby drops his hands to his sides. He looks at me, both pained and defensive. "What *about* Marilyn?"

Lyndon moves closer. "This is getting interestin'," he says. "What *about* Marilyn?"

Bobby looks at him, eyes blazing. "None of your fucking business!" he blurts.

And stalks off.

"Touchy little bastard, isn't he?" Lyndon says.

Pop was a great admirer of Joe McCarthy—not the baseball manager but the tail gunner from Wisconson. By 1950 McCarthy had become the Billy the Kid of Washington, riding down Pennsylvania Avenue, shooting up the town like some one-man outlaw gang. He was shooting blanks, of course, but people didn't realize that; and they were dropping like flies. Soon after I entered the Senate, Pop asked Uncle Joe McCarthy for a favor. He asked him to appoint Bobby chief counsel of his Subcommittee on Investigations.

I was enraged, but there was nothing I could do. Bobby got the job—not as chief counsel, but as an assistant to McCarthy's new superboy, Roy Cohn.

Barukh atah adonai . . .

A frumpy, middle-aged woman is walking by, murmuring a prayer in Hebrew.

"Who's that?" Lyndon whispers.

"I don't know."

. . . elohenu melekh ha-olam . . .

"I'm gonna ask her," Lyndon whispers.

84

He approaches the stoic, sad-faced woman. A moment later he is back. He appears slightly pale, slightly shaken.

"It's Ethel," he whispers.

"It is not Ethel," I say. "I know Ethel. Besides, Ethel is still alive."

Lyndon is still whispering. "Ethel Rosenberg."

"Oh." I watch the woman's passage. I swallow a lump in my throat. "She must have heard me mention Cohn."

He's the one who prosecuted her, convicted her, got her executed.

"With a little help from J. Edgar," Lyndon says.

"She was a Russian spy!" Hoover says, materializing.

"And I'm Santa Claus," Lyndon says. "Why don't you go play with matches, okay?"

He's gone as suddenly as he appeared. I ponder, puzzled. "Why is she still here?" I say. "They were executed in fifty-three."

Lyndon does the arithmetic on his fingers. "Perhaps," he says, "there are extensions. For those whom God was not yet ready to call."

Bobby was twenty-seven when he went to work for McCarthy. He quit after six months. But the association would hound him for the rest of his life.

"Lie down with dogs . . . ," Lyndon says.

"I know. I know."

His first job was to investigate an alleged invasion of homosexuals into the State Department.

"Harrumph!" J. Edgar notes. "Harrumph!"

But Bobby couldn't stand taking orders from Cohn, who was eighteen months younger than him. They fought like little children. In July of '53, Bobby quit. And six months later, when the Democratic minority on the committee asked him to come back as *their* counsel, he agreed. That way he and Cohn could *really* get into it.

By that time, McCarthy was tired of shouting "Commie" in a crowded State Department. His wild charges had cast a chill over the entire country, from writers in Hollywood who found themselves blacklisted to housewives in the Bronx who noticed FBI men talking to their neighbors to find out if they were spies. The Red Menace that McCarthy had created—a piranha the size of King Kong—needed new red meat. To feed it, Joe McCarthy took on the U.S. Army—his fatal mistake. There were few things more sacred to vast Middle America in those days than Joe McCarthy—but one of them was the army. The televised Army-McCarthy hearings slowly turned the country against Joe—and gave the Senate the gumption to realize it had to put a stop to him.

"The time had come in the Senate for some profiles in courage," Lyndon notes.

"You're the soul of irony, aren't you?" I reply.

The trouble was this: in Massachusetts, between his Irishness and his fanatical anti-Communism, Joe McCarthy was the one man alive who could have beaten Archbishop Cushing in an election. Opposing him in public, voting to censure him, could be my own political funeral.

The tension over what to do, as the Senate began to inch toward a censure vote, made my sore back ache. And ache. And ache. To the point where I entered the hospital for difficult surgery to repair it.

There are those who say I entered the hospital to avoid having to cast a vote on McCarthy. The fact is, the doctors warned me that, because of my Addison's disease, there was a fifty-fifty chance I could die on the operating table. And I nearly did.

There are those who say that, recuperating in my hospital bed, I could have arranged by telephone for my yes vote on censure to be paired with another senator's no vote, so I would be on record on the issue. The fact is, they are right; I was the only Democrat in the Senate who did not either vote to censure or get paired off.

But let the word go forth from this time and place as to how truly sick I was. I was so sick that, to cheer me up, Jackie persuaded Grace Kelly—quite possibly the most beautiful woman in the world—to put on a nurse's uniform and come into my room to feed me. And Grace Kelly did that. And I was so sick I just lay there and didn't even recognize her; so sick that, when Nurse Grace Kelly left the room, she shook her head sadly and said to Jackie, "I must be losing it."

"That's mighty sick," the Reverend Dr. King agrees. "That's mighty, mighty sick."

It's a true story; Jackie told me about it afterward.

"Maybe you'd have responded," Lyndon says, "if she'd have sent in Grace *and* Marilyn."

My thought exactly, but I dare not utter it.

"Grace," Lyndon says. He looks sort of pensive, like he's thinking, an unusual aspect for him. "Grace. Grace!"

"What are you doing, Lyndon?"

"Quiet!" Martin says. "He's saying grace."

I wince; I say nothing. It is always difficult when the reverend tries to be funny.

"You don't suppose . . . ?" Lyndon says.

"What?"

"Grace Kelly. Hoover's blackmail tapes. Her and . . ."

"The image has a certain plausibility. There but for the . . ."

"God's gr——"

"She drove her car off a mountain. On a road she had traveled a thousand times before. It's never been explained."

"Nearer my God to thee!"

"You think?"

"The Prince of Peace . . . and a princess."

"An Irish lass. It could be, Lyndon. One must assume He has taste."

"Which casts Prince Rainier as Joseph. It fits. I never understood what she saw in him."

"Where's Bobby? I have to ask Bobby. He's the churchgoer in the family. See if he thinks it's possible. See if he approved a wiretap . . ."

I look around. I can't find Bobby. Then I see him in the distance, in the playground. I drift on over there. Bobby is playing in the sandbox—with Roy Cohn.

"Is it all right, Jack?" he asks. He's got a pail and a shovel and a bucket of water, with which to make mud pies. "Is it, Jack, can I play with Roy?"

I'm a bit disturbed. I try not to let it show; we must be sophisticated about such things; we must be scientific.

"Of course it's okay, Bobby," I say. "Just don't let him bite you, that's all."

While the nation, in 1954, was preoccupied with Army-McCarthy, with the Senate debate over censuring its chief badger, an event was taking place in my family the critical importance of which has been overlooked by virtually all of my biographers. My sister Patricia was getting married. It was not her nuptials that were important so much as her choice of a husband: Peter Lawford, the actor.

Lawford was a member of Hollywood's notorious Rat Pack, that nucleus of fast-living actors and redheaded reincarnees whose members included Dean Martin, Sammy Davis, Jr., Joey Bishop, and Shirley MacLaine. The leader of the pack was, of course, Frank Sinatra. At the vast wedding reception, while the champagne flowed like the river Charles amid islands of caviar, I maneuvered my new brother-in-law into a corner. We watched Sinatra holding court with his toadies across the room.

"Tell me about Sinatra," I said to Peter.

"He's a singer," Lawford replied.

"Yes, Peter."

"He's also an actor. Made a hell of a Maggio. Did you see *From Here to Eternity*?"

"Tell me about his *women*," I said.

Lawford looked at his shiny gold watch. "I've got a honeymoon to go on," he said. "And the Senate doesn't adjourn until—when? August? Catch me when we've got more time."

"Just one," I said. "One story." Pop approached, champagne glass filled with club soda in his hand, to listen to the conversation.

"Okay, one," Peter said. "The only thing that competes with pussy in his brain is a fascination with violence. A few months ago, at a party in Palm Springs, he got so mad at some chick that he threw her through a window. There was blood all over the place. The poor girl's arm was nearly severed. Frank just stood there, sipping his drink, while other people rushed her to the hospital."

"How come she didn't sue?" I asked. "How come it wasn't in the newspapers?"

"Frank paid her off to keep it quiet," Peter said.

As I listened, shaking my head, Pop swallowed the last of his club soda. He wiped his mouth with his sleeve, dried his right hand on his trouser leg.

"I want to meet this man," he said.

We moved across the crowded ballroom to Sinatra's enclave. Lawford made the introductions.

"I've heard a lot about you, Ambassador," Sinatra said, his blue eyes twinkling. "From some friends of mine."

"Friends?" Pop asked, uncertainly.

"*Paisans*," Sinatra said.

He turned to me. "And you're the senator. The one with the bright future. I understand Peter and Pat have bought Louis B. Mayer's house in Santa Monica. If they invite you out there, look me up. Perhaps we can do some hunting together."

Hunting? (My brain was softened from the champagne.) In Santa Monica?

Then I understood.

"I'd like that," I said, as our eyes met, and locked.

In the next few years, Frank and I did a lot of hunting together: in New York, in Las Vegas, in Palm Springs. It was all good sport, though we did not wear plaid shirts, or bright orange vests, or much of anything. J. Edgar Hoover, between framing Commies, kept track of my hunting career, as he had been doing ever since Inga. When Bobby took over the Justice

89

Department years later, he found the following note in its files:

"It is a known fact that the Sands Hotel is owned by hoodlums, and that while the senator, Sinatra, and Lawford were there, show girls from all over the town were running in and out of the senator's suite."

In all my years of hanging out with Sinatra—the Jack Pack, he sometimes called it—what struck me most was not his way with women; I had a cozy batting average myself, long before I met him. It was, more, the implications of the anecdote Peter had told me about the girl shoved through the window. Frank Sinatra appeared capable of doing anything in the world he felt like doing *without having to pay the consequences*.

From the day the first ancient amoeba crawled up onto dry land, I believed, *that* would be the ultimate goal of evolution.

As I create this tome, Sinatra rolls on; while I have paid some prices. Perhaps he was in fact a more evolved species, and I was in over my head: a poker-faced Neanderthal playing cards with a hustling *Homo sapiens*, thinking we were playing stud, not knowing that the game was draw.

It's not always possible, Peter, to see from here to eternity. How would history have been different, for instance, if Pat had married Ernest Borgnine?

"What do you wanna do tonight, Marty?"
"I don't know. What do you wanna do?"
"I dunno. You wanna getta pizza? You wanna kill Castro?"
"I dunno. Whatever. You like anchovies?"
It doesn't seem likely, somehow.

Still I think of McCarthy. Still they don't believe me.

I can see the hospital room: beside my bed, a tank of tropical fish; on the pillow beside me, a Howdy Doody doll (I don't remember why); on the wall across from me, a huge poster of Marilyn Monroe, wearing blue shorts, standing with her legs spread apart. One of the boys had hung the poster upside down, so her spread legs were in the air.

I wouldn't meet her till four years later. Something to look forward to.

The doctors were planning two separate operations on my spine; I told them to do both at once. They said it was too dangerous. I insisted. I was sick of goddamn crutches; I wanted to get it over with, or die trying.

My resistance was low, because of the Addison's disease; they dug a hole in my back the size of a softball; I developed a staph infection, and lapsed into a coma. They called a priest, who gave me the last rites. Pop, I learned later, walked into Arthur Krock's office, sat on a sofa, said, "Jack's dying," and cried. It was the first time he had cried since Joe Jr. died. I suppose I had arrived at last.

Slowly I pulled out of it. Jackie came and went, keeping a wary eye on the nurses. Grace Kelly came and went, unnoticed. On December 2, the vote on McCarthy took place in the Senate. I made no effort to lift the phone, to do anything. How could I vote to censure him for stuff he had done while my brother was on his staff?

So they said I was afraid of McCarthy.

Fuck McCarthy. It was Pop I was still afraid of.

I went to Palm Beach to recuperate. In February there was another operation, to remove a steel plate they had put in, and to graft some loose bones. Then it was back to Pop's villa, to lie in the sun, to heal.

And to think about what I hadn't done.

I became obsessed with a dreamlike counterbalance to my own inaction: with senators through history who had risked their careers by exhibiting political bravery. I had my new staff aide, Ted Sorensen, do some research. And I worked on a draft of a book.

When it was published, *Profiles in Courage* leaped onto the best-seller lists. The profits we poured back into advertising, which sold even more copies. It helped make me a national celebrity, especially when it won the Pulitzer. I appeared on

Ed Murrow's "Person to Person" TV show. Leading more than one wag to mutter: "The senator from Massachusetts ought to show less profile and more courage."

The wags, of course, did not have a hole the size of a softball in their backs.

By spring I was ready to return to the Senate. I was a different person, I think, in two important ways. Most obviously, I was healthier. I didn't need crutches. A combination of injections and exercises greatly strengthened my back. Having survived the operations, I was no longer quite so obsessed with dying.

Which fed an internal change. Once you have shared your hospital gruel with the Angel of Death, you are much more likely to do whatever you want to do—to do whatever you believe needs to be done—and *risk* the consequences.

"Point of Order, Mr. Chairman!"

"What, Lyndon?"

"I would like to clarify this question of consequences, which I suspect goes to the heart of your story. You said before that Frank Sinatra had reached what may be the highest form of human evolution . . ."

". . . however wistful . . ."

". . . however wistful, because he was capable of doing anything in the world he felt like doing, without having to pay the consequences. Now you say that your brush with death led you to *risk* the consequences. Doesn't that actually make you braver than Sinatra?"

"With all due humility, Lyndon, I suspect it does."

"Then what would you call Sinatra's way?"

"You tell me, Lyndon. What would you call it?"

"I would call his way obscene."

I shrug. I raise my eyebrows.

I offer no rebuttal.

A vignette of America, 1954. It's about one of those Jewish ladies in the Bronx. She was fifty-one years old, with a husband

and two growing sons. Her husband sold work clothes, sweat-shirts, dungarees. The woman, to help put her boys through school, worked as a bookkeeper for a stationery store.

"What's all this about Jewish ladies?" Lyndon asks. "In the Bronx? You have some kind of a hang-up? Some retrofamilial guilt about your father's prejudice?"

"It's a symbol, Lyndon, okay? A literary symbol. I don't suppose they have those in Texas. The Jewish ladies in the Bronx stand for all the ordinary, hardworking, common people of America. The ones who are not Frank Sinatra, and never will be. They could be farmers in Kansas. Or shopkeepers in Utah. Symbolically. But this happens to be a true story about a real Jewish lady in the Bronx. Okay?"

"Okay."

The woman was born in 1902, in London, while her parents were emigrating from Russia to America.

"The Alamo."

"What?"

"We have plenty of symbols in Texas."

"I said literary symbols. But never mind."

"Larry McMurtry. The Book Depository."

I hold my tongue. I try to keep my temper.

"Tell me the story," Lyndon says.

As I said, she was born in London while her parents were in transit. They came to America when she was six months old, and settled in New York. Her mother was a seamstress; her father was an inventor, who was not too good with society's little details, such as applying for U.S. citizenship for an infant. A bunch more children were born, native-born citizens, and Anna, the eldest, always assumed she was an American citizen, just like all the others. When she was twenty-eight years old she got married, and went to Europe on her honeymoon. When she returned home she routinely checked a box on some government form stating that she was a U.S. citizen. That was in 1930.

"What does this have to do with nineteen fifty-four?"

One day in 1954, while Joe McCarthy was leering over

America, two FBI men knocked on Anna's door as she was preparing dinner for her family. They served some official-looking papers on her. They told her that she was an illegal alien, that she had falsified a document when she entered the country in 1930, and that she must report to Ellis Island to face deportation proceedings.

"That's absurd," Lyndon says.

But it happened. They told Anna she was a Russian, and might be a Russian spy. She said she'd been born in London. When the FBI checked, it turned out that hospital records in London had been destroyed during the wartime German bombing. This proved to the FBI that she was lying, that she was a Russian after all.

"So what happened?"

They investigated her for months. The most leftist thing they could find out about her was that, according to her neighbors, she thought Adlai Stevenson's campaign speeches in 1952 were brilliant and witty.

"What did you say her name was?" Adlai asks.

They were still trying to deport this lady, who had a son in college and a son in high school, when McCarthy fell from grace, and drowned in a sea of booze. Then the authorities compromised. They agreed to let her go to Canada overnight. When she reentered the United States the next day, she checked the box that said she was not a citizen. And she lived the rest of her life without being an American citizen, registering every January as an alien, as required by law.

"She could have become a naturalized citizen," Lyndon says, "after seven years."

"That's correct," I tell him. "Unfortunately, she died of cancer after six."

We sat in silence for a time.

"The point of the story," I say, finally, "is that that kind of crap, that insidious intrusion into the lives of the most humble, honest people, was going on all across America in the fifties. When I decided to seek the vice presidency in nineteen fifty-six, and the presidency in nineteen sixty, that story should have figured in my goals: to put an end to all that un-American crap. But that's not why I was running at all. I was running out of pure ambition. I was running because that's what Kennedys were for: to run-run-run. To win-win-win. I was running for Pop, out of fear, and for Joe Jr., out of spite, and for old Patrick Kennedy, who came here from Ireland and died of the cholera on the twenty-second of November, to justify his transatlantic passage. Those are not the best reasons to run for president, and after twenty-five years, I am beginning to feel ashamed."

"You ran out of a hunger for power," Lyndon says. "That's why anybody runs."

"Ahem," Adlai says, clearing his throat.

We ignore him.

"Ahem, ahem," Adlai repeats.

We say nothing; we let him think he was different.

It's harmless.

"McCarthy wasn't all that bad," Bobby says.

He's come back from the sandbox, sand on his trousers, pail and shovel in his hand. "He was a lot more sensitive than you think."

Perhaps I shouldn't have let him play with Roy.

I remember a big-deal dinner in 1955. Bobby was being honored by the Chamber of Commerce as one of the Ten Outstanding Men of the Year. Ed Murrow had just done his famous exposé on McCarthy. When Murrow approached the lectern as a guest speaker, Bobby stalked out of his own goddamn dinner in protest.

"I liked Joe," Bobby says. "He wanted desperately to be liked. He was a complicated guy, who just sometimes got a little heavy-handed."

"You remember, Bobby," I say, "that lovely dinner we had one evening with Sharon Tate and Roman Polanski?"

"So?"

"Charles Manson was complicated, too. Not to mention heavy-handed."

"Jimmy Hoffa, too," Lyndon says.

A charge of electricity flashes through my brain. I'm careful not to flinch. Only Bobby, I think, notices.

His continuing defense of McCarthy still rankles me. I have quoted to him often from Ecclesiastes: "There is a time to weep and a time to laugh; a time to mourn and a time to dance; a time to fish and a time to cut bait." But Bobby, the most unassimilated Irishman of all of us Kennedys, the most deeply passionate of us all, always had the most trouble cutting bait.

"Ask Marilyn about Bobby," Lyndon says.

I don't know how he means that; if he is being cruel, or compassionate. In Lyndon's character, the two are entwined, like snakes.

Ask Marilyn, he says. Marilyn died—Marilyn was slain—a year before me. Her quarter century gone, she vanished from this bubbly place a year ago, and the place is harsher for it: as when the sun from distant windswept plains departs.

"I like it," the reverend says. "I like it."

Ask Marilyn! Would that I could. But where is Marilyn now? In the blonde infant crawling on the rug, naked (again) before the photographer? In the black cat howling at midnight for some tom, straddling metal garbage cans in rain-demented shadows of the moon? Perhaps she's in that flower there, blossoming ever so lovely near that rock. Or perhaps—it's just as likely—she's the rock.

These things they do not tell us, even here. These things are stamped FOR HIS EYES ONLY.

A book.

Perhaps sweet Marilyn is a book. She would have liked that, I think. A book. A wise and witty, kind, insightful book.

Perhaps you hold her in your hands, even now.

"The man is shameless," Adlai says.

Says Lyndon: "You don't know the half of it."

□ □ □

When the French garrison at Dien Bien Phu came under heavy siege, when there was talk of sending American troops to rescue the French, I made a major address on the subject in the Senate. Quoth I: "To pour money, matériel, and men into the jungles of Indochina without at least a remote prospect of victory would be dangerously futile and self-destructive. . . . I am frankly of the belief that no amount of American military assistance in Indochina can conquer an enemy that is everywhere and at the same time nowhere."

"What do you call that?" Lyndon asks.

"What do you mean, 'What do I call that?' I call it insight. Foresight: twenty-twenty foresight. What do you call it?"

"I call it half a quote," Lyndon says.

I groan.

"You went on to say that what was needed to fight Communist aggression was a native army capable of fighting their native army."

The bastard's got the memory of a Republican.

"I was the majority leader," Lyndon says. "It went with the territory. I noted quite clearly that you called it 'Communist aggression,' not the 'nationalism' you and Bobby and some consular official had discussed in Saigon."

"In America," I tell him, "nationalism is a virtue only for Americans."

"Precisely, Jack. Precisely. So stop calling it Lyndon's War. Why not start educating people, in this sweet little Marilyn of a book?"

After the '64 election I was going to do it. I was going to bring home the boys from Vietnam. I was going to risk being the most unpopular president in history, but I was going to do it! I was going to end that stupid little war!

"You and what army?" Lyndon says.

Instinctively we both start to turn. Instinctively we check ourselves.

There is, behind us, in the middle distance, a large and

leaden cloud. They lie sprawled upon it in positions of repose that somehow still seem grotesque: the cloud of the recent slaughtered. They are military and civilian, white, yellow, black; they are young and old, men and women, boys and girls. Ours and theirs. Some are in the prime of manly strength, others in the cuddles of infancy. There is no north on the cloud, no south; they sprawl wherever there is room. Intermingled.

Each night, at sunset, it is the first cloud in the sky to run red.

We have been told, Lyndon and I, that they are whole again, that their spirits are as restful as anyone's. Still, we try never to turn, Lyndon and I; we try never to look at them.

It is this, I suspect, that has made us friends.

One evening not long ago they sent an emissary to visit us. She was a dark-haired Vietnamese girl, from the South, I believe. She looked familiar, somehow, and when she said her name was Kim, I knew: I had seen a famous photograph of this Kim, a lovely teenager then, standing naked on a dirt road, somewhere beneath the strafing planes, screaming. A universal, timeless plea for peace.

She was as lovely as ever on her visit, wearing now a diaphanous white gown. She had come, she said, as a representative of all of them. They wanted us to know, she said, that we were forgiven. They wanted us to know that we were welcome: they would like us to visit their cloud.

She had dark eyes and rare beauty and young wisdom. We thanked her for her tenderness. We told her we were grateful for her visit. We told her we were moved by her request.

We watched as she retreated on a zephyr, retreated to the cloud of lead.

We have not yet found the nerve, Lyndon and I, to make our visit.

In 1956, the United States would not be holding an election. It would be holding a referendum on Grandpa. The question before the voters would be, Should kindly old Grandpa be kicked out of the house, made to go sleep in the barn alongside the cows and the hogs, eat what slop the dogs didn't devour?

Chosen to uphold the Democratic affirmative, chosen to run against Ike, would be, again, the man from Illinois.

Sadly with Adlai.

He was, legend has it, perhaps the most intellectual candidate to run for president in this century, and perhaps since Thomas Jefferson. It is my contention that, by agreeing to run again that year, he called into question his very ability to govern.

"I was the head of the party!" Adlai remonstrates, spunkily. "The *titular* head, they used to call it in those days. What would you have had me do? *Someone* had to run against Ike. Or would you have preferred a simple coronation?"

It would have saved a lot of everybody's money.

"Besides, it gave me a platform from which to speak. There were so many things that needed to be said. McCarthy had lost his power, but his spirit still stalked the land. The Russians were testing hydrogen bombs as frequently as we: in the air, on the ground, beneath the ground. We were polluting the very air we breathe with radiation; we were playing Russian roulette with the planet. I called for an end to the testing of nuclear weapons—and got sent to the woodshed for it. But someone had to say those things. Apparently I was ahead of my time."

"A politician has no greater vice," Lyndon says, "than being ahead of his time."

"You don't really believe that, Lyndon," Adlai says.

"I do, sir, I do. What's vision in a statesman is blindness in a pol."

"Nicely turned, Lyndon," Adlai says. "It's cow dung, of course, but nicely turned."

I ponder both views; I seek a synthesis: when its politicians and its statesmen are one is when America as a civilization will truly flourish at last.

That was the image I tried to create for myself.

I nearly succeeded, artifice though it was.

"As I recall," Adlai says, a bit archly, "after you endorsed me that spring, you were hell-bent yourself to be the second half of the ticket. Against good old Grandpa Ike."

"It would have been me against Tricky Dick for veep—in the public perception at least."

I thought, then, that it would be better to make the race and lose than to remain on the sidelines. I'd still be in a strong position for 1960, when Adlai would be nobody's darling. I sent Sorensen around the country, testing the waters for a Catholic veep. He came back with the news that it might really strengthen the ticket, reverse the working-class war-hero tide that had flowed toward Ike in '52. We made this known to the Gladly with Adlai crowd. My father cabled me from a vacation on the Riviera with one of his typical votes of confidence in my abilities: "If you are chosen, it will be because you are a Catholic and not because you are big enough to do the job."

Thanks again, Dad.

My first step was to pick a fight on my own turf. The Massachusetts delegation was controlled by party hacks who hated Stevenson. I began a fight to win control of the delegation. Without delivering my own state, I'd have less clout than a eunuch in a harem.

"Nicely turned, Jack," Lyndon echoes.

It was a brutal, Boston Irish gutter brawl, the kind I'd always avoided, and which my father, once again, counseled against. (Pop wasn't Madly for Adlai himself.) There was political kicking, gouging, knife-stabbing, arm-twisting, and just about every other known tactic short of gang rape, which was omitted only because nobody thought of it. When the last drop of internecine blood finally flowed into the Charles, I had won; I had myself a delegation I could deliver.

Personally, internally, it was a victory of another sort, a kind of Irish bar mitzvah. Without my dad's approval, I had become a man.

Perhaps I had waylaid Joe Jr. as well.

□ □ □

In the incoming tide of history there has always been a confluence of great men and great ideas. In my case the idea was television. (It wasn't my idea, but why quibble?)

"Who was the great man?" Lyndon interjects.

The simple fact is, I was telegenic: the most telegenic politician in the country, the critic for *The New York Times* wrote. With each new appearance—on Murrow, "Meet the Press," whatever—my image began to impress itself upon the retina of the nation: handsome, strong, witty, idealistic, self-deprecating. Television by 1956 had wired America, and that myriad of electronic microdots, all by themselves, created a minor boomlet: Kennedy as a possible choice for vice president.

In return for my early endorsement, Adlai picked me to narrate a film on the history of the party that would be shown at the opening of the convention. The date was Monday, August 13. That afternoon I was still primarily the senator from Massachusetts. By the time the film ended that night, to the thundering applause of 11,000 cheering delegates, I was the third legitimate contender for the vice presidential spot, along with Estes Kefauver—who had contended with Adlai for the nomination itself—and Hubert Humphrey, darling of the civil-rights wing of the party. Estes was known as a crime fighter, Hubert as a libertarian; but after that night I was bigger than both of them. After that night I was a movie star.

"You also weren't burdened with a name like Estes," Lyndon says. "Or Hubert. Or Adlai. America is too *macho* to ever elect an Estes, or a Hubert, or an Adlai."

"You really think so, Chuck?"

I was undecided about seeking the second spot; Pop was dead against it. When Adlai asked me to make the nominating speech for him, I knew it was a consolation prize; I knew I was out as veep. The Stevenson people gave me a speech to read; it was Mother Goose stuff. I made Sorensen stay up all night to write a new one, and when I delivered it before the convention, it was a humdinger.

101

We still assumed that Adlai's choice would be Kefauver. Eleanor Roosevelt, America's second greatest president, had given me the kiss of death the day before when she proclaimed: "McCarthyism was a question on which public officials must stand up and be counted." She had never, she said, heard me express my opinions on that subject.

"I wanted to kill the broad," Bobby says.

Then, to the consternation of the pros, and the delight of the little people, Adlai announced that he was not going to choose his runing mate; he was going to let the delegates decide.

"It was the goddamn stupidest move a politician could make," Lyndon says.

"I failed to see then," Adlai asserts, "and, frankly, I fail to see now, why acting like America is really a democracy is so all-fired stupid."

"Because it goddamn ain't!" Lyndon says. "It's a fucking barroom brawl, and hell take the hindmost."

"Whatever happened to the Great Society?" I ask Lyndon.

"Whatever happened to the New Frontier?" he asks me.

"It was shot down in the prime of life, and you know it!" Bobby shouts.

"Not by Daniel Boone it wasn't," Lyndon replies, calmly.

Anyway, Adlai's action—or inaction—began a twelve-hour free-for-all in search of delegates. The big question was, Should I go for it? Immediately I decided to go. It was heady stuff, this talk. I asked Bobby to phone Pop on the Riviera and inform him we were going for it. As he hung up the phone, Bobby said, "Whew, is he mad!"

Suddenly I was drunk: drunk on my own strength, my own independence, my own power. At thirty-nine the senator from Massachusetts had become a teenage rebel, a rebel with a cause.

The battle for delegates was fierce. On the first ballot, Kefauver led with 483½ votes. But the big story was that I came in second with a strong 304. On the second ballot, New York delivered its huge delegation to me. And then, to the surprise of most of the hall, Lyndon Johnson stood up and announced: "Texas proudly casts its vote for the fighting sailor who wears the scars of battle."

"I said something as cornball as that?" Lyndon asks.

"It was your finest hour," Bobby says.

The stampede to me was on. At the end of the second ballot, Kefauver had 551½ votes and I had vaulted past him with 618—only 33½ votes short of victory. The hour grew late; across the country 40 million TV viewers were glued to their sets, watching. But on the third ballot, when the West and the Midwest stood firm for Kevauver, some of the southerners started switching to him. I had peaked, and it was over. Estes would be the nominee.

I headed for the amphitheater. I mounted lightly to the rostrum. I grinned the grin that everyone called "infectious."

"Like measles," Lyndon says.

And, exuding grace and charm, I moved that the Kefauver nomination be made unanimous.

Then I was gone, leaving the convention—and the nation—cheering for Kennedy.

"It was coitus interruptus," Bobby says.

"Bobby!"

Bobby blushes, in that infectious way of his.

What I had succeeded in doing, of course, by following my own instincts, was both have my cake and eat it.

"Like two secretaries at a time," Lyndon says.

I achieved all that national exposure, made millions of new fans across the country—and still could not be held responsible when Adlai and Estes drowned in the Eisenhower Sea. It was a public relations triumph—achieved squarely against the advice of Pop. That was the sweetest taste of all.

(Sorensen's cadences are marching through my brain. A moment ago, he is saying, you had Eisenhower as a grandpa; now you have him as a sea. You just can't do things like that. To which I can only reply: You win your Pulitzer, Nebraska Ted, and I'll win mine.) (Have they ever awarded one posthumously?)

During the first year of our marriage, Jackie suffered a miscarriage. During that convention summer of '56, she was pregnant again. She endured the excitement of Chicago; then she had to go home and rest. She wanted me to come home with her. Instead I flew off to the Riviera, to soak up some warmth: not so much from the sun as from my father's new respect.

After days of political talk, Teddy and George Smathers and I rented a yacht. We went sailing off the cost of Elba, site of Napoleon's exile. I was real tight after the exhausting convention. I needed some R and R. At each place we docked, a bunch of girls would come on board; we'd drop them off at the next port, and put in a fresh supply. In due course I was completely relaxed again.

At home, Jackie began to hemorrhage. She was rushed to the hospital. Our baby was removed by cesarean section.

It was dead.

They tried to reach me with the news on the Riviera. I was out of touch, at sea.

Finally, in port, I got the news.

Three days later I rushed home.

Our marriage was on the rocks by then. Jackie hadn't fully realized what she was getting into. By then she knew what I was getting into—what I couldn't seem to keep out of. It bordered, I think, on a neurosis: pussymania.

My political career, Pop insisted, could founder and sink on a divorce. He and Jackie had some private talks. Soon after, she was her old self again.

On Thanksgiving, the whole clan gathered at Hyannis Port for a family feast. After dinner, Pop and I went into the study alone to discuss the future.

Pop wanted me to run in 1960—not for vice president, as the press was already speculating, but for the top spot: for president. I played the devil's advocate; I listed all the negatives: I was still young; I was Catholic; I had little support from the party leaders. To all of these, Pop had a positive answer. Which, of course, is precisely what I wanted. When he was through, I stood up.

"Well, Dad," I said. "I guess there's only one question left. When do we start?"

Dad stood and came close. He threw his arms around me. He hugged me tight.

At that moment, I believe, we buried Joe Jr. at last. And set my own clear course.

There is a moment of quiet remembrance. Then Lyndon speaks, softly.

"It was a collision course."

"With you?" I ask.

"With every son of a bitch in America."

As we stepped off the plane, the warmth of Texas in late November was a surprise. We'd been given a chillier forecast. I was concerned, as we moved down the aluminum stairs, that Jackie might be too warm in the clothes she'd brought.

Lyndon and Lady Bird were waiting for us at the bottom of the stairs, as were Governor and Mrs. Connally. We shook hands and climbed into the waiting limousines. Senator Ralph Yarborough, the Texas liberal who'd flown down with us, refused to ride in the same car with Lyndon: part of the petty squabbling going on down there.

The motorcade rolled across the airport tarmac and out onto a highway. We were going first to Brooks Air Force Base, where I was to speak at the dedication of a new air force school of aerospace medicine. The crowds lining the streets between the airport and the base were dense, and cheering wildly— about 125,000 people, the cops would estimate. Kids waved American flags, a nun broke through the police lines to touch me, a sign urged Jackie to come water-ski in Texas. When we reached the medical center, twenty thousand people were trying to squeeze their way into nine thousand seats.

I talked about the space program, told them how committed to it we were. It symbolized, for me, the new frontiers we hoped to reach in every aspect of American life: in defending democracy around the world, in fighting poverty at home, in extending full civil rights to every American. (I didn't mention those other things in the speech, of course; this was Texas, after all.)

The schedule allotted only two hours for San Antonio, but I was curious. After the speech I went to a part of the medical center containing an oxygen chamber that simulated the atmospheric pressure at 30,000 feet. Using a headset phone, I spoke to four young airmen inside the tank. Then I asked the scientist in charge if this work in space medicine might one day lead to better oxygen chambers for premature babies.

The scientist, I think, knew why I was asking. My infant son Patrick had died only a few months before. The second child we'd lost.

There were more cheering crowds as the motorcade wound back toward the San Antonio airport. We'd gotten plenty of warnings not to go to Texas, but as far as I knew the state had not yet seceded from the union. It would still have a bunch of delegates in the next election, and judging from the San Antonio crowds, we would do just fine.

"With me on the ticket again," Lyndon says.

"With you on the ticket again," I concur.

He's still insecure about that, after all these years.

The space program had brought a ton of jobs to Texas. But Lyndon understood its symbolic value as well. As John Glenn had blasted off into space the year before, becoming the first American to orbit the earth, Lyndon had beamed and smiled, and then muttered: "Too bad he isn't a Negro."

"Would of been a helluva thing," Lyndon says.

"Darn right," I agree.

As long as the rocket didn't blow up.

□ □ □

"How did you like my speech?" I said to Raymond as we settled back into the plane. I'd found through the years he was often a good barometer of the common man. Most anybody could shine my shoes; not many would be honest with me.

"I'm sure it was a fine speech," Raymond said.

"What do you mean, you're sure?"

"Tell you the truth, Mr. President, I didn't hear your speech."

"You didn't? That's what you call loyalty?"

"I got my sister living here in San Antone. Haven't seen her for a year. We arranged to have lunch in the airport coffee shop. That's what I call loyalty."

"I didn't know you had a sister down here, Raymond."

"Lots of things white folks don't know about black folks," Raymond said.

There was an edge to Raymond's voice that was unusual. It went beyond our constant bantering, our constant one-upmanship. I could sense that something was wrong.

"Did everything go all right? Is your sister well?"

"Just fine," Raymond said. He was tight-lipped, unsmiling.

"Out with it," I said. "You look dyspeptic. Been reading too much Buckley, or what?"

Raymond looked out the small window. Up front, the hatches of Air Force One were being secured. We'd be taking off in a minute, bound for Houston.

"You won't listen anyway," he said, looking at the seat in front of him. "So what's the point?"

"I certainly can't listen if you don't tell me what you're talking about. Even us Kennedys aren't clairvoyant."

Except maybe Rosemary, I think now, except maybe Rosemary.

Raymond looked at me with a strange and distant look, as if I had read his mind.

"My sister is," he said. His tone was both soft and aggressive.

"Your sister is what?"

"Clairvoyant." His tone was beseeching now. "She reads palms. She reads cards. She makes her living that way. She's got a storefront shop. People bring money, chickens, sugar. Whatever they can spare. She tells the future for them."

I was about to make fun of him, for believing in that kind of crap. The first certainty you learn in the White House is that no one can predict the future.

But he was my friend; I didn't want to hurt his feelings. Or insult his sister.

"What about it?" I asked. "She tell you about your pay cut coming?"

Raymond didn't smile. His eyes were roaming over my face, as if he'd never seen it before.

"She brought the tarot with her. I had her read my cards."

"And she saw something bad for you?"

Raymond said nothing for a moment. Then he lowered his eyes and shook his head.

"What, then?" I asked.

Raymond's eyes seemed almost moist as he looked at me again. "Something bad for a friend of mine," he said. "Something bad for the Knight of Wands. The tarot said my friend the Knight of Wands will die. Tomorrow."

"They didn't teach tarot at Harvard," I said. "Who is the Knight of Wands?"

Knowing full well, of course, what he meant.

"This is what my sister said. The Knight of Wands is shown mounted on a horse, meaning he is on a journey. He is a fairhaired, blue-eyed young man. He is capable of creating conflict, or rivalry. The Death card came up above him. Death is a mysterious horseman who rides slowly across a field. Behind him, the sun shines between two towers. The Knight of Wands is passing by two mounds, or pyramids. Like the towers on the card of Death. That is what my sister said."

"And you think that it's me?" I said. "Maybe it's some other Knight of Wands."

"It's like the magazines always say: Camelot."

"There is no Camelot, Raymond. It's all a fairy tale. A fairy tale that wins us votes."

"My sister—Massie is her name—Massie says you shouldn't go to Dallas." He paused. He spoke softer. "Massie said I should beg you not to go to Dallas."

I projected an air of thoughtfulness. There is a place deep within us, even in the most enlightened of us, that responds to superstition.

"If the cards are correct," I said, "and I don't go to Dallas, won't it happen wherever I go? Or is there a tarot card just for Dallas?"

"I don't know," Raymond said, shaking his head again. "I just know what Massie said. Massie said you shouldn't go to Dallas."

The captain switched on the great jet engines. Air Force One began to vibrate. The speeches had been planned, the luncheons, the dinners. The motorcade route had been announced. Hundreds of thousands of voters would be waiting. We had heard this sort of thing before. Of course we would go to Dallas.

"It's too late to change our plans," I said to Raymond, squeezing the top of his hand. "But I want you to do me a favor. The next time you talk to Massie, tell her I said thank you for her concern." I began to turn away. Then I turned back. "Better yet," I said, "I'll call her and thank her myself. As soon as we get back to Washington."

Raymond nodded and turned away. When he spoke it was as if to the air. "I told you he wouldn't listen," I heard him say.

"Perhaps there should be," Adlai says.
"Perhaps there should be what?"
"A tarot card. Just for Dallas."
Perhaps.

What follows is straight history. But if this were a movie, there would be starting in the background, so low as to be almost

110

unhearable, the faint strains of eerie music: violins, most likely, capable of erupting suddenly into wild flight, or joining with heavy, hidden pianos in an unexpected thunderous crescendo.

Note also the little details so beloved in film noir: the middle name of the central character, for instance. James R. Hoffa. R for Riddle.

Why did the Teamster cross the road?

To plunder the pension fund.

By the start of 1957, as I've said, my own course had been set: a four-year marathon run for the presidency. Bobby had no such course, no such star to guide him. He was still the Democratic counsel of the Investigations Subcommittee, but he needed an issue into which he could really sink his teeth. He found that issue in the outrageous corruption of the Teamsters Union. He sank his teeth into the fleshy butt of Jimmy Hoffa. For the next eleven years they would go through life that way: the corrupt union official alternately running and turning to fight, Bobby hanging onto his bloody butt like a bulldog with rabies.

Bobby heard about the corruption from some newspapermen who were conducting investigations of their own. He went to the West Coast to look into it. One case that horrified him had to do with a rival union organizer whom the Teamsters had warned to stay out of the San Diego area. When the man disobeyed, he was beaten insensible. He awoke with terrible cramps in his abdomen, and was rushed to a hospital. Doctors discovered that a cucumber had been forced into the man's rectum. As he lay there, recovering, he received a message: if he opposed the Teamsters again, the next time it would be a watermelon.

Along with such tales from the street, there were others of corruption at the top: of the union's leaders betraying their own membership by stealing the funds of the rank-and-file workers. Bobby returned to Washington determined to clean the rot out of the Teamsters.

The first person Bobby nailed was the union's president, Dave Beck. It was like taking candy from a baby. Unfortunately, the baby was followed as union head by the bathwater: Jimmy Hoffa. As vice president, it was Hoffa who had been responsible for most of the dirty work. He had made his own pact years before with organized crime in Detroit: the mob would help Hoffa climb to the top of the union; in return, the mob would have access to the Teamster pension funds, which were the largest of any union in the country.

The first face-to-face meeting between Bobby and Hoffa took place the night of February 19, 1957. It was at the home of a Teamster attorney, Eddie Cheyfitz. They were like two boxers sizing each other up before a fight; and it was a strange match: Hoffa squat and strong and talking tough, Bobby short and wiry, but talking just as tough.

"I do to others what they do to me, only worse," Hoffa said, for openers.

(Music intensifies.)

"Maybe I should have worn my bulletproof vest," Bobby replied.

(Sudden crescendo, with piano bass.)

Neither one seemed intimidated.

"You're a damn spoiled jerk," Hoffa said. "You and your brother both. Rich kids born with a silver spoon, who never had to do an honest day's work in your life."

"You're pure evil," Bobby replied. "Part of a wicked conspiracy, using force or the threat of force for extortion."

"Offends your sensibilities, does it, little Bobby? How come when you were a kid you dressed up as a girl? I guess you were a homo, is why."

"I've got a wife and kids," Bobby retorted. "You've got a mistress who sleeps with the mob."

After that, the level of discourse deteriorated.

"I know what I want, and I'll do anything that's necessary to get it," Hoffa proclaimed. "That's the only way for a real man to live."

"You remind me of something rank and slimy," Bobby said.

"I remind you of your father," Hoffa replied.

The antagonists sat down for tea and crumpets, then wended their ways separately into the night.

The judges ruled this first confrontation a draw.

The next morning, Bobby was awakened by a telephone call from Hoffa. "You're not going to make your brother president," the union boss said, "over my dead body."

"I can damn well try," Bobby said.

He hung up feeling pleased with himself.

As a humanitarian gesture, President Eisenhower that year permitted the immigration into the United States of two thousand Palestinian families living in refugee camps. One of the families who entered the country had the surname of Sirhan.

The Sirhans took a boat from Beirut to Naples. From there they took a ship to New York. From there they took a train across the country to Los Angeles, where their sponsors lived; and they settled in Pasadena.

The boy, Sirhan B. Sirhan, who had been four years old when his brother was killed in the war with the Israelis, was now thirteen.

MOMO: Why did Sirhan cross the sea?

HOFFA: To kill himself a Kennedy!

I can't hear their voices as they sit down there in the flames, but sometimes, as just now, I can read their lips.

"Which one is Hoffa?" Dr. King asks.

"The small, squat one between Momo and the ambassador," Lyndon says. "The one shaped like an automobile compactor."

"If he's down there among the flames," the reverend says, "I guess he's really dead. Personally, I kind of liked the mysterious disappearance; like, maybe he was really alive, in Argentina."

"Living under an assumed name," Bobby says. "Adolf Hitler."

What can I tell you; my brother never *liked* the man.

113

□ □ □

My first big step toward the presidency was in losing the vice presidential nomination to Kefauver in '56. Had I been on the ticket, my national career would have been over, and no Catholic would have been nominated for another thirty years.

My second big step toward the presidency was in defeating Kefauver, early in '56, for a vacant seat on the Senate Foreign Relations Committee.

I wanted Foreign Relations badly—

"Sophia Loren?" Lyndon asks. "Gina Lollobrigida?"

Jeanne Moreau would have been more to my taste, I think; but I don't say it. I wanted a seat on Foreign Relations so I could speak out on foreign affairs—

"Brigitte Bardot?" Lyndon asks. "Joan Collins?"

—and sound serious and presidential.

I got the seat with the support of Lyndon.

"You weren't nearly as qualified as Kefauver," Lyndon says. "But your daddy phoned me up. Said how forever in my debt he'd be if I could see my way clear to giving you the seat. I could almost hear the tinkle of your daddy's gold clear across the telephone lines. I figured, what the hell . . ."

"Are you finished, Lyndon?"

"Yes, Jack."

"Thanks, Lyndon, for setting the record straight."

"Any time, Jack. Any time."

Foreign Relations gave me the prestigious platform I needed. I gave a ringing speech attacking the Eisenhower administration for its support of the French war in Algeria. I argued for Algerian independence. "Colonies are like fruit," me and Sorensen said, "which cling to the tree only till they ripen."

The speech won attention nationwide.

Then came the "missile gap." Others were saying how the Soviets had gotten ahead of us in defense and technology, as dramatized by *Sputnik*. At first I hit upon missile gap speeches as a way to garner some defense contracts for Massachusetts.

114

But it soon became clear that the phrase itself touched a nerve in the American psyche.

"Made it sound like America had been castrated," Lyndon says. "Made us feel like we wuz a bunch of eunuchs, and by God, we was gonna get our peckers back."

Lyndon surprises with his psychological insight sometimes. In certain limited areas.

I was also on the McClellan Committee, where Bobby was going after the Teamsters. Pop was against this, saying it would turn organized labor against us in the '60 election. He was wrong again. The televised hearings—Bobby the tousled kid going up against the fat-cat mob-controlled union leaders—won Bobby his own following, both good and bad. The good—those gutsy Kennedys, fighting corruption everywhere they found it—rubbed off on me as well; the bad—charges that Bobby was a ruthless interrogator—stuck to him alone, and clearly did not apply to Smilin' Jack.

The result was a barrage of national magazine articles about the fighting Kennedys unequaled since the fighting Sullivans of World War II. You name the magazine, they wrote us up, complete with pictures. Without doubt the most memorable, the most prescient, was the following paragraph. It appeared in September 1957, in the *Saturday Evening Post*, in an article by Harold Martin called "The Amazing Kennedys":

"Fervent admirers of the Kennedys," the article said, "profess to see in their national prominence the flowering of another great political family, such as the Adamses, the Lodges and the La Follettes. They confidently look forward to the day when Jack will be in the White House, Bobby will serve in the Cabinet as Attorney General, and Teddy will be the Senator from Massachusetts."

How's that for twenty-twenty foresight?

"Amazing," Raymond says. "The fellow's sister must have had a tarot deck."

"Must have," I agree.

And turn.

And stare.

As if I have seen a ghost.

"Raymond! What the hell are you doing here?"

"Just arrived, Mr. President. Just arrived."

"But . . . why? How?"

"A simple heart attack. In the night. In my sleep. I hardly felt a thing."

"But . . ."

"I was seventy-one. I guess Someone thought it was time."

"That's impossible, Raymond. You don't look anywhere near seventy-one."

"Neither do you, Mr. President."

We stand and look at each other. Then we embrace, as we used to do. I'm not sure what to say.

"Under the circumstances," I stammer, finally, "I'm very glad you're here."

"Under the circumstances," Raymond replied, "you ain't nearly as glad I'm here as me."

My gaze still is tinted with disbelief.

Raymond.

Raymond gone.

Sometimes that's hard to accept even here.

Birth and death. God's bookends. So it seems, on earth. Or is mortal existence, more likely, an isthmus of land between two vast, inchoate, deep eternal seas?

There is no answer given here; not, at least, during this first quarter century of memory. Perhaps, in the next phase, there is an answer. Or perhaps, in the next phase, we forget the question: and that *becomes* the answer.

Jackie and I had a child at last. She was born in New York in November of '57. We named her Caroline. In a family that bred like rabbits—see Pop, see Bobby—it should have been no major event. But for us it was exhilarating. After a miscarriage, and then a stillbirth, one begins to question the prices life will charge.

Politically it would be a blessing as well: the family man.

But, looking at that tiny face peering from the blanket, I gave no thought to politics.

I, Jack Kennedy, do solemnly swear.

(Not that we wouldn't give new meaning, later on, to the photo opportunity.)

Bobby and his committee—for so it had come to seem—went after Jimmy Hoffa with two years of on-and-off public hearings. One day during this time, a fellow named Joey Gallo appeared in Bobby's office. He was a New York mobster, the head of an enforcer union. He was dressed, appropriately, in a black shirt, black pants, and a black coat. The first thing he did was kneel down and feel the rug. "It would be nice for a crap game," he said.

(Strains of "Guys and Dolls" in the background. The theme song for Nathan Detroit.)

(Starring Frank Sinatra.)

Someone with unrelated business entered the office. Joey Gallo leaped up, grabbed the man, frisked him thoroughly. Then he explained to Bobby's startled staff: "No one with a gun on him is going to see Mr. Kennedy. If Kennedy gets killed now, everybody will say I did it. And I am not going to take that rap."

It was no idle fear. Gallo was already a suspect in a murder in which the victim had been shot repeatedly in the face.

On the witness stand at the hearings, Gallo took the Fifth Amendment on every single question. In the corridor afterward, he told Bobby: "I'll line up my people for your brother in nineteen sixty."

Good old reliable Joey . . .

The details of the hearings have been related at length elsewhere. Of most interest here, perhaps, are some of the dramatis personae upon whom Bobby pounced. Among them were:

PAUL (RED) DORFMAN

Red took over the Waste Handlers Union in Chicago in 1939, after its president was murdered. Among those picked up by the police for questioning in that murder was the union local's secretary, Jack Rubenstein.

If you haven't already guessed, that worthy gentleman later changed his name to Jack Ruby. And moved to Dallas.

MOMO SALVATORE (SAM) GIANCANA. Aforementioned.

The mob boss of Chicago. Described by Bobby at the hearing as "chief gunman for the group that succeeded the Capone mob." Friend to singer Frank Sinatra. Lover to singer Phyllis McGuire.

Excerpt sample from his testimony:

MR. KENNEDY: Would you tell us if you have opposition from anybody that you dispose of them by having them stuffed in a trunk?

MR. GIANCANA: I decline to answer because I honestly believe my answer might tend to incriminate me.

TONY PROVENZANO

Controlled Teamster Local 360 in New Jersey. Had close ties with the mob. Also had close ties with Jimmy Hoffa, until they had a bitter falling-out.

"Question, Lyndon?"

"Yes. Did Tony Pro, as I believe he was known, ever own an automobile compactor?"

"Bobby?"

"I assume he would have access to one."

My reelection to the Senate in 1958 was a simple matter. Our main goal was to really roll up the vote, and thus attract the attention of politicians across the country.

Pop spent $1.5 million on the campaign. I spoke everywhere in Massachusetts, taking nothing for granted. I rolled up 73.6 percent of the vote—a record for the commonwealth.

"Who was your opponent?" Lyndon asks.

"Vincent Celeste."

"Who the hell was Vincent Celeste?"

I don't really know.

We got the attention not only of the pols but of every kind of organization in the country. Speaking invitations, which had been arriving in a steady stream of mail for two years, increased further; hundreds arrived every week. I accepted as many as possible—building a national constituency, reaching out.

"Time was," Lyndon says, "we thought of auctioning off your chair in the Senate. Since you never were sitting in it."

It was clear to everyone what we were doing, of course, and there was no point being coy about it. As 1960 began, I waited for as long as I could contain myself before making the formal announcement, in the Senate Caucus Room, that I was a candidate for president.

The date was January 2, I believe.

There were, we knew, three main obstacles in the way of my winning the nomination.

1. The party bosses were against me.

"Damn right," Lyndon says.

2. At forty-three, I would be considered too young.

"Damn right," Lyndon says.

3. I was a Catholic.

"Darn right," Lyndon says.

The only way to overcome all these handicaps, we decided, was to enter as many state primaries as possible, and win them all.

Our main opponent in the primaries would be Hubert Humphrey of Minnesota. Lingering around the stage door as a possible compromise candidate would be Stuart Symington of Missouri. Adlai had made clear he would not campaign for the nomination for a third time—but made it equally clear he would gladly accept a draft. But in the end, Bobby predicted early on, our strongest rival would be Lyndon Johnson of Texas.

"You predicted that early on?" Lyndon asks.

"Tarot cards," Bobby says.

The first primary was in New Hampshire, in my own back-yard. Uncontested. No problem. I called Judy Campbell, whom Sinatra had introduced me to three weeks before in Vegas. I'd been phoning her ever since, but we had not yet gotten together. I made a date to meet her the night before the primary—March 7, it was—at the Plaza Hotel in New York. It would be our first real date—and an early celebration of my New Hampshire victory.

So as not to attract attention, I booked a room under a phony name. George Washington. Confidently I strode through the gilt-edged Plaza lobby, along a corridor to the elevators. It seemed to take forever for the elevator to arrive. Finally—

"Get on with it!" Lyndon says.

Finally I was upstairs. The Plaza was not a new hotel; the carpets smelled of must, despite its grand reputation. The room, too, was smaller, less fancy, than I had expected.

"Who the hell cares?" Lyndon says. "Get on with it!"

I had just settled in, taken off my jacket and tie, drunk a glass of water from the tap, when there was a light knock on the door. Eagerly I went to open it. Standing in the hallway, smiling, wearing a white jacket and—

"Was Judy," Lyndon says, impatient.

Was room service, with the bottle of Dom Pérignon I had ordered, and two crystal glasses that sparkled on the tray.

"So how did you give it to her?" Lyndon demands. "Dog style, or what?"

"Listen, Lyndon. I am not here to reveal in detail the sexual intimacies of women who have been kind enough to dally with me."

"You're not? Then what the hell are we doing here? At last, I thought, we're getting to the good parts."

"What are you? A publisher or something? Can't you curb your salacious appetite?"

"Don't worry, Lyndon, he'll talk. As soon as he gets a call from his agent. His agent will make him put in all the good stuff."

I look around. It's Dr. King speaking.

"I certainly hope you're right, Martin," Lyndon says.

Judy arrived. We drank champagne. We spent the night. That's all I have to say.

"Probably because it wasn't any good," Lyndon says.

"As a matter of fact, it was superb. *I* was superb."

"Sez you," Lyndon says.

Silence. They've all run out of banter. Finally it's Bobby who speaks.

"They may have a point, Jack. Maybe you should put the sex in your book."

"Why? Why should I do that?"

"If you leave it out, people will say that Sorensen wrote this one, too."

Peace. I've shooed them all away. Peace at last.

In which to reflect on certain state secrets.

Judy.

Marilyn.

And the events set in motion in A.D. (for Allen Dulles) 1959.

You remember Allen Dulles. Ike's capo?

Ike and Dick in '56. Little did the American people know they were electing Momo and Santo as well.

Peace and quiet. In which, feeling unaccustomedly weary, perhaps I can take a little nap.

Seventy-one years old.

I suppose I am.

In my nap, I have a dream. It is a dream deeply rooted in the American dream. I have a dream that one day this nation will rise up and live out the true meaning of its creed: "We hold these truths to be self-evident; that all men are created equal." I have a dream that one day on the red hills of Georgia the sons of former slaves and the sons of former slaveowners will be able to sit down together at the table of brotherhood. I have a dream that little children will one day live in a nation where they will not be judged by the color of their skin but by the content of their character. This is my hope. This is the faith with which—

A hand rudely shaking my shoulder awakens me. I open my eyes, startled. "What's the matter?" I ask.

"That's *my* goddamn dream!" Martin says.

I rub the sleepies from my eyes. I apologize.

That's what happens when you get old.

Preowned dreams.

From an uncontested victory in New Hampshire we moved west to the first confrontation of the primaries: Wisconsin. It was right in Hubert's backyard, and it would be a real struggle. We mobilized all the troops—Bobby, Teddy, Jean, Pat, Eunice, et cetera. Even Mom. Only Pop stayed home, discreetly out of the limelight, discreetly noncontroversial. (He did send his money, however.) We got ourselves a campaign plane with which to crisscross the state, and dubbed it the *Caroline*. It was a Kennedy blitz. We hoped, by beating Hubert so close to his home state, we could drive him out of the race right there.

Poor Hubert. He was one of the brightest minds in the Senate, one of the most stem-winding speakers, and one of the nicest guys. He'd won national attention for his ringing declarations on civil rights way back in 1948, when half of the Democratic party still owned slaves. But we had him outmanned, outwomaned, and outspent.

"I feel like the corner grocer running against a supermarket chain," he declared one day.

Another time, riding his campaign bus through the night, he heard the sound of a plane passing overhead. He clenched his fist and shook it at the sky. "Hey, Jack, play fair!" he implored.

On primary day, we won a narrow victory. It should have been glorious—but it was sour. The newspapers printed maps of the state broken up along religious lines. They showed that our margin of victory had come entirely from the heavily Catholic areas of the state. It was termed a Catholic victory, and that meant we would have to do it all over again, in every primary, all the way to the convention.

Hubert, buoyed by the closeness of the vote, vowed to press on. It was this decision, in a curious way, that would win me the nomination. If Humphrey had dropped out after Wisconsin, there would have been no more contests in which to show I could win, in which to shake the religious question, in which to prove to the party bosses the voters didn't really fear that a Kennedy win would mean a papal presidency. But Humphrey announced he would take us head-on again, in the next primary. In West Virginia.

"Alas, poor Horatio," Lyndon says. "I knew him, Jack."

At first we were jubilant. West Virginia was only 3 percent Catholic, the smallest percentage of any state in the union— but a poll we'd taken in December had shown us running ahead there by a whopping 70–30 margin. A win like that, in that state, would dispel all doubts.

As we entered the state in the spring to rev up the campaign, we took another poll. This time it showed Humphrey winning 60–40.

"What the hell happened between December and now?" I asked, horrified.

"In December," somebody replied, "nobody here knew you were a Catholic."

Bobby, my campaign manager, nearly went into shock.

"In West Virginia," somebody else put in, "a Catholic couldn't be elected dogcatcher."

I called Pop in Palm Beach and gave him the grim assessment. "Well," he said, "I guess it's a good thing that's not what you're running for."

The lobby of the Fountainebleau Hotel in Miami had sixteen different columns, each covered with a mirror of a different shape and style. As Judy Campbell hurried through it, she could have seen herself reflected back and forth all the way to eternity. But Judy, in a hurry, did not take the trouble to notice.

Sinatra was appearing at the hotel; he'd called her to come down to Florida and see him; she did not know why. They had had an affair a few months earlier, in Hollywood. One day she'd come to his place and he had asked her to get into bed with him and another girl. She'd been very upset; she didn't do that sort of thing. Frank had apologized—but their affair had ended. A few weeks later, in Vegas, he had introduced Judy and me.

123

Now, only a few weeks after our initial tryst at the Plaza, she was in Miami at his invitation. She checked in, found a message waiting for her to meet Frank that evening in the French Room. She appeared on time. Frank greeted her warmly, admired her dress, her hair. And introduced her with pointed casualness to the two men who were with him.

"This is my friend Joe Fish," Sinatra said, "and this is my very good friend, Sam Flood."

She was surprised to see Sinatra go down on one knee, cross himself, and kiss the pinky ring of Mr. Flood.

"Pleased to meet you," Judy said.

Flood was a smallish, dapperly dressed man of about fifty. He was wearing sunglasses in the dimly lit room, and he was sitting with his back to the wall.

"Is dis da broad dats screwing da senator?" Fish said.

Judy was taken aback. Mr. Flood apologized immediately.

"Please excuse the incivility of my acquaintance," he said. "What he meant to to ask was 'Is this the charming young lady who is enjoying a meaningful relationship with the next president of the United States?' Ain't dat right, Fish?"

"Yeah, boss, dat's what I said."

Judy looked from Sinatra to Mr. Flood and back again. She had never seen Frank so nervous. A waiter arrived carrying a small tray with four drinks on it. The waiter, too, appeared nervous. As he began to set a martini on the table in front of Mr. Flood, it slipped out of his shaking hand. The long-stemmed glass toppled on the white cloth of the table. The drink spilled into Sam Flood's lap.

"I'm sorry," the waiter said, shaking, red faced. He fell to one knee, the way Sinatra had done before. "Please find it in your heart to forgive me!"

Joe Fish rose. He pulled a silver revolver from the pocket of his suit jacket. He placed the barrel against the temple of the kneeling waiter, and pulled the trigger.

The waiter keeled over onto the blood red rug.

"Don't let it happen again," Joe Fish said.

Judy covered her eyes, afraid to look at the floor. She

peeked between her manicured fingers. The waiter, looking ill, was beginning, shakily, to stand.

"Next time," Joe Fish said, "I'll use the loaded one."

Sinatra grabbed a white cloth napkin, prepared to wipe the spot in Mr. Flood's lap where the drink had spilled. Flood held a knife at his throat and stopped him.

"Let the lady do it," he said.

The lady did.

Another waiter, as nervous as the first, managed to set a new drink in front of Mr. Flood without spilling it. Joe Fish tasted it, then handed it to Sam.

"So," Sam said to Judy, "tell me about yourself. Tell me what you do."

Judy did not know what to say. She did not know what she was doing here. She looked at Frank for help.

"Judy's a . . . a go-between," Frank said.

"Oh, yeah?" Fish said. "Aside from da senator, whose legs do ya go between?"

"She's a courier," Frank explained. "You know—she delivers messages."

"I get it," Fish said. "Like singing telegrams."

"I already got me a singer," Mr. Flood said. "I already got me two singers. Phyllis and Frank here. Ain't that right, Frank?"

Without rising from the table, Sinatra began to sing his favorite song about how much he loved Chicago.

When he was through, Judy turned to Mr. Flood. "What kind of work do *you* do, Sam?"

"Me?" Sam asked.

In a sudden, swift motion, Joe Fish reached across the table, grabbed the décolletage of Judy's dress, and ripped it downward. Judy didn't flinch. She was not wearing a bra, but she remained at the table, poised as ever, naked now to the waist. She had breasts of which any messenger could be proud. Even a messenger of the gods.

"It's okay, Boss," Joe Fish said, "She ain't wearin' no wire."

"Cross my heart," Judy said, bitterly.

Sam Flood appreciated the pun. "Tell her what I do, Frank," he said.

"Let's see," Frank said. "Exactly what is it that you do? Burglary, assault and battery, assault with intent to kill, carry concealed weapons, bombing, gambling, murder. As well as telling others to murder. Torture with ice picks, cattle prods, and blowtorches. How many murders have you ordered to date? I think the scoreboard passed two hundred last week, didn't it, Sam?"

Mr. Flood eyed Sinatra levelly. "I also kill horses," he said.

Judy Campbell laughed musically. Her fine pale rosé breasts shimmered. "You boys are a gas," she said. "Now tell me what you do, Sam, *really*."

"I must confess, Miss Campbell," Mr. Flood said. "The plain truth is, I am a businessman."

"I knew it!" Judy said. "The minute Mr. Fish pulled his gun, I knew that's what you were."

Sinatra leaned over and whispered, "He's the godfather."

"Mmmmm," Judy said. "I just *love* pizza."

Sam Flood smiled. "You done good, Frankie. She's got beauty and she's got brains. I can tell she's a girl who knows when to keep her mouth shut."

"And when ta open it," Joe Fish said.

Sam Flood stood. "I have to be getting back to Chicago," he said. "To business. It was very nice meeting you, Miss Campbell. I would love to see you again sometime—if I have your permission to call."

Joe Fish came around the table. He pulled out a black revolver—the loaded one—and placed the barrel in Judy Campbell's ear.

"You have my permission," Judy said, seductively.

Sam Flood kissed Judy's hand. Frank Sinatra kissed Sam Flood's hand. Joe Fish kissed Frank Sinatra's hand.

Then they were gone.

A moment later, Fish hurried back into the room. "I forget something," he said. And he reclaimed the black revolver, which hung suspended from Judy Campbell's ear.

When he was gone, Judy turned to Frank. "Who was he, really?" she asked. "I could tell he was important, but I could also tell he's Italian. 'Sam Flood' doesn't sound Italian."

"You want to know his real name?" Sinatra asked.

Judy, pulling her dress up over her naked breasts, nodded.

"Lee Iacocca," Frank said.

All this Judy related to me a few nights later, in my house in Georgetown. Jackie, pregnant with John Jr., was staying in Florida. Judy was reluctant to make love in Jackie's bed, but the bathtub was a bitch on my back.

When we were done, and Judy fell asleep, I lay awake for a long time. I knew who Sam Flood was, of course, even if Judy didn't; from Bobby's committee hearings.

Flood as in *blood*.

Beyond the third-story bedroom window a full moon hung suspended. It seemed to smile a sly smile—then to break out in a broad grin—as I considered the possibilities.

The grin of the man in the moon was—

—all together now (as Bobby, Lyndon, Adlai, and Martin gather around me)—

"Infectious."

West Virginia. The bone crusher of the campaign. How did we ever win in West Virginia?

Let me count the ways.

1. Pop. Pop had one of the most brilliant ideas of his life. He asked Franklin D. Roosevelt, Jr., to campaign for us in West Virginia.

Pop knew FDR's son from the old days. He also knew that in the pantheon of the state, there was no god higher than Roosevelt. He'd been the coal miners' best friend—if you don't count Eleanor—and there were more bridges, tunnels, and streets named after him there than in any other state in the union. Go into the grubbiest shack in the tiniest mountain holler—and we went into hundreds of them—and you were sure to find a faded picture of FDR hanging in the place of honor.

We printed up an endorsement of me by Franklin Jr. and, again at Pop's suggestion, mailed them out from the Roosevelt ancestral home in Hyde Park, New York. Then Jr. came in person and crisscrossed the state, looking and sounding much like his father. As things warmed up, he cited my record in World War II, and claimed that Hubert had avoided service by dodging the draft. This was not true, but it was quite effective.

2. Religion. Our first game plan had been to ignore the religious issue here, and hope it would go away. But I soon realized that it wouldn't. Nobody was mentioning it, but everybody was thinking about it. On one of the first days of campaigning, I was standing on the steps of a building, holding a microphone, speaking to a few hundred people. Someone in the crowd shouted out a question about religion. Instead of shrinking from it, I instinctively met the issue head-on.

"I am a Catholic," I said, "but the fact that I was born a Catholic, does that mean I can't be the president of the United States? I'm able to serve in Congress, and my brother was able to give his life, but we can't be president?"

As I said the words aloud, I felt myself tingle. More important, I could feel the whole crowd tingle. This was what was really on their minds; they wanted to hear me talk about it.

"If I am elected president," I continued, "I will not take orders from any pope, cardinal, bishop, or priest. That is my vow to you. I ask only in return that each and every one of you play fair when you enter the voting booth."

The crowd cheered wildly. We moved on to the next town, and the next. At every speech thereafter, we made sure that someone in the crowd brought up the issue of religion. Then I would answer it. I would stand in the spring sunshine, bareheaded, the wind blowing my hair, and I would look out at the crowd, and up above a glowing white dove would spell out against the clear blue sky, visible only to me, the words of my answer, the words that would still their prejudice, the words that would win their hearts. From this heavenly TelePrompTer spelled out by the glowing Roman dove of the

Lord I would know what to say, how to win their hearts, and—

"What!" Bobby screams. "What! A glowing Roman dove? A heavenly TelePrompTer? What the—"

"Joke, Bobby. It's a joke. Have you ever heard of a joke?"

Bobby sits again, chagrined.

Where was I? The reasons we won in West Virginia. FDR Jr., and turning the religious issue into an issue of fair play, and . . . I thought there was a third reason we won. I can't seem to recall it now.

In a flash, J. Edgar is at my side. He hands me a sheet of paper. Across the top is lettered: MEMO FROM THE FIRES OF MOMO.

"What's this?" I ask.

"Just what it says," J. Edgar says. "A Momo memo."

"A Momo memo?"

"A Momo memo."

"I like it," the reverend says. "It's got a good beat. Good to dance to."

"Where did you get it?" I ask.

"That Sam Flood fellow. Sitting next to your father. He asked me to deliver it. Since no one else commutes."

He always did have pricey messengers.

I open the Momo memo. The words are scrawled in neat letters. Only the edges of the paper are curled with burns.

"The third, and main, reason you won West Virginia," it says, "is because of Frank and me. I gave Frank a bundle of mob money. He disbursed it throughout the state. I sent some of the boys there to make sure it got to the right people. People who knew how to get out the Democratic vote. People who knew how to convince people to vote for Kennedy."

"That's ridiculous!" I say. "Why would the mob support me? My brother was hounding them to death. I'd be the last person they would want as president."

"Unless," Lyndon says, "they had certain friends, who had friends in high places, and those friends figured their friends could call off the dogs. Or call off their brothers. Or something."

129

"I knew it!" Hoover says. "I knew that's the only way you won. With the help of organized crime!"

"I thought there was no organized crime."

"With the help of Sicilian Commies. Whatever."

"John?"

"What?"

The voice is soft, plaintive. I turn to see where it is coming from. It's Hubert, advancing slowly; unbelievable Hubert, who has held his tongue for nearly five full chapters.

"Is it true?" he asks, gently. "You beat me with mob money?"

What can I tell him?

I refuse to answer, on the grounds that my answer might tend to incriminate me.

When we beat him in West Virginia, Hubert was through. (I was watching a porn film in Washington when the returns came in.) From then on we rolled across the country, winning in Nebraska, Maryland, Oregon. When the convention opened in Los Angeles the second week of July, I already had pledged to me 550 of the 761 votes needed to win.

We knew I had to win on the first ballot, or risk losing the momentum and the committed delegates. Words spewed out of Las Vegas that the odds there heavily favored my winning. (No one knew that Pop, on his way west, had stopped there and plunked a million dollars on me, to create just such a story.)

"And to pick up some extra cash," Bobby notes.

At the convention, Eugene McCarthy of Minnesota made the best nominating speech in the history of politics. Unfortunately, he was nominating not me, but Adlai.

"Do not leave this prophet without honor in his own party," he proclaimed.

The convention galleries went wild. They cheered. They screamed. They paraded through the aisles for half an hour while the bands played on. Adlai had their hearts, their minds.

The only thing he didn't have was delegates.

Our real opposition was Lyndon. He'd been haranguing

us all week. He was encouraging votes for Adlai on the first ballot, to stop us; then he'd move in himself. It was the game of a riverboat gambler, and there was no one better at it.

Except me.

Lyndon even attacked my father that week. "I was never any Chamberlain umbrella policy man," he declared. "I never thought Hitler was right."

On nomination night, I watched the balloting on television from a nearby apartment. Wyoming put us over the top. Everyone crowded around, shaking my hand.

"Get Jackie at the Cape," I said, indicating the telephone.

Jackie was not in LA that night, the night the dreams of four generations of Kennedys moved one step closer to being real.

Judy was.

I hurried to the convention hall. I had a private moment with Bobby in the corridor, while everyone stayed back, watching us. Then I mounted the podium, accepted the adoration of the crowd.

I didn't stay long; I was too tired to celebrate; I hurried back to the apartment, where Dave Powers fried me a couple of eggs. Facing me was the first crucial decision every nominee has to make: who to choose as a running mate.

"I can't *stand* the suspense," Lyndon says.

From San Antonio we flew the afternoon of the twenty-first to Houston, where I planned to speak that night at a testimonial dinner for Representative Albert Thomas, the key man in congressional approval of my costly space program. When NASA chose Houston as the site of its new manned space center, it listed all sorts of technical reasons for the choice, but the real reason was to keep Albert Thomas happy. Houston was the congressman's hometown.

The crowds there were even bigger than in San Antonio. I asked Dave Powers how they compared with those on my last visit to the city, in 1962. "Your crowd here today was about the same as last year's," Dave said, "but a hundred thousand more people came out to cheer for Jackie."

It was just what I wanted Jackie to hear. She would, I hoped, be doing a lot more of this in '64.

At the Rice Hotel, where we would be resting, the manager ignored me and stared at Jackie. "Good evening, Mrs. President!" he shouted over the noise. Upstairs, in our suite, I found a spread of champagne and caviar that Jackie had ordered.

"I'm planning to *fight* poverty," I told her, "not induce it."

It was, nonetheless, good stuff. No one could fault Jackie for her taste.

Except, perhaps, afterward.

Aristotle Fucking Onassis.

Zorba the Geek.

It was as if some dark part of her couldn't stand being the nation's stoic princess anymore, and needed to be a frog.

A shipping magnate. Sweet revenge, she must have thought, for all those Kennedy sailing races at Hyannis that she hated.

Or perhaps it was just to change her name. Unlike Ethel, she never really became a Kennedy. If our marriage was a lie—which it was—then her name was, too.

But Onassis? A satyr, after Hyperion?

"Jack?"

"What, Bobby?"

"Don't get too literary. You'll lose the paperback sale."

"What's it to you?"

"The money from your book is going to the poor, right?"

"So?"

"They're my poor, too."

Lyndon is gnashing his teeth, audibly. I turn his way.

"When you going to get on with it?" he asks.

"With what?"

"Your story. About . . . you know. About the second half of your ticket. About choosing your running mate. It's better than *The Three Little Pigs*."

"I imagine," Bobby says, "that you used to root for the Big Bad Wolf."

Lyndon grins. "I didn't even know your father then."

"My favorite," Dr. King says, "was *Little Black Sambo*."

My own, I confess, was *The Little Engine That Could*.

(In our house, it was mandatory.)

(Also at Harvard.)

But Lyndon's right; I must get on with it.

□ □ □

Once upon a distant time, in the wealthy Kingdom of Us, there
was a sweet and beautiful princess, known as Miss Liberty.
She was so fragile she always needed a powerful guardian, to
make sure no enemy stole her away. For eight years, while
Miss Liberty slept uneasily, her guardian was kindly old
Grandpa Ike, a once-fierce warrior who was growing old and
forgetful. When it was time for Grandpa Ike to retire, a new
warrior had to be chosen to guard Miss Liberty.

The leading contender was Grandpa Ike's nephew, Richard
the Stubble-Hearted. For eight years, Richard had served as
Lord Veep, the second in command; now he wanted to become
the king. But some in the kingdom feared that Richard the
Stubble-Hearted had unsavory designs on Miss Liberty, that
she would not be safe in his hands. There were persistent tales
that he had violated some of her sisters in the Land of Orange,
before he became Lord Veep. A faction of the kingdom, therefore, nominated their own candidate to vie for the throne. His
name was Handsome Jack.

("Why are you doing this?" Bobby whispers. "To corner
the kid market?")

("Fairy tales resonate," I reply.)

The contenders would enter the lists each with one mighty
warrior at his side: his choice to be the next Lord Veep. Stubble-
Heart's warrior was Henry Cabot the Large. Now Handsome
Jack had to select his own second in command.

(Lyndon moves closer. He takes off his stocking cap. I do
believe his eyes are watering.)

Among Handsome Jack's advisers there was uncertainty.
Most believed that the best choice would be Stuart of Symington, a distinguished warrior who would give no offense. Other
likely prospects were Sir Henry Jackson, and young Orville the
Freeman. Minstrels throughout the land reported that Stuart
of Symington would be the choice.

The night he was nominated to vie for the throne, Handsome Jack retired alone to his apartment. He'd had little time
to consider his choice for Lord Veep; now he must decide

quickly. Like a bolt from the blue, a wild idea came over him: what if he chose Lyndon, Bane of Texas?

The Bane had been fiercely opposed to Handsome Jack's becoming king. He wanted to be king himself. Most of Jack's friends hated the Bane; they would be sorely upset if he was the choice. But Handsome Jack reasoned thusly: the Bane was one of the most powerful warriors in the land.

"Damn right!" Lyndon says, eyes glowing.

If he became king, it would be far better to have the Bane at his side than as an enemy, Jack reasoned. Also, Jack came from the Northland, and the Bane from the Southland: together, they would have a better chance of uniting the country in opposition to Richard Stubble. And that was the Holy Grail: to make sure that Stubble did not get his dirty paws on Miss Liberty.

"Also," Lyndon says, "if anything unfortunate should happen to Handsome Jack, then the Lord Veep would become the king. And Lyndon the Bane was the best qualified to be king, and to protect Miss Liberty. Isn't that right? Isn't it . . . Handsome Jack?"

Now, Handsome Jack was a sly fellow, slyer than most people thought. For he further reasoned thusly: I will offer the lordship to the Bane; if he accepts, I will have a mighty warrior to enter the lists with me against Stubble. Mostly likely, however, he will decline; most likely he would rather remain the powerful Bane of Texas than the more honorary, but less powerful, Lord Veep. In that case, if he declines, I shall have won his loyalty merely by making the offer, and I can still enter the lists with Stuart of Symington or some other worthy nobleman at my side.

"But the Bane didn't decline!" Lyndon says.

"Are you telling this, Lyndon, or am I?"

"Let me," Lyndon says. "Let me tell my part! The noble Bane consterned everybody—"

"Consterned?" Bobby says.

"—and accepted the veepship. For he reasoned thus and so: as Bane I am very powerful, but I am considered a regional

135

bane; if I ever hope to be king, I will need the national following that as Lord Veep I could acheive. Also, my baneship would be less powerful with Handsome Jack as king than it was under Grandpa Ike. So he sent Handsome Jack a copy of his family crest—the letters *LBJ*—and told him it now stood for 'Let's Back Jack.' And he accepted the lordship."

Bobby is looking sullen. "Fairy tales are supposed to have happy endings," he mutters.

"It does," Lyndon bubbles. "It does. Among Handsome Jack's many followers, the most consterned was his chief aide and brother, Robert the Younger. The next morning, Robert the Younger came to see the powerful Bane. Robert told the Bane that Handsome Jack had only been making a noble gesture, which was supposed to have been declined, that there was opposition to the Bane among the other nobles, that if he persisted in accepting, there would be a terrible, awesome fight at the Round Table.

"The Bane put on an air of sadness, then an air of bravery. 'I love a good fight,' he said. 'Jack and I will fight them together.' And he refused to decline the offer."

"That's what you call a happy ending?" Bobby asks.

"Jack and the Bane went on to massacre Stubble-heart and Cabot the Large, and saved the honor of Miss Liberty. That's what I call a happy ending."

"He's got a point, Bob," I say.

"Some massacre," Nixon says.

What? Who said that? Nixon here? It cannot be!

It isn't.

Sometimes the imagination takes hold. It's a constant battle to stick to reality.

Nixon, of course, was merely defeated, not slain; he would live to paw Miss Liberty another day. That is the difference between life and fairy tales; in life, it's the heroes who die.

"Meaning you, I suppose?" Nixon says.

Of course not meaning me; no man is a hero to himself. (A truth Nixon didn't understand.) Meaning *the image* of me.

"Pop would insist the two are the same," Bobby says.

Yes, Pop would; no, they're not.

"But you *were* a hero, Mr. President!"

Raymond, my valet, is exceptionally kind.

With Lyndon in place as my running mate, I went before the convention to formally accept the nomination for president. It was in this nationally televised address that I first used the term *New Frontier*. Though I didn't much care for slogans, I liked its echoes of Roosevelt's New Deal and Truman's Fair Deal. (In retrospect, it also conjures the image of outlaw gunslingers, an association that escaped me at the time.)

In my speech I sounded a rhythmic, ringing call for the pursuit of excellence in all phases of American life.

Ever since Joe's death I had been groomed to be president someday, with no higher purpose than the pursuit of power, the fulfilling of Pop's hubris. Now it was as if, with the presidency in sight, I needed at last to form a vision of it: to synthesize my dual nature of power and poetry, to conjure what kind of president I was going to be. What I hit upon was nothing less than an American Renaissance, over which I would preside like a Medici prince. I would go down in history as the greatest president since Lincoln, perhaps as the greatest of all.

Such would be my monumental quest.

From somewhere, there is giggling.

I can't tell who it is that's giggling.

The giggling seems to be coming from down below. Hoover, perhaps; Hoffa, perhaps.

I think it is my father who's giggling.

The stale, dank atmosphere of "normalcy." So had I described the fabulous fifties in my acceptance speech. I had only vague hints then that beneath the staleness, the dankness, bubbled a festering stew of deadly corruption. It was as if kindly old Pa Kettle was, back of the barn, molesting his grandchildren.

In 1954, the leftist government in Guatemala had been

overthrown by the Central Intelligence Agency. This was common knowledge to everyone but the American people. I was tempted to bring this up in the campaign, but couldn't; I would be accused of revealing state "secrets," even of treason. What I did not know then was that, even as the campaign began, this same CIA was plotting the assassination of Fidel Castro. After taking office in January I would be briefed on the details, but the plotting began that August.

The scene was the private bathroom in Langley of CIA director Allen Dulles, brother to Secretary of State John Foster Dulles. Publicly, the secretary of state was espousing his questionable policy of containing the Soviets through the threat of massive nuclear retaliation. Privately, his brother had embarked on a personal campaign of picking off baby Communists one by one, like ducks in a shooting gallery.

At the fateful meeting, Allen Dulles sat on the number-one potty, as befit his position as director. Seated on potties two, three, and four, which were arranged in a semicircle around the director's potty, were his three chief aides—Curly, Moe, and Fulgencio. (For historical accuracy, I am using real names here; at the time, of course, they used false identities.) Collectively, the four men were known as "the bowels of the CIA." As in "A new policy thrust has emerged from the bowels of the Central Intelligence Agency . . ."

"All right," Allen Dulles said, calling the meeting to order. "We all know why we are here."

He paused while Curly made a rude noise into his potty; then he continued.

"On January first of last year, Fidel Castro illegally overthrew the legitimate dictator of Cuba, Fulgencio Batista . . ."

"A leader of uncommon wisdom, elegant thumbscrews, and *mucho* money," Fulgencio said. "Or so I have been told."

"Since then," Dulles continued, "Castro has openly declared himself a Communist, and has begun to accept aid from the Russians. This is a situation, ninety miles off the coast of Florida, that we cannot tolerate. We are here today to decide what to do about it."

"Kill the bastard," Moe said.

"Good," the director replied. "I am glad we are all in agreement. The next question is, how best to accomplish this."

Curly raised his right hand, which was clutching a wad of about to be used toilet paper. "I have a letter from a little girl in Kansas," he said. "She suggests that we fill a box of Castro's favorite cigars with depilatories. This will cause his beard to fall out, and he will lose his macho image. The whole island will rise up in laughter, and Castro will die of embarrassment."

"I like it, I like it," Moe said. "But we need a backup plan. A lady in California writes that we should fill his cigars with botulism. In case his beard doesn't fall out quick enough."

"Now we're getting somewhere," Fulgencio said. "But suppose he gives up cigars. We have to have a waiter in Havana slip a poison pill into his food."

The suggestion was greeted by a thunderous outburst in the potties. This was commonplace whenever the talk at such meetings turned toward outright violence; it was the reason the meetings were held where they were.

"Very good," the director said, when silence had returned. He pressed an ominous-looking black button on the wall beside him. Large, phallic intrusions of Airwick rose from the floor near each seat. "However," he said, "should those attempts happen to fail, I have another idea."

"What's that?" the other three asked in unison, as they wiped.

"Shoot him," Dulles said.

Curly, Moe and Fulgencio looked from one to the other, nodding sagely. This was why the director was the director.

"I'll do it gladly," Fulgencio said.

"No, me," Curly said.

"Me-me-me-me-me!" Moe insisted, shooting his hand into the air, waving frantically.

"Hush," Allen Dulles said, impatiently. "It won't be any of you. This cannot be tied to the agency. It's a secret that must remain in the bowels."

"Oh," the others said, disappointed.

"What we must do is hire someone from the outside."

"The Jackal!" Curly said.

"We can place an ad in *Soldier of Fortune*," Moe suggested.

"No," the director said. "We will pay money for an assassin, of course; but the money will go through several middlemen, so it cannot be traced to us. Even more important: we will employ someone who has his own independent motive for killing Castro. That way, if he is caught, the blame will fall on him alone, and we will not be suspected."

"Brilliant!" the other three said in unison. And another wave of thunder filled the bowls.

"Who is it that you have in mind?" Fulgencio asked.

"You shall see," the director said. "Shortly."

They all stood up and adjusted their pants.

"One more thing, before you leave."

They all waited expectantly.

"Don't forget to flush," the director said.

A few days later, the director boarded a plane to Las Vegas, Nevada. To avoid attracting attention, he was wearing his favorite disguise. He was traveling as an American eagle, in a suit of feathers and beaks.

"Look at the big bird!" a little boy in first class said to his mother.

"Don't be rude, Jason," his mother said. "I'm sure the director has a perfectly good reason for traveling like that."

At the Las Vegas airport, the director spent half an hour losing money in the slot machines. There was a covert operation in Honduras that he hoped to finance this way. But all he could get was cherries and lemons; the three machine guns never came up. The director noted his losings in his expense-account ledger, then took a cab to Circus Circus.

Still wearing his eagle suit, he slipped into the second seat at the baccarat table. The first seat was occupied by a man dressed as a large fingernail.

"Is that you?" the fingernail said to the eagle.

"Shhhh!" the eagle said. "Act natural."

They played baccarat for twenty minutes. Then the director in his eagle suit casually led the way to a twenty-one table, where they sat and began to play. The director told the fingernail the nature of his business. He knew that the fingernail was not really a fingernail, but was a chief aide of reclusive billionaire Howard Hughes.

"You want me to find you a hit man?" the fingernail asked.

"Hit me," the director said.

"Hit you? Why do you want them to hit you?"

"Not you. Him."

The dealer slipped the eagle a card. The fingernail, who was a Mormon and had never played twenty-one, was confused.

"You want us to hit him?"

"Not him," the director said. "I want you to hit Castro."

Now the dealer was confused. "Which one is Castro?" he asked. He shrugged and gave the fingernail a card.

"You're busted," the director said.

"What is this, some kind of joke?" the fingernail said, angrily.

"Maybe we should talk somewhere else," the eagle said.

They climbed to the second floor of Circus Circus, and jumped into a safety net below the trapeze; there they could talk with no interruptions.

"Okay," the director said. "This is why I wanted you to meet me here."

"I know why," the fingernail said. "Because the CIA is known as the Circus."

"Wrong," the director said. "The CIA is known as the Company. The British secret service is called the Circus."

"You're British?" the fingernail asked. "George Smiley or somebody?"

"George Smiley is a fictional character," the director said. "I am very real, and I am American." And he explained the plan.

"Got it," the fingernail said. "You are putting out a hundred-and-fifty-thousand-dollar contract on Fidel Castro of

Cuba. You want me to act as middleman, to line up a hit man from the Mafia. In return for this favor, you will give my boss . . . ?"

"A year's supply of empty Kleenex boxes."

"Done," the fingernail said.

The director was in a good mood. He was whistling an old Carmen Miranda tune as he left the casino. A little boy, entering the hotel with his mother, saw the man in the eagle suit and asked, "Why is the director whistling?"

"Don't be rude, Jason," his mother said.

At the airport, the director inserted his last quarter into a slot machine. First one window, then the second, then the third shuddered to a stop with a machine gun in it. Ten million dollars in quarters poured out of the slot.

The director pocketed the money joyfully. He would be able to do some things in Honduras after all.

The man in the fingernail suit took off his disguise. He made a telephone call. Half an hour later he slipped into a booth in the lounge of the Sands Hotel. A moment later a man wearing a low-cut dress joined him.

"Hi, Bob," the man in the dress said.

"Hello, sweetheart," Bob said.

"I'm not no sweetheart," the man in the dress said. "It's me. Johnny Roselli."

"Why are you dressed like that?"

"You said it was a strictly pervert operation."

"That's *covert*," Bob said.

"Shit," Roselli said, struggling out of his taffeta.

Bob explained the nature of the hit. Johnny Roselli smiled. "My boss is gonna love this one," he said.

"Your boss?"

"I know just what he's gonna do," Roselli said. "He's not gonna give the hit to one of our boys. He's gonna subcontract it out to Santo."

"Who's Santo?"

"Santo Trafficante. In Miami. He used to control the casinos in Havana. Till Castro shut them down. He hates the son of a bitch. He'd gladly kill Castro for nothing. That way they won't trace the hit to us. And Momo will keep the dough."

"Who's Momo?"

"Me."

Sam Giancana, looking dapper as ever, slipped into the booth with them.

"Where's the broad?" Roselli asked.

"How many times do I have to tell you? She ain't no broad. Her name is Judy. She's taking a shower."

"Good," Roselli said. "Because we got to talk. This guy here wants—"

"I know what he wants," Momo said.

With an exaggerated motion, he reached across the table and removed the swizzle stick from Roselli's Shirley Temple. The swizzle stick, which was shaped like a tiny microphone, was, in fact, a tiny microphone.

"You got yourself a deal," he said.

Johnny Roselli beamed. "What we gonna do with the money?" he asked.

Momo put the microphone in his pocket. "I'm thinking of buying some property," he said.

Bob racked his brain, trying to think of what in Las Vegas was for sale. "The old frontier?" he asked.

Sam Giancana shook his head. "The New Frontier," he said.

There is silence when I finish the story. Adlai, in particular, seems shocked.

"It's all true," Lyndon confirms. "I read the files personally, after Jack here was shot."

"The fucking incompetents," Bobby says. "Bad enough the agency got involved with the mob. You'd think the least somebody could do was pull it off. If they'd succeeded in killing Fidel, everything might have turned out differently."

The reason they didn't succeed, of course, was because of the tapes.

"What tapes?" Nixon asks, excitedly.

"What tapes?" Adlai echoes.

"The little boy," Bobby explains. "Jason. He wasn't a little boy at all. He was a midget, from Cuban counterintelligence. He got all those conversations on tape, and sent them off to Fidel."

"How do you know that?" Adlai asks.

"The FBI intercepted the tapes," I explain.

"Intercepted? Then how did Castro get them?"

"Hoover made copies of them. For his private files. That gave him something on Dulles, on Bob the Fingernail, on Roselli, on Giancana. Even on me. Then he sent the originals back on their way to Cuba."

"Why did he do that?" Raymond asks.

"He didn't want Castro to know he'd made the midget."

"Brilliant, wasn't it?" J. Edgar says, materializing. "That's how we do things in the spy game. Very close to the vest. In the next three years we surreptitiously entered the midget's apartment every two weeks, and made copies of more than three hundred tapes."

"Unfortunately," I point out, "Fidel apparently retired him upon receiving the Vegas tapes. The only thing he ever taped after that was three hundred Chicago Cubs games."

"It's neat," J. Edgar says. "Very patriotic."

Bobby stares at him, eyes blazing. He's about to leap at his throat.

"I think you should leave now," I say.

Hoover looks at me, then at Bobby, then back at me again. "Touchy, touchy Boston fans," he says.

This iceberg of madness lay, of course, below the tranquil surface; all the American people saw that autumn of 1960 was me and Nixon running for president: a lapsed Catholic versus a devout Paranoid.

There were three critical moments during the campaign: my appearance before the Houston ministers, the first debate, and my call to Coretta King.

"Amen!" Martin says.

Bigotry is one of the two great engines that drive the American reality. (The other being violence.) While I crisscrossed the country speaking of hopes and dreams, the engine of bigotry continued to grind among the electorate. One typical example was a statement in early September from the good Baptists of Arkansas: "We cannot turn our government over to a Catholic president who would be influenced by the pop and—"

"That's pope!" Bobby corrects.

"—who would be influenced by the pope and the power of the Catholic hierarchy."

Jackie found the issue highly ironic. "You're such a lousy Catholic," she used to say. "Now if it was Bobby . . ."

When the issue wouldn't go away, we decided we had to confront it head-on. One way would be to follow Jackie's line of reasoning. I could, for instance, distance myself from Catholic dogma by confessing to all my adulteries. Somehow that didn't seem like the high road. Instead I agreed to answer all questions about religion at a televised meeting with a group of ministers in Houston. I gave a dramatic speech about the separation of church and state, declaring that I would resign the presidency before I would permit religious pressure to violate the national interest or my own conscience.

"What conscience?" Hoover asks.

The issue did not go away, of course—it still hasn't—

"Amen!" Martin says.

—but it was driven deeper underground; right-thinking people could no longer make an honest case for it.

When the teleivison networks first suggested a debate between me and Tricky Dick, I accepted immediately. Nixon was ahead in the polls; after eight years as vice president, he was better known nationally; and he was presenting himself as much more experienced in foreign affairs. I had nothing to lose in a debate—and a lot to gain if I merely came off as his equal.

The first debate was held on September 26. It would not only turn the election around but also turn American politics around. It was from that night on that what a politician stood for became far less important in winning elections than how he looked on television.

The things we said that night are of little consequence; in fact, most people who heard the debate on the radio felt that Nixon had won. Most pundits the next morning, paying attention to the words, called it a draw. But 70 million people saw the debate on television—and the images they saw were Smilin' Jack versus Uriah Heep. My hands were shaking, but I could hide those behind the lectern, or grip it tight. Nixon had put on a lot of makeup to hide his jowls—and beneath the hot lights he began to sweat like a horse. I looked calm and confident; Nixon looked almost pathetic. The next morning, as I resumed the campaign, people began to rip at my clothing, my cuff links. I had become overnight the James Dean of politics.

"Jack."

"Yes, Martin?"

"You forgot something. You left out the call to Coretta."

"I didn't forget. I'm merely pausing. For effect."

"Oh."

"I have an idea. Perhaps you'd like to tell about it."

"Me? Would that really be okay?"

"Be my guest," I say.

Martin clears his throat. He rises to his full, imposing height. He stares out majestically at the vast and sweeping eternity of clouds.

"I have a dream!" he intones.

"Martin?"

"Sorry, Jack."

He begins again.

"The date was October nineteenth. I was attempting to integrate a department store in Atlanta by sitting in. Predic͘ ably, I was arrested by the Atlanta police. The authorities soon released me. But six months earlier, I had been put on probation by a judge in De Kalb County for a traffic violation. That judge took this new opportunity and had me arrested for parole violation—and he sentenced me to four months at hard labor.

"Now, that might not sound like much nowadays. Especially to you folks up north. But in those days, in the South, sentencing an uppity black man to hard labor was pretty near like sentencing him to death. They woke me up at four thirty in the morning, they put me in handcuffs and leg irons, they took me from the county jail out dark, dirt country roads to some obscure jail deep in the rural outback. Once them white prisoners learned who I was, a shiv in the back was likely; if not, a necktie party by the decent white folks was a strong possibility.

"Coretta was near hysterical. Her friends knew it. Somebody got word to the Kennedys, suggested that a call from Jack—some reassurance from the presidential candidate— might help her to calm down. Jack's advisers warned him against it; told him a call to Coretta just then, three weeks before election day, would cost him the whole South, and the presidency. But Jack disagreed. He got Coretta on the phone and he talked to her.

"Bobby was also worried about the political implications. But he was even more worried about me. He got that judge from De Kalb County on the phone and expressed some opinions about the notion of hard labor, instead of bail, for a traffic violation. I wouldn't be surprised if he also hinted that the judge might be looked on with disfavor should the Kennedys win the election. Whatever he said, I was released the next day.

"The best part is, it didn't cost Jack the South. Instead it won him the solid support of black people throughout the land. And without all those black votes, he would not have been elected. All of which proves there are times when the politically expedient is the morally wise. Right, Jack?"

Yes, Reverend. Once in every great while.

The campaign approached its climax. I hopscotched across America, working as hard as any mortal could.

Bobby, my manager, worked harder. He's the greatest man I ever knew.

"Stop it, Jack," Bobby says.

Over and over, showing I could be as tough as Nikita Khrushchev, I told the American people, "The world cannot exist half slave and half free."

Subtly comparing myself with Lincoln.

Even more subtly conjuring Nixon, who was out there campaigning half shaved and half frizz.

I spoke of the need for expanding educational opportunity to everyone; I spoke of the need to end poverty; over and over I played the theme of getting America moving again. And America responded.

Such talk, now, makes me uncomfortable. It is bad enough for the living to blow their own horns, worse for the immortal. Let me quote, instead, one paragraph written back then by the nation's most insightful journalist since Mencken, Murray Kempton.

> *Suddenly this is no longer an election campaign to John Kennedy. It is the blowing of bugles. . . . He has been captured by an urgency which is not political but national. A great part of it comes from the contempt for Richard Nixon which he has developed over the last few weeks and the assurance he feels that the election of this feeble, fumbling, hollow man would be a national disaster. Some of it comes from the faces he sees in his crowds; he believes at last that the country can be awakened, that the last eight flaccid years are finally over.*

That's the way it was. Precisely.

"Jack." It's Bobby. "Do you ever have any regrets?"

"About what?" Though I know what he means.

"Quoting Kempton, and all. Regrets about the journalist you didn't become."

"No," I say.

Lying.

□ □ □

148

On election night we all gathered at the compound in Hyannis Port to watch the returns. Bobby's large house had been turned into Election Central, with dozens of TV sets, telephones, calculators. Wires crisscrossed the floors, being chewed on by dogs and kids. The whole family and some of our closest friends were in the house, munching sandwiches, staring at the TV sets as the returns began to trickle in. Upstairs, in the pointy attic, Pop manned his own battery of private phones, like a Boston Irish fiddler on the roof.

"An ethnic simile he would not appreciate," Bobby says.

In a small cottage at one end of the compound, unknown to the others, Judy Campbell awaited my appearance.

In a small cottage at the other end of the compound, Marilyn Monroe did the same.

The early returns looked good. By 8:00 P.M. the central computer we'd installed in Bobby's living room was predicting I would win the election with 51 percent of the vote. The family was jubilant, my sisters jumping up and down, the servants handing out drinks. I knew it was too early. The returns were mostly from the East, the region of my greatest strength.

The Pennsylvania returns came in—a solid majority for us. The industrial states began to come in—and they appeared strong for us.

"Oh, Bunny, you're president now!" Jackie cried.

I looked around the room; who the hell was Bunny? But when she came over and kissed my cheek, I knew she meant me.

"Don't buy any White House china yet," I warned. "We sitll have the West to hear from."

A few minutes later came the word that Ohio was going for Nixon. And then Kentucky, Tennessee, Wisconsin, the whole damn Farm Belt. The victory was disappearing before our eyes.

Upstairs, in his private attic, the fiddler on the roof fiddled with his private phones.

The mood was growing ominous. Texas and Illinois were

running too close to call—and we'd probably have to win both to win the election.

The telephone in the den rang. One of the kids answered it. It was for Uncle Jack. I went to the phone and listened over the din.

"Mr. Kennedy?"

"Yes?"

"This is Judy from *Time* magazine. We're having a special election night subscription drive—a one-year subscription for just thirty-three cents an issue. As a bonus, you get a free Polaroid camera . . ."

I said I was not interested. I was about to hang up, when the woman said, "And if you act immediately, you also get a lovely blow job."

"Oh," I said. *"That* Judy."

I told Bobby I needed to get away from the crowd; I needed to walk on the beach, to collect my thoughts.

In the oceanfront cottage, the only light was from a kerosene lantern, the kind that the wives of sailors used to keep burning to await their husbands' return from the sea. Judy was wearing a new negligee for the occasion. It was black and very sheer, except for three appliqués sewn on in strategic places. Covering each breast was a small donkey. Covering her nether region was a campaign slogan: ALL THE WAY WITH JFK.

The negligee had been a gift, she said, from her thoughtful friend Sam Flood.

Judy wasted little time. I'd barely stretched out on the four-poster bed when her educated tongue, her suction-cup lips, were plying their wondrous skills.

Just as I thought I couldn't stand it any longer, the Princess phone beside the bed rang. (Bobby had been kind enough to have one installed for the evening.) It was Lyndon, being patched through from his ranch.

"Yes, Lyndon," I said.

I pushed at Judy's dark head; Judy didn't stop working.

"I just wanted to tell you, Jack," Lyndon said. "Texas is gonna be close—but safe."

The magic instant he said *safe*, I came.
Lyndon Baines was stealing Texas.
(His cronies would swallow the evidence.)
(Just as Judy was.)

It was well past midnight when I got back to Election Central. The kids had been put to bed, but everyone else was still there. The mood was quiet, weary. The election was still up in the air. Winning or losing, it appeared, would depend on Illinois, where Nixon and I were neck and neck.

I ate a sandwich and drank a beer. I asked Bobby where Pop was. Pop still was up in the attic, he said. Fiddling.

At 3:30 in the morning I had 261 electoral votes. But I needed 8 more to win, and there was no guarantee that I would get them. Nixon went on television from the West Coast, looking worn as an old cloth coat. We hoped he might be conceding. But he didn't.

I told the others I was going to bed; win or lose, I would still be alive in the morning.

Tired and alone I walked down the beach, to the isolated cottage in the dunes. There I did go to bed—with Marilyn.

Or tried to.

At my request, she was wearing her "Runnin' Wild" dress from *Some Like It Hot*. She had recently split with her husband, and this would be our first time alone together, our first night of love. The dress would honor that afternoon we had first met, more than two years earlier.

Marilyn was sipping an aperitif. I took her hand; I kissed it. We let our lips touch, lightly.

I slumped into a chair, weary. Marilyn could see that I needed stimulation. She bent over, opened my zipper, providing breathing room. Then she backed away. She stood about eight feet in front of me. And in the dim light, ever so slowly, she began to undress herself; to remove, as slowly and excruciatingly as a stripper, the sequined dress, under which there was nothing but herself—the world's sexiest movie queen.

I had the strangest thought: If my dad could see me now!

Slowly, ever so, Marilyn's flesh appeared. First one soft, glowing breast, then the other. Slowly, ever so, she wriggled the gown down over her hips. All the while her eyes were trained on me—not on my face but on the appendage protruding from my pants. I could see where her eyes were; they burned there like a laser beam—on my own renewing strength.

The phone rang. I reached across for it. Marilyn, as if petulant, speeded up her undulating wriggle.

It was Bobby on the phone. Pop had just talked to Mayor Daley, he said. We were going to carry Illinois, Daley had said—with a little help from our friends.

Just as he spoke the word *friends*, Marilyn dropped her dress. In the pale light I was staring at the hitherto forbidden brownness, goldness, of her.

With a little help from our friends . . .

Untouched by human hands, I came.

Marilyn continued her dance, not disconcerted, just smiling, smiling, as she watched the milky stream.

"I'm sorry," I said a moment later, stroking her hair as she crouched beside me.

"That's okay," Marilyn said, in her whispery voice. "It always happens . . . the first time."

Her words cheered me. Quickly I shook off my embarrassment, my guilt. It was, I told myself, the most natural thing in the world to happen, the first time you're elected president.

"Jack."

"What, Lyndon?"

"Thanks."

"Thanks for what?"

"For taking my advice."

"What advice is that?"

"About not leaving out the good parts."

I awoke in my own cottage, at 7:30 in the morning, and was informed officially that I was president-elect of the United

States. I stepped outside into the crisp November air; the house was surrounded by agents of the Secret Service. I took a stroll along the beach, watching the cold blue waves roll in; the beach, too, was lined with agents.

I breakfasted with Jackie and Caroline; the president-elect as loving husband, loving father. Then, for most of the day, Bobby and Pop and a few of the others analyzed the vote.

In the electoral college, I'd received 303 votes to Nixon's 219—an apparently solid victory. But if Texas and Illinois had gone the other way, I'd have lost the election.

A more stunning indication of my mandate was the popular vote. Out of more than 68,000,000 votes cast, I won by 118,550. I won 49.7 percent of the popular vote; Tricky Dick, the man you love to hate, won 49.6.

It would be full speed ahead for the New Frontier.

The people, after all, had spoken.

In the vast and glorious state of Texas, I had won by the width of a mosquito's ass: 46,000 votes. And this, as I've mentioned earlier, only after Lyndon's people got a whole passel of Nixon votes disqualified.

"Mosquito's ass my ass," Lyndon says. "We won, didn't we? Lyndon Baines Johnson won you Texas; not to mention Georgia, Missouri, South Carolina, and Alabama. Had Robert the Younger succeeded in ousting me from the ticket, Nixon would have met his Watergate ten years sooner."

I allow the truth of it.

"Mosquito's ass," Lyndon says again, apparently taken with the phrase. (I picked it up from Henry Cabot Lodge.) "Sheeet! In Illinois all you got was a mosquito's pecker."

I allow the truth of that, too. My margin in Illinois was only 8,858 votes. How many of those were the votes of dogs, cats, canaries, wharf rats, and the honorable deceased I cannot say for sure. All I know is that every time a bloc of Nixon votes came in from the Republicans downstate, Mayor Daley countered with a bigger bloc of his own. Till Daley said he was through—and the Republicans produced their final winning tally. Only to discover that Daley was playing possum—he'd snuggled away a passel more Kennedy votes, which at 5:00 A.M. he produced, to put me over the top.

The winning votes, it turned out, came from Chicago's West Side River Wards. Mayor Daley was the boss of Chicago—but he was not the boss of the River Wards. In the 1920s, the only boss there had been Al Capone; in the 1930s, Frank Nitti. And onward through the begats of Murder Incorporated, until, in 1960, the one and only boss of the River Wards, the man who told people how to vote—and how often to vote—and how to count the votes—was none other than Salvatore Giancana. (Aforementioned.)

Momo.

If I was celebrating modestly that morning, Sam Giancana was ecstatic. His most powerful enemy in the world, who had been harassing him in Congress for two years, was Robert Kennedy. Momo had just helped elect Robert's older brother president. His dear friend Judy Campbell was sleeping with me—a fact we would rather the nation's press not ascertain. In addition, he was under contract with the government itself—through the CIA—to kill Fidel Castro, another fact the government would prefer remained secret. If ever in the history of the universe a mobster could feel free of the threat of further harassment, it was Sam (Momo) Giancana that day.

Right, Bobby?

No response.

I repeat: Right, Bobby?

"In a mosquito's kazoo!" Bobby says.

In the days after the election, there were widespread reports of shenanigans in Illinois. Nixon was urged to contest the election. He never did. People assumed it was because he was a good sport, because he did not want to hurt the country.

If you believe that, you believe in Tinker Bell.

(As my first witness, I call Deep Throat.)

The most obvious explanation is usually the truest. And

the most obvious explanation is that the downstate Republicans of Illinois, with Jimmy Hoffa's Teamsters in their corner, were just as committed to voting suburban graveyards as Sam Giancana was to voting urban ones. If you doubt the likelihood of this, ask Daniel Ellsberg, John Dean, John Ehrlichman, Edmund Muskie, et cetera.

Whatever the five-o'clock-shadowy reason, Richard Nixon did not protest. The election landslide stood.

I glance down among the fiery flames, to see if I get any response, any disclaimer, from Jimmy Hoffa. The squat, subcompact figure is motionless. Only his right taillight is blinking.

The third happiest man in America that day was my father, of course; the Kennedy manifest destiny he had charted so long ago had come to pass. And the fourth was Frank Sinatra. Old Blue Eyes had a friend in the White House—or soon would— a rat-in-law, so to speak. (He actually called me his brother-in-Lawford.) By spreading mob money in West Virginia, by raising legitimate money at Hollywood fund-raisers, he had made his personal godfather happy. No more horses' heads in this singer's bed. There were two great powers in America—the federal government and organized crime—and Frank saw himself as Ozymandias, with one great leg of stone in each camp.

At his huge California estate he had entertained me on campaign trips to the West. At other times he had played host to Momo. The gold-plated faucets had emitted hot and cold running girls on both occasions—perhaps some of the very same ones. Now, the day after the election, Frank began drawing up plans. A month later, a construction crew arrived at his villa at Palm Springs. They began to build a huge new guesthouse on Sinatra's estate, which included a dining room that could seat forty people. They broke ground for a private heliport. Frank paid hundreds of thousands of dollars in overtime so the workers would get it done in a hurry.

What he was building, he told himself and his friends, was

the place where President Kennedy would stay when he needed to get away from Washington. What he was building, Frank Sinatra thought, was the Western White House.

Bobby is seized with a severe coughing fit. I pound him on the back till he stops.

"Fat chance," he mutters, red faced.

And so it came to pass that on a cold day in January 1961, I was sworn in as the thirty-fifth president of the United States. As I took the oath of office, my right hand on the family Bible, I could not help thinking of my great-grandfather, Patrick Kennedy, who left Ireland a pauper and came to America in steerage class, and who died of the cholera . . .

"Yes, Jack, we know," Adlai says. "On the twenty-second of November."

Robert Frost, at my invitation, read a poem he had written for the occasion. Cardinal Cushing, at Pop's invitation, delivered a long-winded prayer. Then I approached the lectern to make my inaugural address.

"Kennedy's First Inaugural," I assumed they would call it.

A bright sun was glaring, a cold wind was blowing as I spoke to the thousands of people spread out before me in the capital—and to the entire world. The speech was short. Still, only bits and pieces come back to me now.

"We observe today not a victory of party but a celebration of freedom . . . ," I began that day.

"Let the word go forth from this time and place . . ."

"Et cetera," Lyndon says.

For the four hours following my speech, I stood in the biting cold and watched the long inaugural parade roll by. I enjoyed every minute of it. Thinking, over and over again, with wonder: "I am the fucking president of the United States."

Little realizing that, word for word, that is precisely how history would remember me.

For the third time that penultimate day we were airborne, droning through the Texas night from Houston to Fort Worth. The dinner for Albert Thomas had been deeply moving to the old congressman, bringing a hint of tears to his eyes; for the rest of us it had been, as such affairs always are, mostly somniferous. I am not sure if the young honor the old out of duty, generosity, or foresight. Say this for the space program, though: we would get whatever we wanted.

I retired to my cabin on the plane and summoned Raymond, to assist me with the day's third changing of shirt and tie. It would be nearly midnight when we arrived in Fort Worth, but I knew there would be throngs to greet us, both at the airport and at the hotel. In the history of the republic, from Washington to Barnum & Bailey to Gypsy Rose Lee, no mortal had better advance men. The father of the need, again, was television, which was broadening the deceitful craft of public relations from the press release to the flesh market.

"How did the dinner go, Mr. President?" Raymond asked, while removing a television shirt, pale blue, from the wardrobe.

Our arrival would be too late for film at eleven, but it would make the morning newscasts in the Dallas–Fort Worth area.

"You telling me you missed that one too?" I asked. "Don't tell me you've also got a sister in Houston. One who reads crystal balls, maybe?"

"Fish entrails," Raymond said. "We were much too poor for crystal balls."

I laughed. He was a tonic to have around. I could easily have changed my own shirt.

"Fact is, I wasn't invited to the dinner," Raymond said.

"I know. You and Senator Yarborough. Count your blessings."

I removed my suit jacket, my tie, the white shirt that was wet in the armpits. Raymond handed me a towel and some Mennen spray.

"That gives me an idea for something you could do, Raymond. In nineteen sixty-nine. After we leave the White House."

"What's that, sir?"

"Fish entrails. You could go back to Cambridge. Set up shop in Harvard Yard, reading fish entrails for the undergrads. For the law students, too. Tell them whether they're gonna pass or fail."

"Be more money in it," Raymond said, "if I told them what the questions on their exams would be."

"There you go, Raymond. Now you're talking. That's the difference between you and me. You've got a better head for business. Growing up rich, I didn't have your advantages."

"I can see where that would be a handicap," Raymond said, holding the blue shirt for me to slip my arms through. "A rich person doesn't have to learn any skills to feed his family."

"It's no joke," I said. "In sixty-nine, when Bobby becomes president, you can always go back to shining shoes, if it comes to that. But what can Jack Kennedy do? The one thing I was trained for, the one thing I became an expert at, was running for president. Well, that's something you can only do twice. Where does that leave me afterward?"

Raymond handed me a striped tie—red, white, and blue; in Texas you don't go paisley, or they think you're queer. "Perhaps," he said, "President Bobby could find you a position. Something simple, that doesn't take much training. Ambassador to England, maybe."

I eyed him narrowly, wondering if he was cutting Pop. I chose to take the remark as innocent.

"Maybe he'd make me attorney general," I said.

"Don't despair." He stuffed my soiled shirt into a laundry bag bearing the presidential seal. "There's lots you can do in the future. If . . ."

He stopped. I finished his sentence for him.

"If there is a future?"

"You can still turn the plane around, sir. Head on back to Washington. My sister called me at the hotel. She begged me again to warn you not to go to Dallas."

"I haven't forgotten," I said, peering into the mirror above the dresser, straightening the knot on my tie. "The Knight of Wands will die tomorrow."

Raymond nodded, almost as pale in the glass, at that moment, under the fluorescent lights, as a white man seeing a ghost.

"You know what I figure, Raymond?"

He shook his head from side to side, wordlessly. I turned to face him, shrugging into the jacket of my suit.

"I figure they're gonna kill Lawrence Welk."

I grinned and moved past him, toward the door of my dressing room. Raymond did not seem amused. Hand on the knob, I turned to face him again.

"In the war," I said, "on *PT-109*, I could easily have been killed. I made it through. In 1954, they cut me apart in the hospital to fix my back. I came so close to dying, they gave me the last rites. The way I figure it, every day since then has been a gift. The other day, Jackie was afraid. I'll tell you what I told her. If somebody wants to kill the president, they can do it. A rifle from a high window. There's no way that could be stopped.

159

It's one of the risks of the job, that's all. But I can't stop being president because of that."

Raymond stood silently, then nodded slowly with understanding.

"There's one thing I want you to promise me, though," I said, approaching him again.

He tried to speak, but his voice was caught in his throat.

"I don't want my boy to grow up as disadvantaged as me. Not knowing people like you. So I want you to promise me. If anything should happen to me—tomorrow, or anytime—you'll go on being an uncle to John-John."

Raymond swallowed. He spun around, went to the small sink, turned on the tap, began to wash his hands.

I stood there, looking at his back. An ancestral back, I thought, that had helped to build the nation, but had yet to share in its fruits. I left him there and returned to the main cabin. Nothing would happen tomorrow. I still had too much work to do.

Besides, I thought, who would want to kill such a fine and charming fellow as me?

The only one with sufficient motive was Jackie.

After the election and a few days of swimming in Palm Beach, my thoughts turned toward the staffing of the new government. I instructed my aides to scour the land; I wanted none but the brightest and the best. First I would deal with the FBI and the CIA, then choose a cabinet.

Most people, including my closest friends, urged me to get rid of Hoover, and assumed I would. The FBI needed a new electric broom, so to speak; it needed to be swept clean. I agreed with all my heart—and I made J. Edgar my first reappointment.

"An act of high patriotism and pure intelligence," J. Edgar says, flitting up to listen.

An act, more accurately, of high treason and self-preservation. Hoover still had, at the tip of his pudgy fingers, the secret Inga tapes. And God knows how many others.

160

"Thirty-seven," J. Edgar says.

"Fifty-four," says the passing white cloud.

The lady barely pauses in her prowling. "For shame. For shame," Ethel Rosenberg says.

Most people, including my closest friends, also urged me to get rid of Allen Dulles at CIA, a stodgy holdover from the old guard. Quickly I reappointed Dulles.

"To the consternation of us all," Adlai says.

I presented the two appointments as a gesture of continuity to our enemies abroad and at home. The government, under President Kennedy, would continue to root out evil wherever it could find it.

(Except, of course, in the offices of the two directors.)

What no one knew was what Dulles had told me in a top-secret briefing after the election. He told me that the agency had for months been secretly training an army of anti-Castro Cubans. This army, he said, would soon invade Cuba; the faithful populace there would rally to its side; Fidel Castro would be toppled, and a government friendly to the United States would rise like Old Glory in his place.

As Dulles revealed this plan to me in the Oval Office, it sounded like music to my ears; like "The Star-spangled Banner," to be precise. Only later did I learn that a CIA microstereo, implanted in the director's right testicle, was in fact playing the national anthem all through our discussion, at a pitch too high for the human ear to hear, but not too high for the human gut. The invasion plan—since it would merely set Cuban against Cuban, and cost no American blood—sounded, against the stirring (if inaudible) anthem, like a fine idea. Worthy, in fact, of Pop. Getting rid of Castro as my first act of foreign policy would be a political tonic at home, and a warning to the Commies around the world that Kennedy played tackle, not touch. In addition, like some military Visa card, the plan had been preapproved: by Ike. Who was I to countermand the hero of D day?

But I want to make one thing perfectly clear (Nixon comes

automatically to mind when pleading ignorance): at no time during our conversation did Dulles brief me on the other plans afoot to kill Castro. He made no mention of depilatories for his beard, botulism for his cigars, poison for his food, or Mafia bullets for his brain. Historians have suggested that, because the director came to the second briefing dressed as a large, feathered bird, I should have asked more questions. My failure to do so I can only chalk up to inexperience. I hadn't even taken office yet; the head spook in an eagle suit was an awesome sight.

"I still think it was a good plan!"

I turn around, to see who spoke. It's Ike, himself. The general has wandered over from the Republican side; a rare visitation indeed.

"You still think the invasion of Cuba was a good idea?" I ask, incredulous.

"Invasion of Cuba, piffle. The plan to put Mamie in a clinic. To dry out. So I could have more time with—"

John Foster Dulles, emerging from behind the general, quickly clamps his hand over Ike's mouth.

"Golf!" Dulles says. "To have more time with his golf."

Ike wriggles free. "Of course golf," he says. "What did you think I was going to say?"

Dulles leans over, whispers in the general's ear. Ike's eyes widen. He peers at me, at Bobby, at Lyndon, at Adlai, at all of us.

"Democrats?" he asks. "These whippersnappers? Up here? I didn't think they allowed Democrats up here."

Dulles shrugs, as if to say it's not a perfect world. I wonder in passing if it's painful to the Lord, having, sometimes, to separate brothers.

"Who's that?" Ike asks, as the reverend approaches our group. Dulles leans over, whispers in the general's ear.

"Oh, a caddy," Ike says. "I suppose it's all right, if he's a caddy. For a moment there I couldn't believe my eyes."

Dulles moves closer, whispers to me now. "Please excuse the general. He thinks he's at the country club." To the others, aloud, for Ike's benefit, he says, "We're just playing through, gentlemen. Has anyone seen my ball?"

"Does it play 'The Star-spangled Banner'?" Lyndon asks.

Doing the arithmetic, you may have gathered, is one of the pastimes here. I remember clearly that John Foster Dulles passed away even before I was elected, which makes him several years beyond his time. I pose the question to the group.

"It's clear," Dr. King says, "that the Lord takes powerful note of those who die. But it may be that even He isn't current on those who pass away."

"Or it's possible," Bobby suggests, "that secretaries of state get an extra measure of purgatory. To fulminate at the tables of the Lord. To purge the bullshit."

"Or maybe," Lyndon asserts, "that peckerwood brother of his, just like Hoover, somehow still has clout."

Most likely, I decide, it's a simple mistake in bookkeeping.

The thought brings to mind some patter from the past: a little ditty I wrote, and performed, for Powers, O'Brien, and the boys while we drank green beer one fine St. Patrick's Day. I called it "The Cardinal's Son":

> He was a cardinal sin,
> He was the cardinal's son,
> He was a holy terror,
> He was a clerical error . . .

The issue in the song, as I recall, was the result of an affair between the cardinal and a nun. The key line in the refrain went: "He's getting into the habit now."

You may have noticed, in our expressions, what seems like disrespect at times. Even toward Him. It's calculated mischief; an attempt to stir His ire. An attempt at being *noticed*.

Here we huddle, amid the cosmic truths: still babes in toyland.

□ □ □

But back to my cabinet. I sought suggestions for the key cabinet posts, and the first list I was handed was from Pop. For Secretary of State, he recommended Benito Mussolini; for Defense, Hermann Goering; for Treasury, Hirohito.

My response was less than enthusiastic.

"Something wrong?" Pop asked.

"It's a bit on the conservative side," I said.

Pop pursed his lips, thinking it over. Then he pulled out a pad and quickly scrawled another list. It read as follows:

State—Jack. Defense—Teddy. Attorney General—Bobby. Treasury—Rosemary.

"I can't help noticing," I said, "that you've got me down for the State Department. Who did you have in mind for president?"

"Not to worry," Pop said. "I can handle it."

I assured him I would give his suggestions serious thought. I turned to a list that Sinatra had sent from the coast: Secretary of State—Ray Milland; Defense—Humphrey Bogart; Treasury—George Raft; United Nations—Gregory Peck; Peace Corps—Jimmy Stewart; Attorney General—Sam Giancana.

Except for the AG, I found his list oddly appealing. A cabinet to enthrall the country. It had one fatal flaw, however. In the Kennedy administration, it was I who was to be the star.

Frank's friend Shirley MacLaine sent in some suggestions that were equally intriguing: for State, Alexander the Great; for Defense, Genghis Khan; for Treasury, Rumpelstiltskin. A good list; except, I feared, communication might be a problem.

"Easy as pie," Shirley said, but I had my doubts.

From the Vatican, Pope John also sent a list of suggestions: for State, Dean Rusk; for Defense, Robert McNamara; for Treasury, Douglas Dillon.

In the end, of course, I made my own selections.

164

Bobby is apoplectic. "Don't *say* things like that about the pope," he implores. "People will *believe* you."

"It's a joke," I tell him. "Everyone can see that."

"Not the Baptists," Bobby warns.

How could she do it?

Aristotle Fucking Onassis!

It is a little-known fact, but true, that in his younger days, when presumably he could get it up, Onassis had a fling with Gloria Swanson. The same Gloria Swanson who was my father's mistress for three years.

Jackie professed to love my father. Now I was dead; Pop was in a wheelchair, speechless, the victim of a stroke; and Jackie starts screwing around with a jerk who had shared a mistress with Pop. On the face of it, it was simply vulgar. Was there, beneath the surface, something Freudian?

The truth is, I think not. But could she do it only for the money?

I am reminded of a joke. A millionaire asks a young woman if she will sleep with him for 10 million dollars.

"For ten million dollars?" the woman says. "I'll have to think about it."

"Will you sleep with me for five dollars?" the man asks.

The woman becomes enraged. "What do you think I am, a whore?"

The man replies calmly: "We've already established what you are. Now we're just haggling about the price."

Appreciative laughter greets my story. Lyndon likes it especially.

Aristotle Fucking Onassis!

When he and Jackie were about to announce their engagement, he sent an emissary to visit Miss Swanson. The emissary allowed as to how it would be difficult and embarrassing were she to reveal her ancient fling with Onassis, given her well-publicized relationship with Jackie's father-in-law. That classy lady replied that the very notion that she might

165

make the ancient fling public "flatters my memory even as it insults my integrity."

If Onassis were subtle enough to realize that he had been skewered by the remark, he had this consolation: the emissary had not even had to offer the considerable sum of hush money he had brought with him.

Jackie Oh!

"Remember that scene a while back?" Bobby says. "When Jackie was creating herself? I think that was exactly right. She was creating herself for you. To be first lady. Once you were gone, and she'd played the grieving widow for as long as she could stand it, there was nothing left. Beneath the pillbox hats there was no *her* left. And so she floundered."

Leave it to Bobby to defend her. Loyal to the end, and beyond. But perhaps he's right.

Jackie O.

Jackie Zero.

Loyalty. That, of course, was the main reason I named Bobby my attorney general. (That and the fact that he was unemployed.) When I'd filled out my cabinet, only the post at Justice was left. Pop had been lobbying for Bobby for months; had, in fact, been insisting on it. But Bobby wasn't interested. He did not want to spend his whole life in my shadow, he said. He did not want to work in the White House, taking orders from me. Or in the cabinet. What he wanted to do, he said, was go back to Massachusetts, run for governor, carve out a career of his own. Besides, he said, all hell would break loose if I named him the AG. People would cry nepotism (with mild justification); they would say he was too young, that he was not qualified.

All this I understood. But in the end I decided I needed him. Most of the others I'd picked were not cronies; I didn't know them. By reputation, they had brains, and talent; but I also needed someone I could trust. Completely. And so, one fine December day, I twisted Bobby's arm, almost literally. I made the announcement in front of the Georgetown house,

Bobby standing beside me, his little boy's tousled hair blowing in the wind.

"You had the guts of a burglar," Bobby says.

The ensuing public relations storm was predictable, and short-lived. Surprisingly, Bobby got most of the flack. As if he had demonstrated his unfitness for the job by accepting it.

Historians since have noted that it was probably my best appointment.

It was also a fateful one. What a conflagration swept through the underworld! Here, they reasoned, they had used good mob money, good mob singers, to elect Jack Kennedy president. They didn't like me, but they figured they could live with me; they figured they understood me; they figured they could use me. Especially since Judy had plenty of cleavage in which to carry messages. But Bobby? As attorney general? That they hadn't counted on. Bobby was their Public Enemy Number One.

In Chicago, when Sam Giancana heard the news, he jumped out the nearest window. (Unfortunately, he was in the basement at the time.) In Las Vegas, Johnny Roselli strapped himself to a roulette wheel and tried to double-zero himself to death. (Sinatra unhooked him, bloody but still breathing.) In Miami, Santo Trafficante jumped naked into a pool of hungry sharks. (The sharks turned out to be dolphins, who nuzzled him and whispered sweet nothings.) In New Orleans, Carlos Marcello tried to immolate himself. (His flame of choice, alas, was Cajun peppers.) You'd think such experienced killers might have done themselves in more successfully. But all of the worthy gentlemen survived.

Much, of course, to my ultimate chagrin.

So Bobby took over as head of the Justice Department, and he made the prosecution of organized crime his number-one priority. After his years with the Rackets Committee, he had spent much of 1959 writing a book about the mob and how its tentacles reached into almost every stratum of American life. *The Enemy Within*, he called it; he believed that organized crime was a greater internal threat to American freedom than Communism was. Since Hoover's official stance at the FBI was still that the mob was, like the unicorn, a mythical beast, Bobby created the Organized Crime Task Force within the Justice Department. He staffed it with the best investigators he could find, and he drew up a list of the men they needed to go after. Right at the top was Sam (Momo) Giancana. Followed almost immediately by Johnny Roselli, Santo Trafficante, and Carlos Marcello. Bobby told his investigators he didn't care what they got them for: if it wasn't murder or extortion, get them for tax evasion, for traffic violations, for pulling the DO NOT REMOVE tags off mattresses, anything they could make stick.

Pop was of the opinion that Bobby was being a poor sport. A man makes a sizable contribution to your campaign, you can overlook a few businesslike murders. But Bobby was tenacious; once he took the job, he was going to be the damndest AG in history.

While Bobby was chasing gangsters, Hoover sent over to my office, every few days, a secret FBI report on the sexual escapades of some senator or congressman. He thought the reports would amuse me, he said. In fact, of course, each was an implied threat. "Bobby may be my boss," J. Edgar was saying with each file he sent over. "And he may be closer to the president than I am, which is a situation I can't stand. But just remember: push me too far and I've got the same kind of reports on you."

"Effective, wasn't it?" Hoover says, grinning his toothless, mealy grin.

The passing white cloud has paused, is listening; I don't know why it can't make up its mind.

The Oval Office. Mine. Quickly I made it seaworthy: pictures of sailing ships on the walls, a replica of *PT-109* on the mantelpiece, a miniature full-rigger, gift of Chairman Khrushchev. I always felt the sea was a part of me, the salty bearer of my fate. It laps the shores of Ireland from whence my ancestors came; it supported the boats on which they sailed to America; it created Boston Harbor, where they lived; it caresses the sandy beaches of Hyannis Port, where we grew up. Into its arms I spilled when the Jap destroyer cut us in half, and its arms supported me during the four-hour swim to shore. By sea came the booze that made Pop's final fortune, and on sailboats did we as growing youngsters play. And yet a simple plaque on the wall of the office, a gift from Admiral Rickover, said it best: OH, LORD, THY SEA IS SO GREAT AND MY BOAT IS SO SMALL.

Lyndon leers. "Is that true, Jack? I always suspected you had a small boat. You wanna compare boats?"

His lewdness, I sometimes believe, is congenital. As if he were bred in a pasture, from a virgin and a Texas bull. A modern Minotaur.

And yet it was me they slew, amid the labyrinth.

Seated behind a large desk that Jackie found in the White House basement and had refinished, I turned my attention to foreign policy. All through the campaign I had attacked the Republicans for the mess they had gotten us into around the world. On taking office, I discovered the mess was as bad as I had claimed. In my State of the Union address at the end of January, I tried to warn the nation of what lay ahead. "The tide of events has been running out and time has not been our friend. . . . There will be further setbacks before the tide is turned."

In time of trouble, the sea again.

While Ike slept.

Some critics found my message too pessimistic. How could I know there would be further setbacks before the tide was turned?

Hell, that was the easy part. We were planning them ourselves.

Foremost among these was the abortive invasion of Cuba, which has come to be known as the Bay of Pigs. It is time now to reveal the truth about both the plan and its curious appellation.

"Apalachin?" Hoover interrupts. "There was no Apalachin. It was just a bunch of guys playing pinochle. A typical afternoon in the Catskills. Ask anybody. Ask Jackie Mason."

Hoover still doesn't know his Catskills from his Apalachins. I choose to ignore him.

I have already taken the blame for the fiasco. I did so as soon as it happened. But the real story, for security reasons, has not till now been told.

The critical fact is this. In the suburbs of Washington, D.C., there are two different institutions that go by the initials CIA. One, located at Langley, is the Central Intelligence Agency. The other, a few miles down the road at Boondock, is the Criminally Insane Asylum. In this instance, all the time we thought we were dealing with one CIA, we were actually dealing with the other.

That explains why the director came to see me wearing a large feathered suit. That is why he was playing the national anthem on his balls. That is why they asserted that Castro's well-equipped army of 120,000 men could be conquered by an invasion band of 1,400 expatriates; and if that failed, they asserted, the expatriates would disappear into the hills and begin a guerrilla war, much as Castro himself had done against Batista. That is why, when I made clear that the U.S. Air Force would not become overtly involved—that the vast might of the United States could not be seen before the whole world as picking on little Cuba—they asserted that the expatriates could triumph anyway.

In the face of such assertions, I agreed to let the invasion plan proceed. Not realizing my fatal mistake—that the plan had been conceived, and was being carried out, by the *wrong* CIA. I thought we were dealing with the Criminally Insane Asylum. Instead, the whole thing had been the brainchild of the Central Intelligence Agency.

Little wonder that not a single part of the plan worked right.

A bunch of old unmarked planes were supposed to destroy Castro's air force on the ground. Even the insane would have realized that the rubber bands on the planes would break. But the other CIA didn't. The insane would have realized that the population of Cuba—since the anti-Castro part of it had long since fled from the island—would not rise up against Castro. But the other CIA didn't. Most important, the insane would have realized that Castro would have a counterplan with which to meet such an invasion, which had been widely rumored in the press for months.

The Cuban defense plan was a simple one. Against the mighty Goliath of the United States, the Cuban dictator would use a young shepherd boy, David Gonzales.

All along Cuba's coastline, Castro had built enormous holding pens. These pens were filled with hundreds of thousands of pigs. As the invasion fleet, having set sail from not-so-secret bases in Guatemala, began to enter Cuban waters, the shepherd David moved along the line of pens, opening the gates. As each gate was opened, tens of thousands of pigs spilled out onto the beaches and into the shallow waters. Before long the entire bay where the invasion fleet was to come ashore was a grunting, squealing mass of slippery pigs. There was no room for the landing craft to enter: they kept bumping into masses of four-hundred-pound pigs. There was no way for the invaders to cross the beaches; instead of sand underfoot, there were massed pigs. The invaders could get no purchase on the backs of the wet, slimy hogs; they kept sliding off, and getting trampled. They had brought plenty of ammunition, but it was being absorbed by the fleshy pink porcine flanks. By nightfall, not a single invader had crossed the beach, and the only Cuban casualty was a BLT.

The Cubans protested the attempted invasion to the United Nations. Adlai, our ambassador, made a ringing denial that the United States was in any way involved. We had never told poor Adlai; and now, how could we? How could we admit that this ludicrous operation, supposedly spawned by the insane, had actually come out of the bowels of the Central Intelligence Agency? The whole country would be a laughing-stock.

In the war room that night, the agency argued for further escalation of the plan. Drop napalm on the Cuban pigs, they argued. Throw the fat into the fire. (Or vice versa.)

I refused. By this time, I knew which CIA I was dealing with. I called the whole thing off. And took the blame.

That is the first thing I learned as president, and the most important thing. It is the very lesson that Nixon refused to learn, and which brought him down. It should be rule number one in the guidebook for presidents: If you don't want the truth to come out, *take the blame*!

So I took the blame for the Bay of Pigs. So much so that it has become almost a generic term now. Rare is the man who doesn't, somewhere, have his Bay of Pigs, under one name or another.

Like Chappaquiddick.

"Like Watergate," the reverend says.

The sea, the sea. Always the eternal sea.

"Like the Tit Offensive," Lyndon says. "All them beautiful Asian girls, walking down out of North Vietnam, out of the jungles, opening their shirts; coming toward us, their luscious breasts erect in front of them, like naked shields. How did they expect our boys to fight? Shoot those sultry girls in the boobs? That was my personal Bay of Pigs; it brought me down. The goddamn Tit Offensive."

"That's *Tet*," Bobby says.

"Whatever."

I turn and look over my shoulder. At the cloud of lead. They are still there, waiting.

Diaphanous.

I had developed, from the moment I was elected, the image, the concept, that I wanted for my presidency: historic, great, even mythical in the profundity of its thought, in the grandeur of its accomplishments, in the symbology of its devotion to the right and the good and the eternal. I would sit not only with Roosevelt, not only with Lincoln; I would walk with Apollo.

Now, not three months in office, I had stumbled into a bay of pigs' knuckles, of hog jowls. I prowled the moonlight in the Rose Garden, alone, thinking, or with Sorensen, talking. It was the first real defeat of my life. I thought of Adlai, quoting Lincoln in another context, about the boy who stubbed his toe: he was too big to cry, but it hurt too much to laugh.

I analyzed what had gone wrong. The culprit was virginity, newness. I didn't yet know which advisers I could trust and which were blinded by their own biases. I hadn't yet learned that my instincts were superior to their "facts." Most of all, I hadn't yet drawn the distinction between Boondock and Langley; hadn't yet accepted the notion that while some things might be insane, others were downright wrong.

Unlike Sinatra with his injured girls, I couldn't pay Castro to keep the invasion out of the press. I had to accept the consequences.

In need of succor, I arranged a rendezvous. Death take the hindmost now; I had a rendezvous with Marilyn. It wasn't love, it was mythology. My private life, too, when the biographers unearthed my bones, would prove to have been monumental.

We met at the Carlyle (a hotel chosen, too, for its historic resonance). When I opened the door she was as I had requested—supine on red silk, the living image of the calendar which, years before, had made her famous. I stripped off my clothes and snuggled into the warmth of her; the whitenesses; the perfumes; the pinks, the blues, the fleshy creases. We cuddled for hours and then we fucked for just as long. No election-night jitters this time; I buried the Bay of Pigs in her recesses.

There was aggression without violence, passion without guilt. The only thing missing, I realized later, was the White House photographer.

When we were through she wrapped us in the silk. Silent we huddled, compact, cylindrical, pungent, like a good Havana cigar. A woman is only a woman . . . I forget what wise man said that. The surgeon general, perhaps.

With her permission I did, in time, produce a cigar. She took it from me, bit off the end, insisted on sucking air with her wonderful lungs while I toyed the flame of my lighter around the business end. Forever Marilyn, flaunting hints of next time before I could make my getaway.

The cigar lighted, she handed it over, asking, before I could exhale: "Why did you do it?"

I had no idea what she was talking about, and told her so.

"The Bay of Pigs," she said.

Political Marilyn. I always tried to suppress her bluntness in that arena. And usually lost.

"To get rid of Castro," I said.

"Why?" With that little-girl, wise ingenuousness. "What's he ever done to you?"

The pro forma rhetoric lit up like a slide show in my brain: saving the world from Communism . . . preventing a Russian foothold in the Western Hemisphere . . . thwarting the exporting of revolution . . .

These are difficult things to enunciate when the tender palm of Marilyn Monroe is cupped around your balls.

"Did you ever hear of the Monroe Doctrine?" I asked.

"I practically invented it," Marilyn said.

"Oh, I see." Puffing on the cigar. "And how does *yours* go?"

"Do unto others," Marilyn said, sliding down inside the red silk sheet, her head disappearing into the cylinder, into the cocoon, until I felt an exquisite softness upon me, and then a moment's gasp, and muffled words, up from the cylinder, ". . . as you would have them do unto you . . ."

And then no more words again. Only a snakelike, impossible wriggling. Until, her head still buried deep in the silk cocoon, what was presented to me was a lovely triangle. A damp invitation of curls. And droplets.

In an ashtray on the bedside table I set the cigar.

We were wet and heaving and wanted no silk when that round came to an end. Limp and naked we lay on the bed, exhausted. But Marilyn wasn't finished yet. With politics.

"James Monroe was a distant relative of mine," she said.

"That's ridiculous. Your real name is Norma Jean Baker."

"So was his," Marilyn said.

I pondered that one for a while. Marilyn was non sequitur

174

made flesh. Unless you held your breath and dove deep for meaning. More often than not it was there. Before I could puzzle that one out, however, Marilyn spoke again.

"That was way back in the eighteenth century. Do you still think it's relevant? In a world of jet planes and missiles and television? That this hemisphere is all ours? Then why isn't that hemisphere all theirs? We've got them surrounded by missiles and bombers, in Turkey, in Greece, in Spain, all over Europe. Their country's been raped by war a dozen times, and they live with that. With being surrounded. And we've never had a single foreign soldier on American soil, and we turn to jelly over a guy with a beard in Cuba. Can you explain me that, John Fitzgerald Kennedy?"

I reached for my cigar and got it lit again.

I couldn't explain her that.

Marilyn spoke again, earnestly. "You're the best-looking president we've ever had. You've got the best sense of humor. A detached irony that's very rare in politicos. Maybe the most intelligence, though I've heard good things about old Tom Jefferson in that arena."

"Is that so?" I said, trying to sound offended. "Tom Jefferson? Where did you hear that?"

"It's in the presidential papers of my great-great-great-great-grandfather. Norma Jean Monroe."

"I see," I said, sorry I had interrupted. I wanted her to go on. And she did.

"You've got everything it takes to be a great president," she said. "But that alone is not enough. There's one thing more you need."

"Dare I ask?"

I was trying to feel amused, even offended, at this lecture from a sex goddess. The truth is, I was enthralled.

"You have to act great, Jack. I don't mean playact, like me. That's not enough, not for a president. For a candidate, maybe; maybe it's enough for your dad. But not for you. Not to be great. History won't be fooled by images. Not mine, not yours.

175

To be great you have to do great things. Just like a writer has to write great books, or a painter paint great paintings. A president has to perform great acts."

"I thought I did pretty good just now," I said, puffing.

Marilyn frowned, though not, I think, in anger. "You can start by stopping your patronizing of women. Your using of them. But you know what I'm talking about. Public acts."

I couldn't help myself. "You want to go down and do it in the park?"

"Go ahead, make jokes," Marilyn said. "Maybe you'll get into the comedians' hall of fame. Georgie Jessel will speak at the ceremony. Frank will sing. But what about the nation's hall of fame? The world's? History's, for Chrissake! That's your goal, Jack. You know it and I know it. But to get there will require great acts. Great moral acts."

I started to smile. She saw it and plunged on. "Go ahead, make some dumb joke about great immoral acts. But I'm serious. Politics as usual won't fool anybody. You've got to transcend that. You've got to make some great internal leap of personal moral vigor."

I interrupted again. "Is that like vigah?"

She said nothing. She saw the truth of it, as she often did. I was playing the clown to hide the wounds she was inflicting. Inflicting with malice toward none, but to energize me to a higher calling.

"You see the presidency, then," I asked, "as a morality play?"

"Not as any kind of play. As a moral stance. A moral symbol, yes, but a symbol of a moral real. You don't have to live very long to realize there is no morality among the gods. But why is that? Perhaps so that men will discover it for themselves. And become proprietary. And make it human."

I was struck by an idle thought: Did Mae West ever talk like that?

"Go ahead, scoff if you like," she said. "But history will prove me right. Regardless of the current wisdom, the current power fields, the current consensus. Go ahead, kill Castro, if you think that will make you a hero. But kill the part of you that needs to kill Castro, and you can become . . ."

"A saint?"

"You'll never pass the physical. But you can become . . . I don't know . . ."

"Another President Monroe?"

"Another Churchill, maybe. Will that do?"

That will do fine, I thought.

What I said was "I don't want to be another anybody."

"Great. Be yourself then. That's all anybody can be, I suppose. The best damn Willy Loman you can be, or whatever the hell play that was from. But do you know who the real Jack Kennedy is, under all the imagery? Find it, Jack, find it before it's too late. You might be pleasantly surprised. Now, for Chrissake, call room service and buy a lady a drink while I take a shower. So I don't have to wonder who the real Norma Jean really is."

With that she leaped from the bed and ran into the bathroom, not bothering to cover herself. I thought I heard the sound of two loud sobs before the shower drowned them out.

I could not be sure.

Not then, not now.

I reached for the phone and dialed room service and ordered the drinks. I replaced the receiver and lay there, my heart throbbing in my chest, my mind in wild turmoil; and my guts.

Above the sound of the muffled shower there were distinct sobs now. Distinct and unmistakable.

This time they were mine.

Silence surrounds me as I conclude. No wisecracks from anyone. Each, I think, for the moment, is looking inward. Finally it is Bobby who speaks, a hoarseness, a hint of pain, in his voice. He asks why I am doing this, why I am being so personal.

An unexamined death, I reply, is not worth dying.

On the trip back to Washington, I pondered deeply what Marilyn had said. I had gone after her as a world-class dalliance, nothing more. But she was threatening to become my Golden Muse; life giver, spirit giver, to the Good Jack.

"An odd choice of words there—*threatening*," Adlai notes.

By the time I got off the plane I was excited. The hell with invasions, the hell with killing Castro. I had a better idea. I would fight Castro *with* Castro. I had toyed for several months with the idea of a concerted economic development of Latin America. An Alliance for Progress, we would call it. The al- ianza. Now I sketched some quick notes—and they went far beyond mere economic aid. If the Communists were exporting revolution, then we could do the same with democracy. With the same fiery passion; even bearded and cigar smoking, if necessary. In the marketplace of ideas, even in the marketplace of revolutions, democracy could triumph on its own human terms. That must become our belief. That must become our passion.

I invoked the alliance a few days later, and it was not merely about economic aid, the stuff that puts people to sleep. It was about the future of the region, and the world.

"Let us once again," I implored, "transform the American continent into a vast crucible of revolutionary ideas and ef- forts."

It was a new Monroe doctrine, shaped for the modern world, built on passion and morality instead of guns.

What I dared not call it—though it would have been the truth—was the Marilyn Monroe Doctrine. But for the discern- ing historian, for the subtly annotative, I included a few hints. By building, for instance, the key sentence of the entire speech around the word *crucible*. It was a wink to Marilyn across the continent; she caught it and winked back. Among the thou- sands of telegrams that poured in after the speech were a dozen red roses with a card attached. The card said: "From the real Norma Jean."

"You see!" Hoover says. "That's why she had to die. She was making the president soft in the head. Soft on Communism. I'm not saying she was a spy, the Manchurian Pussy, nothing like that. Don't get me wrong. Marilyn Monroe was as American as cantaloupes. But if she was turning the president to mush in the face of the evil Communist menace, then something had to be done about it. In the national interest. For the national survival!"

I glare at him in silent fury, filled with the hatred of the ages.

That is something we are supposed to give up, in our twenty-five years here: the hatred of the ages.

At the moment I am filled, however, not with God but with Goya: "The sleep of reason produces monsters."

What is Hoover doing here!

I cannot speak to the unspeakable.

If Marilyn was my golden Muse, I had of course my dark Muse as well. It was not that Judy was corrupt, or evil; she wasn't. But through the nether darkness between her legs I was communing with the underworld. The devil as godfather. Sam Giancana, who had his men hang enemies alive on meat hooks and poke their naked balls with cattle prods, was sharing the same moist box. Judy the person almost ceased to matter; she was an innocent whose perfect vulva, whose inviting labia, had become a repository for the contending forces within the American nature, within the American soul. There in her eternal tubes two armies of contending sperms did clash by night; did fatal, fetal battle, as on a darkling plain; as blonde and dark did battle, warring for my contentious Self.

The next round went to darkness. Not six weeks after the Bay of Pigs, on the thirtieth of May, we killed Trujillo.

By *we* I mean the CIA, of course. With my unspoken—

"Unspeakable!" Adlai says.

—approval.

It was almost another disaster. But I had learned something from the Bay of Pigs: to be more careful, to read the fine print. And so it was that, a week before the murder, I found the following sentence in a memo: "As approved by the highest authority, on the 30th of May, during the second game of a

Memorial Day doubleheader, Dominican nationals armed and trained covertly shall enter Candlestick Park and gun down Rafael Trujillo, the shortstop of the San Francisco Giants."

I nearly hit the ceiling. I called McGeorge Bundy into my office double quick and threw the memo in his lap.

"The fucking shortstop of the San Francisco Giants!" I screamed. "What the hell are they talking about?"

Bundy read the memo. He turned to the cover sheet. "It's Langley!" he said. "Why are we dealing with Langley? The assignment was for the CIA at Boondock."

"Damn right it was," I said. "You better get it straightened out, or heads are gonna roll!"

By the time he left the office, one head had already rolled. Allen Dulles, I decided right then, was out on his feathered ass.

Bundy straightened things out. The Criminally Insane Asylum got it done. Rafael Trujillo, the fascist Dominican dictator, was shot and killed by his own nationals, and a puppet government friendly to U.S. interests took his place. And few suspected, and none could prove, that we had done it.

That same afternoon, I was happy to report to a meeting of the NSC, Rafael Trujillo of the San Francisco Giants went three for four with a walk.

As a matter of private conscience, I quickly endorsed a bill providing increased economic aid to the Dominicans.

They have been successfully growing shortstops ever since.

Ivier.

"*Ivier?* That's no word," Martin says. "Is it, Adlai?"

"I don't think so. I suppose it could be a gardener who specializes. But I doubt it."

"Sure it's a word," Boby says. "Look it up."

"We don't have a dictionary," Martin says. "If it's a word, use it in a sentence."

Bobby grins. "Although both Brown and Harvard are in the Ivy League, Harvard is Ivier."

180

Heavenly Scrabble. What can I tell you? Some people are less introspective than others.

On the third of June, four days after the assassination of the correct Trujillo, I was in Vienna for a face-to-face meeting with Chairman Khrushchev. I was interested for literary as well as political reasons, my own congenital mix of poetry and power. It was like stepping into the pages of Orwell, for a chat with the head pig. Also like flying Air Force One into my dreams.

Jackie was with me, looking ravishing in a wardrobe by Cassini. She was an asset in any meeting with foreign leaders, most of whose wives were built like dachas. Jackie could have charmed the pants off any of them, had she been interested in that sort of thing. Looking back, however, I sometimes wish she had been less attuned to fashion and more to the proper pursuit of modern first ladies. Then she could, perhaps, have suggested a better date for the meeting; just as the old actress chose the proper date for Bitburg. (One should never honor Nazis when Mars is in the house of Jupiter.)

"Or Venus, for that matter," says a friend of the passing white cloud.

It was not a true summit meeting, in the sense that we had no formal agenda, no accords to reach, no treaties to sign. It was a get-acquainted session, a feeling out, like boxers in the first round; in the hope that we could avoid stumbling into a nuclear war because of miscalculation by either side. If knowledge of each other's personalities could not bring friendship, it might at least avert catastrophe.

I brought the chairman a gift: a leather-bound volume of the poems of Robert Frost. And he brought me a gift: a leather-bound Soviet tractor.

"Please excuse the ungainly size," Khrushchev said, as the huge tractor was unloaded. "I told them to give you a Soviet tract. A small mix-up. It happens."

I thought immediately of Langley. "I understand," I said.

(When we got home I told Lyndon the tractor was for him.

He was much impressed with the chairman's thoughtfulness.)

After the opening pleasantries, our talks were wide-ranging: on the exporting of revolutions, on Cuba, on Laos, on Iran. I warned the chairman that the Russians could not expect to take over the world for Communism. He replied that they had no need or desire to do so, but that the United States must not hold Russia to blame every time an oppressed people rose up to overthrow a fascist dictatorship. In Iran, he warned, the shah would eventually be toppled—and it would not be by the Russians. I warned him that America would stand up for its national interests everywhere. He did not back down; he seemed to me as tough as any of Bobby's mobsters.

I suspected that we might do better if we cleared the room of advisers, if we talked alone, one on one. The chairman agreed to try it. As the last interpreter left and the door closed behind him, Khrushchev relaxed visibly. But I knew I must remain on guard.

"So," he said, leaning back, clasping his hands on his large belly, "how is Marilyn Monroe in the sack?"

I felt that was none of his business. "Maya Plisetskaya is just an illusion," I said.

I apparently touched a nerve. "Fuck Babe Ruth!" he said.

I considered storming out right then. But in diplomacy, what is not said is often more important than what is said. It could have been worse, I realized. He could have said, "Fuck Carl Yastrzemski."

I decided to change the subject. "The pen of my aunt is on the table," I said.

"Why does your director dress like a bird?" he asked.

We continued in that vein for some time. "A useful exchange of views," as the joint communiqúe would say. Then I pressed him on the single most important issue that divided us, the one that could most quickly lead to a nuclear war: Khrushchev's announced plan to sign a peace treaty with East Germany, and thus seal off the West from Berlin. I warned him he could not do that.

"What are your plans for Berlin?" I asked.

He declined to answer, on the ground that it might tend to incriminate him.

I pressed him again; again he did not respond. "Enough of power," he said. "Now some poetry." He handed me the gift I'd brought him. "Read me one of your brother Bobby's poems."

"Robert Frost," I said. "He's not my brother." I flipped the pages until I found a favorite, and I began to read.

"That's it!" Khrushchev said. He jumped up from his chair, and he came around the table. "That's it, that's it, that's it!"

"What's it?" I asked, puzzled. "That's what?"

When I stood, he hugged me tight, like a brother. "Your poetry is wonderful," he said. He took the book from me, and there was rapture in his eyes as he began to read aloud what I'd just read.

"Something there is," Nikita Khrushchev intoned, "that doesn't love a wall."

I was pleased, yet puzzled, by his enthusiasm. It was a pretty good line, I agreed, but not a *great* line.

November 21 became November 22 at the Texas Hotel in Fort Worth, where we arrived shortly before midnight. Jackie, tired from the long day of campaigning, retired directly to her bedroom as always. Her lady-in-waiting, Minerva Cheevy, unpacked her suitcase, hung up the pink suit she would be wearing in the morning, placed her favorite stuffed horse on her pillow. At my end of the suite I kicked off my shoes, put my feet up on an ottoman, quaffed a cold bottle of Corona while Raymond drew my bath. Raymond seemed edgy, perhaps, I thought, because we were already in the voodoo vibrational zone of Dallas, to which we'd be heading in the morning. It turned out that was only partly the cause of his restlessness; he was eager to get out to a late date he had with Minerva.

"Cheating on your wife?" I chided him.

"We're just gonna have a drink in the lobby," Raymond said.

I couldn't really blame him; I could appreciate the trim cocoa cuves of Minerva Cheevy myself. Unfortunately for both of us, she was only eighteen, echoing the fate of her poetic forebear in this: she'd been born too late. Once, finding her alone in Jackie's bedroom in the White House, I'd asked about her name. "Minerva was the goddess of wisdom," she'd replied, blushing a hot chocolate.

"Also of the arts," I'd said, wanting to touch her cheek, but not daring to; this child.

Energized by the moment that had slipped away, I crossed to Jackie's room, hoping to catch a glimpse of Minerva now. She was already gone, primping, perhaps, for her drink with Raymond. Jackie, in a white peignoir, was propped on her pillows, glancing through a magazine.

"*Vanity Fair?*" I asked, nodding.

"They stopped publishing years ago. *Cosmopolitan.* There's an interesting quiz in here, actually. 'How to Tell If Your Husband Is Cheating on You.' "

"And?"

"You don't want to hear it," Jackie said.

I sat on the bed beside her; I squeezed her hand. It was the only way I knew to say I love you.

Bobby snorts. Bobby frowns. Bobby, dear heart, is trying not to say something. He always, of course, loses these battles. "What was wrong with telling her in words?" he says.

"Words? Words? How would it have looked? Me and Jackie naked on the sheets, twisting, moaning, and Sorensen beside us in his suit and tie, riffling through his *Bartlett's.*"

Bobby gives me his best you're-hopeless look. "It didn't seem to stop you with Marilyn," he says.

I look at him, surprised; shocked, almost. This is something we never discussed in life.

"I never loved Marilyn," I say. "Not like that. I never told her I loved her."

"I know," Bobby says. "You told her that *I* loved her."

"What's wrong with that? It was the truth, wasn't it?"

"That was for me to know and for her to find out."

"Why?"

"Because I couldn't *do* anything about it."

"Why not?"

"Because I loved Ethel. I didn't *want* to do anything about it."

"How could you not want to? Even Hoover said it a minute ago: 'She was as American as watermelons.' "

"Cantaloupes."

"What?"

"As American as cantaloupes, is what Hoover said."

"Right. Toward the end she drooped, but only a little. Cantaloupes, then. So how could you not want to? Especially if you were in love with her?"

"Of course I wanted to, in my fantasies. Those last few months, every night, when me and Ethel made love, it was really Marilyn I was fucking. In my mind. Right up her ass from behind, with my hands clasped tight to her honeydews."

"Cantaloupes. Every night? You were married for twelve years by then, you had about seven kids, and you and Ethel fucked every night?"

"Of course."

"That's preposterous. That's downright sick."

"The only thing that made it sick," Bobby says, sadly, "is that sometimes in my mind it was Marilyn I was fucking."

"That's not what made it sick, Bobby. That's what made it at least a little healthy. That's what made it good for you."

"It's funny," Bobby says. "That's exactly what Ethel said."

"Ethel? You told Ethel that? You told Ethel that all the time you were making love to her, you were really screwing Marilyn?"

"Not her. I told Ethel Rosenberg. Yesterday. She told me it was all right. 'Whatever gets you through the night,' she said. Julius wasn't very good in bed, she said. What she did, she would lie there and think of atomic bombs going off. It worked every time."

"Aha!" J. Edgar says, sidling nearer, taking notes.

"Aha what? What are you doing?"

"Taking notes. Gathering evidence. In case they give the Rosenbergs a new trial."

"They've been dead for thirty-five years," Bobby points out.

"With these liberal judges, you can't be too careful," Hoover says.

We stare at him with focused eyes, until he melts away. (Would we could have done that in life!) I see him down among the flames, talking heatedly with Pop. Sharing his new evidence, no doubt: orgasms and atoms.

It is a welcome diversion. Between Bobby and me there is an awkward silence. Discomfort, the first since our early years. The truth has been spoken at last: I used to fuck Marilyn without really loving her; Bobby truly loved her, without ever fucking her. I was the rake, as always, heedless of consequences; Bobby was the puritan, as always, mindful of a higher god. But in this case my sexual thrusts were daggers into Bobby's heart.

And still he loved me.

"Or did he?" Lyndon asks. "Passion is a rat poison. He had all those contacts with Hoover. With the CIA. With the mob. Perhaps it was Bobby who was behind it all! In Dallas. Be like him to pick Dallas, to embarrass me."

For a moment I do not grasp what Lyndon is saying. Then it strikes me with the impact of a steamroller. I draw my right arm back to smash his face. The reverend, anticipating my move, grabs me from behind in a bear hug.

"Nonviolence," he says, as I struggle in his powerful grasp. "Remember?"

It's taken Bobby even longer to understand what Lyndon was saying, so alien is the notion. A flush that must have started at his ankles now rises like a rash across his face. He leaps at Lyndon, who ducks his large frame. Bobby lands on Lyndon's back, his arms around the fleshy neck. Lyndon struggles to free himself from the burden of Bobby, even as he did in life. As if this Kennedy nettle is his karma. They struggle that way, like bucking bronc and jockey-sized bareback rider. Lyndon ducks, trying to throw Bobby over his head; for an instant they are one, like a centaur. Then as Bobby starts to slide it's Raymond by his side, half to pull him off Lyndon, half to cushion his fall. With Raymond as fall guy each can claim victory.

The action has cooled my anger, but only a little. Martin

still is holding me. I glare at Lyndon. I see that Bobby is glaring at me. As if resentments long buried, never given expression, have risen now to the surface. Red faced, breathing hard, he is trying not to speak. But the bitterness bursts forth in an angry torrent.

"I loved her. I loved her with all my heart! How could you keep seeing her, after you knew that? You had an endless supply of women. Angie Dickinson. Jayne Mansfield."

"Speaking of watermelons . . ." Martin says, loosening his grip a little.

"Not to mention Fiddle and Faddle."

"Fiddle and Faddle?" Adlai asks.

"Two secretaries from the White House pool," Raymond explains.

I note that the notion of privacy, if not of loyalty, seems to dwindle up here. Right quick, in Raymond's case. As if officially now he's one of us. Neither race nor position of servitude a burden in the afterlife.

"Do you have a problem with that?" Martin asks.

"I didn't say I had a problem with that, Reverend."

"Why, Jack, why?" Bobby implores. "Why didn't you give her up, when you knew I loved her?"

"Why didn't you ask me to?"

"I couldn't do that. I was loyal to Ethel. I was going to stay loyal to Ethel. I would have looked ridiculous. But you should have known what I was feeling."

What can I tell him? That I didn't understand what he was feeling? That, incapable of true love, I could not fathom it in others? Such is the barren truth, painful even now. I see no point in delving into it.

"Delve!" an ominous voice says.

I spin around in a thicket of apprehension. No one is near but the passing white cloud. Can such a fearsome order, such a fearsome voice, emanate from such a wisp of innocence?

Shall I say she was my Muse, my glistening golden conscience? Shall I say I was planting my seed in her to save my soul? Eating her for God and country?

"Melts in your mouth, not in your hand." Lyndon quivers.

"Say what is the truth!" Bobby screams.

"Done!" I shout back. "This is the truth. She was an over-grown child without a father, who never had love. I was the ultimate authority figure—and yet incapable of love. We were the perfect match. Searching for love in each other's thrusts and parries. Secure in the knowledge that we would never find it. The ultimate turn-on, the ultimate aphrodisiac—the knowledge that you will never be sated, no matter how much you grunt and sweat and spill fierce liquids. Neuroses that coalesced; that assured us that though we could never truly love, or be loved, at least we were not alone. The King of Power, the Queen of Passion, entwined in skin and vigah, secure in the knowledge that love would not be born. And so . . ."

I pause. I stop. I should spare him that, at least.

"And so?" Bobby urges, wild, agitated.

And still I hesitate.

"And so?" says the passing white cloud.

Surely, the white cloud knows.

"And so, in time, she began to yearn for what I couldn't give. She began to yearn for love that was pure and true. And undemanding. She began to yearn, in short, Bobby, for you."

The cry from Bobby is unearthly. Free of Raymond, he hides his face in his hands. "I knew it," he says, muffled. "I knew it." He pulls his hands clear of his face. "I knew it," he shouts, "and I did nothing!"

The torment in his eyes is unspeakable. That at least I have to assuage.

"But you couldn't do anything, Bobby. Don't you understand that? That's the part of you she loved. You were Don Quixote, to her Dulcinea. Loving pure and chaste from afar. If you were different, if you had come on to her, if you had taken her to bed, you would have destroyed her love in an instant. You would have become, in her eyes, just like all the others. A use of her body, nothing more. You would have become"—I cannot rid the sadness from my voice—"you would have become, to her, nothing more than me."

"But I loved her truly!" Bobby exclaims, mournfully.

"Precisely what she could not accept. Except through messengers. Intermediaries. Go-betweens. Except through me."

There is a broken silence. Lyndon finds it embarrassing. "Jesus, Bobby," he says. "And all that time, you didn't know how much fun you were having."

Bobby looks at him, then at me, then at him again, with a tinge of hatred. The silence among us is throbbing like spent passion as we each remember Marilyn. Even the white cloud is throbbing.

"She was a bridge," Bobby says. "In body and mind. You could almost define it, a bridge over troubled waters. In the fifties she was the quintessential woman, as created by man: Diamonds are a girl's best friend. By the end she was the career girl, the band singer, the self-made alcoholic; the misfit. *Some Like It Druggy.* She was a flower child, in a way; the very first flower child, trapped in a woman's used body. An innocence that wanted to do good in the world, a body that wanted to love freely. But, like them, she didn't have the power to do good, even if she'd have known how; and, like them, loving freely didn't make her happy. So, like them, she turned to chemicals."

"You don't think the flower children did good?" the reverend asks.

"They did drive Lyndon from office," I say.

"Hell, no," Lyndon objects. "They did no such thing. Squirrelly little cunts and their filthy boyfriends with hair down to their dicks. I wasn't in trouble till the parents out in the suburbs turned against me."

"After the Tit Offensive," the reverend says.

The eyes from the cloud of lead are crawling on my neck like prickly heat. I see no point in rehashing Vietnam. Raymond, my friend, senses this. He brings the subject back to Marilyn.

"Is it true what they wrote in the tabloids?" he asks Bobby. "That Marilyn wanted you to divorce Ethel and marry her. So she could become first lady when you became president?"

Bobby seems suddenly weary; he wants to end the matter.

His words sound empty now, matter-of-fact. "She knew I couldn't love her—make love to her—while I was married to Ethel. She also knew I wouldn't divorce Ethel. She had no false hopes; those would have kept her alive. She had no hope at all. That's what led to the drinking, the pills, her fears that she might go mad. People can't live without hope. But she didn't want to be the first lady. She already was the first lady; first lady of the whole American century. Certainly more than Jackie ever was.

"Marilyn knew that, and found it empty. Unlike Jackie, she'd had a surfeit of fame, of adoration. Of the roar of the crowds. What she heard at the end, I think, were all the little voices. Of the abortions. Of the miscarriages. The tiny hands, the tiny feet, the tiny mouths that weren't saying I love you, Mommy."

"Did you talk to her about that stuff?" I ask.

"She was too busy filling your bed."

"Not then. Later. Up here. You had plenty of time to talk up here."

"Twenty years," Bobby says. "But up here there was no need to talk. We just sat together, side by side. Looking down at the blue-green earth, winking at the passing white cloud. Holding hands. Smiling at each other, shyly, when the passing white cloud winked back."

There is awe in our silence now, even in Lyndon's. In all our years up here, none of the rest of us has known this: the passing white cloud winking back.

On August 13, barely two months after Vienna, the East Germans began to erect, by dark of night, the Berlin Wall.

To say that it is Robert Frost's wall, inspired by his imagery, is not to malign the poet. Quite the contrary, the wall itself has been much maligned. It is in its way a solid symbol of the confinements that all nations impose—that the very concept of nationhood implies—to one degree or another. More important, it is a monument to man's stubborn will to survive. The truth is, the wall may well have saved mankind.

The Russians were being sorely embarrassed that year by

a steady stream of émigrés crossing from East Berlin to the relative freedom of the West. It was to cease this flow that Khrushchev was threatening to sign a treaty with East Germany. If the East Germans then sealed off Berlin, we would have to deal with them, and we did not recognize their statehood. Relaxing our commitment to defend the freedom of West Berlin would undermine our commitment to all of Western Europe, and to all of our allies everywhere. This I made clear to Khrushchev at Vienna: Berlin was one of our vital national interests: he should not miscalculate; we were prepared to go to war, if necessary, over Berlin.

And so, inspired by my gift of poetry, the wall. This concrete barrier by which the Communists themselves proclaimed Communism to be a prison. Oh, we in the West wailed and beat our breasts over what a terrible thing it was. Suggestions of what we should do about it landed on my desk like an avalanche. Most of them were simple, direct: we should go in there and knock it down. The fact was, the wall was in East German territory; the East Germans had every right to build it (every legal, if not human right). Other suggestions were more exotic. One in particular I remember was to drop Bob Mathias and the Olympic pole-vaulting team behind the wall by parachute, to secretly teach the East Germans how to vault their way into the West. (As an added incentive, successful émigrés would get their pictures on boxes of Wheaties.) Another was to send a trompe l'oeil artist to Berlin, to paint holes in the wall through which people could escape. After considering all the options, I did nothing. The wall still stands today, a monument, some say, to my cowardice.

The fact is this: the wall successfully cut off the flow of refugees. If the Russians could live with the ignominy of the wall, but not with the ignominy of the exodus, so be it. With the exodus stopped, Khrushchev abandoned his plans for a treaty. The access of the West to Berlin was not threatened. A military confrontation—perhaps even a nuclear one—was averted. Human existence itself may have been saved.

I call it proudly, therefore, the poet's wall: an image cast in stone, a symbol incarnate. If, indeed, there is something that doesn't love a wall, consider this: consider the road not taken.

The reverend has been pondering the matter of posthumous popularity, of the relativity of reputations. "If Jackie had taken a bullet with you in Dallas," he observes, "she would have died a queen."

What he says is true, of course, and its implications are somewhat sad: most people live long enough to disgrace themselves.

One of the rare, if not exemplary, exceptions, was Pop. In December of '61 he suffered a stroke. His left side was paralyzed. He was confined to a wheelchair. He couldn't speak, except to mouth at times indecipherable animal noises. He was barely continent, and he drooled. In Hyannis, in Palm Beach, wherever we happened to be, he was simply parked in the shade, like a pram. Painful though it was, we recognized the truth: Pop had lived to the point where he could no longer disgrace himself.

The stock schemes, the booze running, the real-estate scams, the whoring, the Nazi worship, the string pulling, all still dwelled inside him, one assumes, like past lives. Whether he recollected them we couldn't tell. If time, as some say, is the fourth dimension, then there he dwelled; there was nothing else left.

It must also be the worst dimension: mortal powerlessness, with nothing but time on your hands, and in your mind. For even down there among the flames, where I see him now, Pop has risen. Now he has cronies again, and laughter.

"Do not make light of it!"

There is, in the voice of the white cloud, this time, the screech of lizards, the sting of scorpions, a sound I have never heard.

"Do not make light of it—or you shall pay a visit."

There is a shudder in my very essence. It is not a visit I care to make.

□ □ □

And yet . . .

On September 18, 1961, the crash of a light plane in the Congo claimed the life of Dag Hammarskjöld of Sweden, the secretary general of the United Nations. The former Belgian colony had been transformed into a comic-opera jungle in which real blood was being let. Lumumba had been assassinated; Tshombe, Mobutu, Kasavubu were warring for power. Hammarskjöld had gone there to lend his personal prestige to a U.N. presence that was maintaining a perilous peace.

His death led to his winning, posthumously, the Nobel Peace Prize. It also led to a crisis at the United Nations; the Russians wanted to replace him with a troika, a political move that we managed to defeat. Much more important to me personally, however, was the fact of his premature death. He was here to welcome me upon my own arrival two years later; he was here to be my guide.

In life we hadn't known each other. In his position, he could not befriend national leaders, or he would forfeit the vital appearance of neutrality. Privately, I later discovered, he also had few real friends. A major player on the world stage, he was, in the depths of his soul, a lonely man.

As are we all.

There was, to Dag, as I came to call him, an internal elegance beneath a gentle strength: in death as there had been in life. We took, in those early days, long, thoughtful strolls among the clouds, discussing philosophies: an attempt to ease my transition. His assignment to be my guide was not an accident. (Nothing here is, I suppose.) In life he was a spirit who seemed to have passed beyond carnal knowledge. And this troubled him deeply; he experienced it as a weakness, an emptiness.

"I would imagine," Lyndon says.

"Quiet," Adlai says, listening, intent.

In fact, it was something much more profound: a kind of rehearsal. This he didn't learn until he was here. When I jokingly remarked that I was not the ascetic type, he seemed al-

194

ready to know this. His tone became that of a mentor. His words were cautionary: "You cannot play with the animal in you without becoming wholly animal, play with falsehood without forfeiting your right to truth, play with cruelty without losing your sensitivity of mind. He who wants to keep his garden tidy doesn't reserve a plot for weeds."

When he said that, I paused among the clouds, transfixed. It was as if he had seen right through me, had penetrated all of my secrets, both of state and of nature. It was as if he had written my epitaph.

It was as if some prayer were expected of me, right there, on the spot. JFK's Prayer:

> Forgive me, O Lord, because I have played with the animal in me, and become wholly animal.
>
> Forgive me, O Lord, because I have played with falsehood and I have forfeited my right to truth.
>
> Forgive me, O Lord, because I have played with cruelty, and have lost my sensitivity of mind.

I thought of such a prayer, but I did not say it; I did not utter the words. Not then. Not ever.

And yet it was many years ago that Hammarskjöld said those words to me; and try as mightily as I could, I have not forgotten them.

They have led, indirectly, to this book, this confession, this naked narrative, this summing-up. They even contain its only true title: *Weeds.*

One night years later, a particularly restless night when I was haunted by his words, I went to see him. I protested his epitaph for me—though he had never claimed that that was what it was. I tried to maintain a detached demeanor, tried to suppress my anguish."It wasn't all weeds," I said. "I did a lot of good works. A lot of damn good works."

His reply was without condescension. "God sometimes allows us to take the credit—for His work. Or withdraws from it into His solitude. He watches our capers on the stage with an ironic smile—so long as we do not tamper with the scales of justice."

At first my anger flared; he would give me credit for the weeds, but not for the good works! It was unfair bookkeeping, by any reckoning. Only later did I see, did I accept with gratitude, the implication of his comment. Weeds though there were, countless, countless weeds—I am showing you now the entire garden—still, in the end, *I did not tamper with the scales of justice!*

This he was allowing me. How many politicians, how many presidents, how many leaders of nations, how many *commanders in chief*, can say that?

This remark, too, led to my summing-up. It gave me the courage to tell all. Let the lesser truths be naked, so long as the larger truth prevails. It may be negative, but it is awesome: I did not tamper with the scales of justice.

"Try mightily though you did," Lyndon says, smirking.

Lyndon had little use for Hammarskjöld. "The Adlai Stevenson of the afterlife," he called him once, behind both of their backs.

It is a comparison that Adlai, now, hopes to be worthy of.

Two years ago—a little more than two—on the eighteenth of September 1986, Hammarskjöld's twenty-five years expired. There are many different ways to depart this vale of years. Some go quietly, alone, into whatever night or day or dawn awaits. Some have small gatherings of friends to see them off; upon occasion there is a party. Most anything tasteful is permitted. The traveler knows not, in any case, where he is going; what, if anything, lies beyond. But with Dag, something special was afoot. It was not announced, not formal, and yet it was clear to all.

Precisely what was different is hard to define. A private man, as I've said, he had no close friends to bid him adieu. As his pupil, I was privileged to be among the last to wish him well. More than a spiritual handshake, a kind of spiritual clasping to the bosom is what it felt like. But the difference was in his departure. Most, simply, at the appointed hour, vanish.

196

Dag Hammarskjöld *ascended*. It was not something that we physically saw, no rising in the sky to join the stars. But it was something that we knew, all of us, as surely as if we had witnessed it. Whatever lies ahead for most, Dag was going somewhere else. I heard no heavenly music, but I thought of Horatio's benediction over the fallen Hamlet. Flights of angels, I knew, were singing Dag Hammarskjöld to his eternal peace.

If there have been other such ascensions in my many years here, I am not aware of them.

In introspective moments, I sometimes feel less like Hamlet, more like Prufrock, who heard the mermaids singing, each to each. I do not think the angels will sing for me.

(Though the family will spread the word, of course, that they did.)

While I was preoccupied with foreign policy, Bobby, over at Justice, was pursuing his attack on crime. His first major move was against one of the most vicious and most powerful, but one of the least known, mob bosses in America. His name was Carlos Marcello.

Carlos, based in New Orleans, was the godfather of the South and Southwest. He owned half of the sheriffs, mayors, and judges in Louisiana, and a good many in Texas as well. His organization did a billion-dollar-a-year business in heroin, cocaine, prostitution, hijacking, and modern jazz. He lived on a sprawling, 22-million-dollar estate surrounded by hundreds of bougainvillea bushes and thousands of Dobermans.

Bobby, of course, terrier that he was, could not resist going after Carlos Marcello.

Born in Tunisia of Sicilian parents, Marcello had been brought to the United States as an infant. But he had never become a naturalized citizen. He lived under a Guatemalan passport, which he reportedly had gotten by bribing a Guatemalan leader with a hundred thousand dollars. He was, therefore, an illegal alien—and Bobby moved to get him deported.

In the spring of 1961, when Marcello showed up for his quarterly check-in with the local immigration office, he was arrested and handcuffed. He was taken directly to the airport, where a U.S. Border Patrol plane was waiting, its engines revved. The plane flew him to Guatemala City, where he was left with no luggage and little money. Soon after, the president of Guatemala ordered him expelled, and had him flown to the jungles of El Salvador. There he was deposited, among the silent vines and the chattering monkeys, in his Italian silk suit and his two-tone shoes, thirty miles from the nearest village.

Marcello began to walk. The swampy jungle floor oozed into his shoes, causing blisters on his feet. As luck would have it, he happened upon a jungle stream, in which an alligator was dozing. Marcello, using the stealth he had learned years before as a wise guy on Bourbon Street, sneaked up on the alligator unawares and bit off his tail. After sucking the blood to quench his hunger and thirst, he sat on a moss-covered log and made himself some alligator shoes.

While Marcello plied his father's old craft, the tailless alligator slithered around behind the log and bit off a piece of Carlos Marcello's ass.

As the mobster groaned in agony, a monkey began to chatter in the trees above. He was making monkey sounds, but Marcello, in what he would later describe as a religious miracle, understood the instructive words.

"If you want to get an alligator's tail," the monkey said from the treetops, "you don't bite off his tail. What you do is bite off his head. Then the tail will die."

Marcello pondered these words of wisdom in the halo of an epiphany. A great smile split his face. He donned his new shoes and began to walk. His spirits rose with each passing liana. He started whistling "Dixie." Then he switched to the funeral march from *Aida*. By the light of a full moon he emerged from the jungle and saw before him a small coastal town. As he approached it, he was a terrible sight to the villagers. His face had been scratched by vines and thorns. His Italian suit was in shreds. His head was crusted with the droppings of seventeen different kinds of parrots.

"It's the devil himself!" an old woman wailed, and, crossing herself, hobbled into the town's only church.

"It's Theodore Roosevelt," said the town loony.

"Nah," said a Dominican pilot, drinking tequila at an all-night cantina. "It's just some half-assed gangster from the States."

Marcello was impressed by the pilot. He quickly arranged a trade: his new alligator-tail shoes, and a few Doberman puppies, in return for a midnight flight to Florida.

So it was that, on a small rural airfield, in a plane without lights, Carlos Marcello once again entered the United States illegally. He carried with him no drugs, no contraband, only the monkey wisdom of the jungle: "If you want to get an alligator's tail, you don't bite off his tail. What you do is bite off his head. Then the tail will die."

"So the question is," Bobby says, "whose monkey was it?"

"I beg your pardon, Bobby?"

"The monkey. Was it one of our monkeys or one of their monkeys? That's the real question, it seems to me."

Perhaps my mind has been wandering, back to the departed Dag, to the knowledge that I myself will probably not ascend, not this time. My puzzlement is in my face.

"It's obvious what the monkey meant," Bobby says. "Right? Marcello was furious at me, for harassing him. For having him deported without warning. He blamed me for his ignominious exile in the jungle. I'd have thought that was his natural element, but no matter. He was in a rage against me. He wanted to see me dead. Then this monkey, which just happens to be sitting in a tree beneath which Marcello just happens to be passing, tells him how to go about it. I'm the tail, right, and you're the head, Jack. If he has me killed—the attorney general—you as president will just go after him with even greater vigah. You'll bite off the other half of his ass. But if he kills you—the head—then Lyndon will take over. And I will be powerless. He'll get the head and the tail both by killing you. Thus spaketh the monkey. Correct?"

"Let's assume your interpretation is correct. For the purposes of this discussion."

"Assume? What else could the monkey have meant?"

"It just as clearly could have been referring to the Commies," I point out. "Marcello hated Castro. He and his buddies in Florida, Meyer Lansky and Santo Trafficante, had lost a fortune in gambling money when Castro shut down the casinos in Havana. We know they'd been trying, without success, to kill Castro—at the instigation of the CIA. Suppose this is what the monkey is telling him: if you kill Castro, some other revolutionary, like his brother Raúl, or Che Guevara, will take his place. You won't have gained a thing. But if you kill the head—if you kill the puppet master, Khrushchev—then the puppet will wither and die. That interpretation makes just as much sense."

"Except," Bobby says, "that it is not borne out by history. Nobody killed Khrushchev."

"Okay. I said I'd accept your interpretation. So what about the monkey?"

"Well, whose was it? Who put it there?"

"I don't think anybody put it there. I don't think it even existed. I think it was an imaginary monkey. A metaphorical one. Carlos Marcello is stuck out there in the jungle, with a dozen parrots shitting on his head, and he starts hallucinating. He hears voices. He had this insight that he doesn't even really understand yet. So he attributes it to a monkey."

"That's really what you think, Jack? That gangsters talk to imaginary monkeys? Then they come home and tell their buddies they talked to a real monkey? I don't think so. I know them better than you, Jack. I think if Carlos Marcello told Sam Giancana he talked to a monkey, then he talked to a real monkey."

"But—if I may," Raymond says, "monkeys don't talk—not English."

"There you go," Bobby says. "Monkeys don't speak English—unless they are trained to do so. They also don't plot to kill the president—unless someone puts them up to it."

"What you're saying," I ask, incredulous, "is that the monkey was planted there? And that the monkey was *using* Carlos Marcello?"

"Exactly! And the question is, who was using the monkey? Was it a Russian-trained monkey? Was it a Cuban monkey? Or, like I said before, was it one of ours? Was it an FBI monkey? Or a CIA one? The CIA controlled the government of Guatemala; they trained the whole Bay of Pigs army in Guatemala; they could easily be training monkeys down there. It was the president of Guatemala who expelled Marcello into the jungle in El Salvador. Perhaps it was no accident where they put him. Why did they put him in the jungle anyway—unless it was precisely for him to run into this monkey?"

"And they got lucky?"

"Maybe they didn't get lucky. Maybe they trained a thousand monkeys to speak the same few sentences. Maybe they trained every goddamn monkey in the jungle to say in English how you get an alligator's tail."

"I discussed this at great length with Momo," I say, wearily, "in the sealed envelopes that Judy Campbell used to carry back and forth between us. It was Momo's opinion that Carlos had merely hallucinated the monkey. 'Don't believe too easily in conspiracies,' Momo used to write, over and over again. 'It is easier for a man to go crazy than to conspire.' "

"That's great!" Bobby says, his tone dripping with ice. "Put your trust in Momo. Now as you did then. May I point out," he says, pointing, "where Momo is now?"

"He's with Pop," I say.

"That's beside the point!" Bobby says, almost screaming.

I wait till Bobby calms down. I've been playing the devil's advocate, in search of a new insight. I know for a fact, of course, that the Dominican pilot who flew Marcello back to the States was employed by the CIA.

"It was really Rafael Trujillo, wasn't it?" Lyndon says.

"Trujillo was dead by then," the reverend notes.

"Not him," Lyndon explains. "The other one. The shortstop for the Giants."

Lyndon is correct. He's seen the files.

We all fall silent, pondering the conspiracy. In a world in which everybody always uses everybody, who was using whom? Then Adlai, of all people, startles us.

"You know what Marilyn used to tell me, up here?" he says. "I remember, because she said it several times. She said: 'You know Lee Harvey Oswald, who killed Jack? To me he always looked like a monkey.' "

We let ourselves think back upon the scene. There can be no denying the resemblance.

I do not want this memoir, this accounting, to sound frivolous. The presidency is a serious business. Nuclear testing, poverty, race relations, astrology—these are all weighty matters. If at times I seem to dwell more on personal than on political subjects, it is simply because my host of biographers, both within the clan and without, have dwelt at length on my public persona, on my accomplishments and on my failures, on the Kennedy legacy. I tried heroically, during my two years and ten months in office, to keep an opaque wall between my public life and my private life, and for the most part I succeeded. It was my view that the nation had elected a president, but not a husband; a national leader, but not a father or a son or a brother. And certainly not a preist. The things that went across my desk in the Oval Office were public papers, public policy, and I tended to them with all the intelligence and all the skill I could muster. And if, beneath my desk at the same time, Fiddle or Faddle was crouched naked, playing with my zipper, that was nobody's business but our own.

In my lifetime, as I've said, I mostly succeeded in keeping the public life and the private life separate, and it is probably for the best. But sometimes I wonder. In public, in 1962, I watched John Glenn become the first American in orbit, and I pledged we would put a man on the moon by the end of the decade. I had, in truth, no real interest in space; but when I died, they named the Kennedy Space Center after me. In public, Jackie and I entertained Pablo Casals at the White House, and Robert Frost, and countless other cultural heavy hitters. Given my druthers, I'd rather see Beverly Sills hit a high C while being mounted from the rear than listen to her onstage; but my speeches called for an artistic renaissance in America, and so when I died they named the Kennedy Center for the Performing Arts after me. All this is probably as it should be. But sometimes I think, wistfully, that I would rather they had renamed the Mayflower Hotel after me, or a brothel on K Street. Let the monuments reflect the man.

On the other hand, perhaps not. Treat every man according to his deserts, as Hamlet said, and who would escape a whipping?

"Whipping?" J. Edgar asks, appearing from nowhere, breathing hard, leather thong in hand. "Who is it wants a whipping?"

"Over there," I say, inspired, pointing. "I think that passing white cloud . . ."

"Oooooh, he is a cute little cloud, isn't he?" J. Edgar says, prancing in place, then gamboling off in pursuit.

"Yes, He is," I murmur, softly.

We watch in awed silence as Hoover chases the cloud, his thong held high.

I can only assume we have seen the last of him.

The point—to get back to it—is this: I was raised on a motto well known to us all: "All work and no play makes Jack a dull boy." In the Kennedy iconography, there was no sin greater than dullness. And any sin was permissible in its avoidance. My father lived by that motto, and he was only Joe. Imagine the terrible pressure on Jack himself! And if the presidency is the hardest job in the nation, it only follows that the president must play the hardest as well.

"Jack be nimble, Jack be quick, Jack jump over the candlestick!"

Many's the hot twat I jumped in obedience to this other parental advice.

As the twig is bent, they say . . .

"First it was a small boat, now it's a twig," Lyndon interjects. "You sure did have a problem with your masculine equipment, Jack."

"Speak for yourself, Lyndon," I retort.

(And wonder, secretly, if there is anything to what he says.)

The one place where public policy and private pussy came together, of course, was at the intersection of the thighs of Judy C. Mistress to the president. Flame of the godfather. A rather combustible intersection, I concede. It was our own little secret—mine and Judy's and Momo's—and a few of my lackeys', and a bunch of Sam's lackeys', and Frank Sinatra's, and . . .

If the *Washington Post* knew about it, or *The New York Times*, they didn't print it. Not in those civilized times, when men were men and reporters knew their place.

"The good old days," I can hear Nixon muttering.

Did you know that when Tricky Dick used to go out on Bebe Rebozo's yacht, they'd pack it stem to stern with stewardesses? There was safety at sea, Nixon used to think. Not realizing that, in his special case, a little well-publicized pussy would have been laetrile for his malignant image.

Bobby didn't know about me and Judy. Puritan that he was, I invited him into every room of my presidency except the bedroom. He didn't know until one day in the spring of '62, when J. Edgar took him to lunch at Horn and Hardart's. There, between the escargot and the Boston baked beans, the head of the FBI gave the attorney general the lowdown on his brother, the president.

Bobby, crestfallen, heartbroken, said he didn't believe it.

Hoover offered to produce the wiretaps.

Bobby said that wouldn't be necessary.

After lunch, he took a taxi from Horn and Hardart's to the White House. And he puked baked beans all over my crowded desk. (Luckily, no one was under it at the time.)

Bobby wasn't happy with me.

He told me I had to stop seeing Judy.

In my heart, I knew that in *his* heart he really wanted me to stop seeing Marilyn.

And that I wouldn't do.

And so, in the interest of national security, I agreed to give up Judy.

Bobby left, unhappy. I watched him go, unhappy.

Every week, Judy used to carry a sealed letter from me to Momo. And every week she'd bring one back. We were playing chess through the mail—we could hardly sit down at the Harvard Club together—and now the game would have to end. Just as my knight was closing in on his queen.

"Little knowing," Bobby mutters, righteously, "that you were really playing chess with Death."

I fear that I am falling short of my goal.

I had hoped to make this a masterpiece—the *Moby-Dick* of memoirs—win another Pulitzer Prize, at the least. Ahab would pale before the skipper as president; Moby-Dick himself would pale—or darken—before the monstrous, cruising, spouting Ship of State. Lashed together, harpooned by fate, we would cruise the roiling, shark-filled waters, beset, perhaps, by nuclear piranhas.

But I sense that, aiming high, I've once again sunk low. I keep getting stuck on the short hairs.

So it was in life. So it appears to be in afterlife.

Perhaps I need some educated filler. Two hundred pages of discourse. Scholarly elucidation. Not on whales, of course; that was Melville's subject, not mine. Not whales but two hundred pages of description and comparison, from firsthand experience, of the relative merits of certain lengths and widths, moistnesses and drynesses, wiriness and silkiness, shallowness and depth, virginity and voraciousness, Caucasian and Oriental, Indian and black, triangular and nondescript, easy and forced, oily and suedelike, pink lipped and white lipped . . .

"Jack?"

"Yes, Reverend?"

"I don't think that's really necessary."

"Perhaps not, Reverend," I say. "Perhaps you're right."

Thinking: that's what they told Melville, too.

"Jack."

"Yes, Lyndon?"

"I think it's time we went. Time to go and make our visit. To the people on the cloud of lead."

He doesn't want to go, of course; it's the last thing in the universe he wants to do. His statement is a simple ruse: he wants me to push ahead with my story.

I understand. His ruse works, nonetheless.

Late in the spring of 1962, my forty-fifth birthday was celebrated with a massive, star-studded, as they say, fund-raising party in New York's Madison Square Garden. The surprise of the evening was when Marilyn stepped out of the shadows and into the spotlight—her last wild, symbolic act—to sing "Happy Birthday" to me. She stood not ten feet from me in the center of the boxing ring, before twenty thousand people, wearing a low-cut white evening gown, flaunting our unspoken affair before the world.

It was that outrageous act, I suspect, that pushed them over the edge. All of them.

It happened two months later. August 5, 1962. One of those typically American nights when everyone, afterward, for the rest of their lives, would remember what they were doing.

I was screwing someone, I recall. (It's just her name that escapes.)

In California, it was a hot and sultry night. Some like it hot, but not Marilyn. Oppressed by the heat and humidity, she was walking about naked in the secluded cottage on the secluded estate where she was staying. No one would find her here, no one would intrude on her privacy; she could be the nature girl that was a part of her, let the evening moisture have its way. In a glass pitcher on the table beside her bed was a batch of vodka and tonic she had mixed, dozens of ice cubes floating on the surface like a flotilla of PT boats. Beside the pitcher was a worn copy of *Anna Karenina*, one of the Russian novels she loved so much.

As she emerged from the bathroom, she heard a faint knock on the door. She was surprised, but not startled. She had heard no one approach, and the cottage appeared on no map, was far from any public roadway. If she had been Lady Chatterley—a book she had recently read—she would have assumed it was the gamekeeper, come for another tumble. As it was, she assumed it was a servant come down from the main house a quarter of a mile beyond the rolling hills and lawns with a message that someone, somewhere, felt was important. Marilyn, that summer, felt that little in life was important. She was trying desperately to wean herself from tranquilizers, less desperately from alcohol. It would later be put about that she had tried suicide several times in the preceding months—put about for obvious reasons. These reports I tend not to believe—because she had so much to give the world, and because she told me they weren't true.

At the second light knock, she grabbed a thin robe from the back of a chair and slipped her still fine body into it. This was more an act of propriety than of modesty; the robe consisted of two filmy layers of pale blue chiffon, which concealed almost nothing. A barefoot California girl, weary before her time, she moved toward the door, then stopped as it began to swing open. She hadn't locked it, saw no need to in this secluded place.

A reading lamp was on in the living room. By its dim glow across the room she saw two figures moving in behind the slowly opening door, women who seemed to be trying to be stealthy and yet who also were stumbling over each other. They reminded her of people from the past, a thought she could not pin down. Her normal response with strangers was politeness; she was taken aback, however, by this quiet barging in.

"I beg your pardon," she said. "Are you looking for someone?"

"For you," the first woman said, as the second closed the door behind them. Together, side by side, they then moved closer to her. Marilyn, seeing their faces, stood transfixed. The night was young; she'd only had a drink or two. Three at the most.

"I'm Jackie," the first woman said.

"I'm Ethel," the second said.

Marilyn stood wide-eyed, her mouth open, speechless. Then

she stammered, "Yes, I see," and added a moment later, "Won't you come in?" And then, like a character from one of her films, "But you're already in, aren't you?"

Like most Americans, she had seen countless pictures of Jackie and of Ethel. But she had never met either of them before. She could only guess at how they had found the place, or what they wanted from her.

She didn't have long to wait to find out.

"I understand you've been sleeping with my husband," Jackie said.

Marilyn looked with astonishment at the first lady, who seemed dressed for a cooler evening, in purple slacks, a pink, long-sleeved blouse, white gloves, and purple heels. But she was a quick study. If they were really going to play this scene, she thought, it could only be played for laughs.

"Actually," she replied, all sweetness and innocence, "we haven't found much time for sleeping."

"You know what I mean," Jackie said. "You've been fucking him all over the East Coast."

The common obscenity sounded dirty the way Jackie said it. Marilyn preserved her sweetest tone. "Somebody has to," she said.

Marilyn turned toward Ethel. "And you?" she said. "The other Mrs. Kennedy. What is your complaint?"

"My husband loves you," Ethel said.

"Yes," Marilyn replied. "More's the pity."

"Then why don't you sleep with him?"

"A good question," Marilyn said. "I've pondered it often myself. Is that what you would like me to do? Sleep with Bobby?"

"You're damn right it is," Ethel spat. "Get this obsession out of his mind once and for all. Let him see that your pussy isn't a damn bit better than mine."

Marilyn stood there, looking from one to the other, nonplussed. "If you ladies could get your act together, and come up with a suitable plan," she said, "perhaps we could work something out."

Now it was Jackie and Ethel who looked at each other.

Jackie spoke first. "As a matter of fact, we do have a plan. That's why we're here."

"Now hold on a minute, Jack," Lyndon says. "The way I hear it—the way I *saw* it—Jackie and Ethel hated each other. They couldn't work together for the March of Dimes, let alone on some private business."

"If you'll let me continue," I reply, "the story will illuminate itself."

"Yeah, let him continue!" Raymond says.

"Yeah!" Adlai echoes.

When they are silent, I resume.

Jackie and Ethel began moving toward Marilyn, as if, indeed, by some prearrangement. Marilyn slowly backed up, toward the bedroom. As she did, she had the same fleeting thought she'd had earlier: that she had seen these people before. They exuded menace as they moved her into the bedroom; at the same time, they were comical in their walk, as if they weren't used to high heels.

"They're men!" Lyndon blurts, excited.

The precise thought that Marilyn suddenly had. They were men in drag, like Tony and Jack in the movie! They were merely wearing Ethel and Jackie masks. She could see that now in the bedroom, where the overhead light was on. And they clearly meant her no good.

She thought of screaming, but didn't; no one would hear from this isolated cottage. She continued to back away from their advance. The back of her legs touched the bed. Jackie moved forward, shoved her roughly onto it. Ethel grabbed her head, held it in a powerful grip. Jackie reached for the pitcher on the table. Ethel forced open her mouth. Marilyn gagged and swallowed and gagged again as Jackie poured the icy vodka tonics down her throat.

She tried to struggle away, but couldn't. They were stronger than she. Her robe came open, leaving her half naked. The others didn't seem to notice.

"The pills," she heard Ethel say.

Jackie reached into her purse, pulled out a prescription

209

bottle. She opened it, began to pour a stream of small white pills down Marilyn's throat.

They held her in a tight grasp, till Marilyn no longer struggled, till her eyes closed, till she went limp. They let go of her then, and left her there like a beautiful corpse on a paperback cover, sprawled across the bed.

Jackie lifted the reciver from the Princess phone by the bed. She placed it on the floor, near Marilyn's dangling hand. They looked around, making sure that everything was in order. As they did, they heard footsteps outside.

"Who's that?" Jackie whispered.

"Let's beat it!" Ethel said.

They floundered on high heels across the living room, burst out the door, ran as best they could into a copse of woods behind the cabin.

A small, slim man, who had been walking on the gravel path toward the cabin, stopped suddenly when he heard the commotion. He saw two figures burst through the door and disappear out back; in the moonless night, all he saw was their shapes.

He waited till there was silence, till they were gone. Till the only sound was a whippoorwill singing in the brush behind him. Then, quietly, he slipped in through the open door.

"And?" Lyndon says, impatient at my silence.

"And what?"

"What happened next? Who was the man? Why did you stop?"

"This is the end of a chapter," I reply.

"What? You can't do that. You can't just leave us hanging like that."

I'm gratified to learn that even Lyndon doesn't know the truth of *this* scene.

"Sure I can keep you in suspense," I tell him. "All the good *Geschreibers* do."

210

On the last day of my life I arose early. I was scheduled to address a crowd in the parking lot across from the hotel before Jackie and I attended a Chamber of Commerce breakfast. I was in a good mood while shaving; the crowds so far had been large and enthusiastic, in part no doubt because of Jackie's rare presence. And Jackie seemed to be enjoying herself, or at least giving a good imitation of it.

My mood darkened when I turned the pages of the *Dallas News* and came upon an advertisement surrounded by an ominous black border. It was signed by something called the American Fact-finding Committee; it had been paid for by the local John Birch Society and Nelson Bunker Hunt. It was a vicious and insane attack, accusing me of being pro-Communist. Me, the eldest living son of Joseph P. Kennedy.

"Why," the ad demanded, "have you ordered or permitted your bother Bobby, the Attorney General, to go soft on Communists, fellow-travelers, and ultra-leftists in America, while permitting him to persecute Americans who criticize you, your administration, and your leadership?"

I could not help wondering to whom they were referring. Hoffa and his bullyboys? Carlos Marcello and his dope-pushing monkeyshines?

"They were raising a valid question," J. Edgar says.

I can hardly believe it. He chases the little white cloud with a whip, yet here he is.

"It was you who suggested the placing of the ad," I tell him. "To muddy the subsequent waters."

"I've never admitted that," Hoover says.

Another ringing denial from Crime Fighter.

"Why," the advertisement continued, "has Gus Hall, head of the U.S. Communist Party, praised almost every one of your policies?"

Perhaps, I figured, they were still smarting over the roll-back I had forced in steel prices, after the steel magnates had pledged to me they would not raise prices, then did it anyway. Dumb shits didn't care what an inflationary spiral would do to the country, as long as they lined their own pockets first. It was then that *The New York Times* astounded the country by finding fit to print—on the front page, no less—my comment that most businessmen were "sons of bitches."

What I had actually said, of course, was that most businessmen were pricks.

"Why," the advertisement went on, "have you scrapped the Monroe Doctrine in favor of the 'Spirit of Moscow'?"

The essence of politics is self-control. You can't let the bastards get to you. When, a few minutes later, Kenny O'Donnell entered my suite to show me the newspaper, all I said was "We're heading into nut country today."

I spoke to the crowd across from the Texas Hotel, then went to the ballroom. Jackie was twenty minutes late for the breakfast. I used my standard line for such occasions: "Mrs. Kennedy is organizing herself. It takes longer, but, of course, she looks better than we do when she does it." When she did enter, the breakfasters stood and craned their necks to get a glimpse of her. "Why is it," I asked, "that nobody wonders what Lyndon and I will be wearing?"

What she was wearing was what I had picked out in Washington: the pink.

After the Chamber speech we returned to the suite to relax for an hour before making the short plane trip to Dallas. We could have driven there, but airport crowds are always good copy. While waiting, I placed a call to Uvalde, Texas, where John Nance Garner, Roosevelt's first vice president, was marking his ninety-fifth birthday. I saw a glimpse of myself in the future: wheelchair ridden, or bedridden, drooling, tubes coming out of every orifice. I did not, I decided, ever want to be ninety-five. But when Garner came on the line, his voice was strong and robust. He offered me some advice, the wisdom of his years. "Don't take any shit," he said.

As we prepared to leave, Roy Kellerman, the head of the Secret Service detail, entered the room. He said the Dallas papers had predicted rain, but that the weather there seemed to be brightening. His men there wanted to know if I wanted the bubble top for the limousine on or off.

Contrary to later speculation, the bubble wasn't bulletproof. It might, however, have altered a bullet's trajectory, or distorted a gunman's aim. I knew that Jackie liked it on, so the wind wouldn't muss her hair. But this was a political trip; we had come here specifically to be seen. And so, of course, I made a political decision.

"If it's not raining," I said, "have the bubble top off."

"Is that it?" Lyndon asks, when I pause. "I mean, there's not much irony in a bubble top, one way or the other."

"That's it," I say. "For now."

"Good. You wouldn't want people to think you were still preoccupied with your own death. Martyrdom, as your people like to call it. Much as that charbroiled word used to be reserved for saints. You're not claiming sainthood, are you, Jack? I mean, not *here*."

"Whose death *should* I be preoccupied with, Lyndon? Bobby's, perhaps?"

"Hell no. Six of one Kennedy, half a dozen of another. If

213

you'll recall, you were in the midst of recounting the death of Norma Jean whosis, alias Marilyn Monroe, when the previous chapter came to an untimely end. Now, that is a death about which folks are genuinely curious. Personally, of course, never claiming to be a gentleman, I preferred brunettes. Gimme the Jane Russell type anytime. A genuine Texas-sized gal. Bosoms designed by Howard Hughes himself. But, Miss Monroe's being the cantaloupes under discussion, I thought you might get on with it."

Lyndon always fancied himself a connoisseur, in the produce department. Which is one reason his Viet shoeshine girl raised eyebrows. Slim in the mammaries, those folks. Comes from a rice diet. Unlike the wholesome, cheese-fed Scandinavians.

"Like Inga," Hoover says.

Like Inga.

"You people are disgusting," Bobby says. "Both of you."

I offer no rebuttal; I do tend to degenerate. The scene that Bobby found there was traumatic.

"Scene? Bobby? Where?" Lyndon can't contain himself.

"At the cottage. It was Bobby, of course, who came walking up the gravel path, just as the two Neanderthals dressed up like Jackie and Ethel burst out the door and disappeared."

"I knew it!" Lyndon says. "There was always scuttlebutt that Bobby snuffed her. To keep her from going public about you and her!"

I turn to Bobby. "Shall I dignify that with a reply? Or would you like to tell it yourself?"

Bobby pulls at his ear, that old, shy mannerism of his when he was about to speak in public. His hands and knees no longer shake, however. Say that much for death.

"I was in California that weekend," Bobby begins. "It's common knowledge. I had some free time, and I was hungry to see Marilyn. Do you know the pain of unfulfilled passion, either of you? I doubt it; you both could find fulfillment in a knothole. Well, it hurts, it hurts like hell. There's not much in life that hurts worse. I'd made her into a goddess; that's what romantic love does, though neither of you would know about that, not with Jackie and Lady Bird. Hell, it wasn't just me, the whole world had made her into a goddess; maybe she *was* one; maybe God Himself had made her one. I loved her, and she loved me, but the Catholic in me was so screwed up I still couldn't touch her. I'm not sure what I planned to do that night. I just wanted to be alone with her and see if the veils—the goddamn walls—would fall. If not, then I needed to tell her good-bye. Wrench her from my heart, like uprooting a tree."

"A tree?" Lyndon asks. "I thought it was twigs that ran in the family."

I feel like busting him one. But Bobby hasn't heard; he's almost in a trance as he continues.

"I called Frank to find out where she was; Frank always knew stuff like that. He hadn't spoken to me for a year, because after he built a whole Western White House on his estate, complete with a heliport, I wouldn't let Jack go near it. The president can't do that, I'd said; Sinatra hangs out with the mob, and everyone knows it, and the president of the United States can't be his guest. Reluctantly, Jack had agreed. On his last California trip he'd stayed up the road. At Bing Crosby's place. Another singer. A *white* one. A Republican! Sinatra probably hated me for that as well. Can't say I blame him. Still, when I called him, he told me where Marilyn was. He always called her Norma Jean, with contempt. I don't know what he had against her; maybe she was the only woman in Hollywood that Jack had gotten to first."

Bobby is suddenly winded, suddenly pale. The image of me and Marilyn batters him still. I think we ought to change the subject. But Bobby gamely goes on.

"I drove to the estate, parked off the road, climbed a low fence, to avoid the gatekeeper. Security wasn't all that good; it was just a private residence. I kept to a path along the bottom of a hill, away from the main house, till I saw the lights of the cottage Frank had described. As I drew nearer, the dim lights seemed to expand inside my chest. What would happen that night, alone in this lonely cottage with Marilyn? I had no idea—

215

but the conflicting possibilities were ripping me in half. I did not have Jack's curious detachment about sex. Sex with Marilyn Monroe would be, for me, monumental. It might also be religiously—and therefore psychologically—impossible.

"The night was moonless, and that fact seemed to speak to me; it seemed to say that God had closed His eyes, that God wasn't watching, and that therefore anything was possible—or at least forgivable. This was a new thought to me, though I had come to understand it was the rule by which Jack was governing the country (except that for "God" he substituted *The New York Times*). (The Woodward and Bernstein era had not yet dawned at the *Washington Post*.) I paused at the spot where the dirt path forked into a gravel walkway leading to the cottage. Ahead lay Marilyn; behind me lay a long stand of bushes in which two whippoorwills were having a dialogue; behind, also, lay a lifetime of faith and faithfulness.

"As I started up the gravel path I saw a shadow, then another, through a window. Marilyn was not alone. My heart dropped like a stone in a well. My daydreams and my apprehensions, as is so often the case, had both been merely wasted energy. I stopped, took a few more steps, then stopped again. I did not want to be seen here; if Marilyn was not alone, what was the point? I was about to turn and retrace my steps when there was a commotion inside; two shadows stumbled past another window, then burst out the door, leaving it open behind them, and fled around behind the house. In the dark I could only form the briefest of impressions, and they were contradictory: awkward female forms fleeing, amid the sound of male voices. I hesitated, uncertain if there were more people inside; perhaps I had stumbled into a party. I waited till the night was still; then slowly, carefully, I approached the cottage. Through the open door I could see no one; quietly I stepped inside.

"The first room was furnished like a country living room, with wicker chairs, a wicker settee. It was vacant. I moved toward a brighter light beyond a doorway. There, in the bedroom, was Marilyn: naked except for a twisted negligee, sleeping, or unconscious—or, possibly, dead.

"I had the sensation of my heart stopping as I moved toward her; I had never seen her this way, this glorious, godly nakedness upon which, I knew, Jack feasted. But desire was quickly fused with fear. The way she was sprawled across the bed spoke of something deeper than sleep. I remembered the fleeing figures; her rapturous flesh had for a moment driven them from my mind. Quickly I moved closer, and surveyed the room. The phone receiver was dangling near her hand. Had she been trying to summon help? On the table was a nearly empty pitcher; beside it a vial of pills, also nearly empty. I felt her limp hand, searching for a pulse; I couldn't find one, only my own fear and excitement fed back to me.

"It looked like suicide. I scanned the room for a note. With two motives. The first was to see if it really was suicide. I couldn't believe that Marilyn had reason to kill herself, unless I read it in her own words. The second, perhaps shameful, also leaped quickly to my mind: what if she'd left a note that mentioned Jack? Their affair becoming public knowledge could destroy the carefully crafted image of Jack and Jackie, of Camelot; could even destroy his presidency. I saw no note.

"The fleeing strangers leaped to my mind again. It could not have been suicide; she had not been alone. But it could have been murder—murder made to look like suicide!

"That, I told myself, made no sense at all. Who would want to kill Marilyn Monroe? It would be like killing Jiminy Cricket. It would be like killing Bambi.

"Still, I'd seen the figures flee. Perhaps, I thought, she'd mixed alcohol and pills and had overdosed, accidentally. And two friends, coming to visit, had found her that way and had not wanted to get involved. Or perhaps she had really killed herself—and the visitors had taken the note! If so, what did it say? Was I in it? Was Jack? If it surfaced, we would have to deny its authenticity.

"All these thoughts raced through my mind at the scene

of the crime—or whatever it was. And they fused into one dominant thought: I'd better get out of there, for my sake, for Ethel's, for the kids', and for Jack's. There was nothing I could do for Marilyn now.

"I took a long, lingering look at her form, almost as sexy in death as it had been in life. Then, careful not to touch anything, careful to leave no fingerprints, I hurried out the door into the night.

"Fearful of being seen on the path, I hurried around the back of the cottage. In the dark, I stumbled on a rock and fell to my knees. My hand landed on something soft, something rubbery. Thinking it might be a clue, I took it with me as I circled around the estate, and gradually made my way back to my car. I drove back to Beverly Hills, to the place I was staying, which belonged to a friend of Peter's. Alone inside, I switched on a light, and looked for the first time at the rubber object I had stuffed inside my shirt. It was a face—Ethel's face—staring up at me.

"I couldn't believe the coincidence. What would a mask of Ethel, that someone might wear to a costume party, be doing back of Marilyn's cottage? I turned the mask inside out, examined it closely. There was no label. But inside the left nostril, I found the telltale sign—a small z inside a circle. There were only half a dozen people alive who would know what that z meant—and one of them was me."

Bobby stops. We all wait, breathless, though I know what he means. I and one other.

"Well?" Lyndon says.

"Well?" Adlai says.

"Well?" Raymond says.

"If Jack can keep you in suspense, then so can I," Bobby says.

The others grimace. They begin to move toward him, with menace.

"Okay, okay," Bobby says. "The z was like a trademark. It meant the mask of Ethel had been made in one specific place. It had been manufactured in the laboratory of the FBI."

□ □ □

All Bobby knew was that Marilyn was dead, perhaps murdered. He'd seen her corpse; he called me on a secure line late that night. By the next afternoon it was all over radio and television, on the front page of the newspapers. The nation would not be shocked that much by a death until more than a year later, until my own. An overdose of pills, perhaps accidental, the reports said, though there were implications that it may have been suicide. Bobby had told me alone about the mask with the z, but he wasn't sure what had happened in the cottage.

Bobby was deeply depressed. Though I knew much more than he did, I was in a rage. Every such clandestine action provokes an equal and opposite reaction. My reaction was to move once more against Castro. I ordered full speed ahead on Operation Mongoose, with Bobby in charge. It would take his mind off Marilyn. It would channel my bitterness. It would divert the agencies to political—not personal—mischief. If my golden Muse was gone, I would give vent to the darker side.

The CIA again began working with Roselli and Momo to get the bastard assassinated. A huge covert operation was established in Miami and New Orleans to devise plans to undermine the Cuban regime. I made no inquiry into which CIA was handling it—I didn't care, as long as someone got the job done. We let the Cuban refugees know they would get another crack at an invasion. We built up the naval force in the Caribbean. In charge of all of this I put not the Defense Department, or State, or the joint chiefs, or even John McCone, whom the pope . . . whom I had named to replace the disgraced Dulles at the Langley CIA. In charge of it all I put Bobby. By day he worked at Justice, intensifying his war on the mob. That year he would put 288 mobsters on trial; the year I took office only 35 had been indicted. By night he worked on Mongoose, checking plans, reading reports, firing up the Special Group (Augmented), as we called our own little Death-for-Castro committee at the highest level of the government. And somewhere in there—I think it was between 3:00 A.M. and 3:05—he would even turn his attention to civil rights.

"It was between three and three-oh-one," Martin says.

While all this was going on, Castro, coward that he was, got the notion that he ought to defend himself. He turned for help to his Uncle Samovar in the Kremlin. Khrushchev responded with generosity. He gave Castro an autumn solstice gift of 20,000 Russian troops, 150 jet fighters, 350 tanks, 1,300 pieces of field artillery, and 700 antiaircraft guns. Not to mention a series of huge crates being unloaded in Havana Harbor that could have been pear trees, but probably weren't. Our war against him was a great secret to the American people. Bobby and I felt it was gauche of him to go public in such a material way.

Then the trouble started. Senator Keating of New York, being fed secret information by one CIA or the other, announced that the Russians were putting missiles in Cuba. Bobby talked to the Russian ambassador. He was assured that only defensive missiles were being placed there. It was hard to explain to the American people why Castro should need defensive weapons, since we surely meant him no harm. So we painted him as paranoid. And I made a ringing speech declaring that we would not tolerate offensive weapons in Cuba.

A few weeks later, we sent a U-2 spy plane to snap some pictures over the island. When we got them back from Fox Photo, there were some neat shots of suntanned Hispanic girls in bikinis. But among them was one shot that appeared to show construction sites for offensive, surface-to-surface missiles. The photos were pretty small; I wished immediately that we had sprung for the four-by-sixes, instead of settling for the three-and-a-half-by-fives. But, with the aid of a magnifying glass, the missile sites were pretty clear—and off across the ocean, headed toward Cuba, was a fleet of Russian freighters with large, tarpaulin-covered cylinders on their decks. These were either huge baseball bats—we knew that Castro liked baseball—or medium-sized dildos, or offensive missiles. Since the Russians had said they wouldn't send missiles, I subscribed to the dildo theory myself. But we had to act on the assumption that they were missiles, just in case.

What followed is well-known: the thirteen tense days that have come to be known as the Cuban Missile Crisis. The Special Group (Augmented) was split down the middle. Half wanted me to send in the air force to knock out the missile sites. The other half favored a blockade, to prevent the missiles from arriving. I opted for the blockade, and told Khrushchev we would board his ships if they approached Cuba, and turn back any that carried missiles. Any that refused to be boarded, we would sink.

I went on national television to explain to the people what was happening. If we sank a Russian ship, Khrushchev would have to retaliate—and the result might be nuclear war. But this risk, however grave, we had to take, I said. We could not allow Soviet offensive missiles in Cuba, only 180 miles from my father's compound at Palm Beach.

The only thing I inadvertently omitted from my speech was the fact that we had been making covert war on Cuba for many months; that we had, therefore, precipitated the crisis ourselves; and that it was all a result of the death of Marilyn Monroe. (I alluded, as all presidents are required under oath to do, to the Monroe Doctrine; only Bobby knew what I really meant.)

Khrushchev fumed and blustered in public about the right to defend his allies—a right which, of course, has been granted to the United States alone. But in private he was scared shitless. He didn't want a nuclear war any more than I did—especially over a bunch of medium-sized dildos.

For that is a truth that has never been revealed till now: that is what they were, dildos. The brand known in Cuba as Macho Marauders. This Khrushchev revealed to me in a secret letter. "How will history remember us," he asked in poetic Russian, "if we destroy the earth over a bunch of mechanical cocks?" Six hours later a second letter arrived, in which Khrushchev flaunted Russian power and said they were really missiles after all, and that if we sank his boats he would pull the plug out of the whole damn bathtub.

This left us in a quandary. What to do? Which letter to

believe? Then Bobby came up with the idea that saved the world. Ignore the second letter, and respond only to the first, he said. Which we did. "Surely," I wrote back, "the Kremlin would not want the embarrassment of the U.S. Navy revealing its dildos before the world."

The chairman agreed. He ordered his ships to turn back. But not before there were several sleepless nights in capitals around the world.

For a president to be touched with greatness, he must seize such moments as are offered. Thus did I seize mine. I kept the hemisphere safe for penile intercourse.

When the radar screens showed that the Soviet ships were, indeed, turning around, we in the White House rejoiced. I telephoned former Presidents Truman and Eisenhower to tell them the news. It was my finest hour as president. I couldn't help thinking of Lincoln.

"This is the night I should go to the theater," I told Bobby. Bobby laughed, but his response was strangely prophetic. "If you go, I want to go with you," he said.

J. Edgar's face is red with rage (as opposed to his normal touch of rouge). He's waving his arms like a windmill in heat. He's sputtering, trying to jump-start his voice. Finally he blurts out what's on his chest.

"They were missiles!" he says—roars—gurgles—all at once. "They were not dildos. They were killer Russian missiles, able to destroy America!"

Bobby smiles. Even Lyndon smiles. Hoover is nonplussed, still livid. Bobby, of all people, takes pity.

"Of course they were missiles," he says, softly.

"Then why the blarney is he talking about dildos?" Hoover demands. "Makes the whole thing sound like a joke. Like the Russians aren't a threat at all. Talk like that undermines the entire free world. And also Mississippi."

"Mississippi?" the reverend asks.

"He's trying to be modest," Bobby explains to J. Edgar.

"To soft-pedal his achievements. You never did understand Jack's style. Jack's subtlety."

"Subtle as a crotch," J. Edgar says.

"That's *crutch*," the reverend corrects.

"That's *crotch*," Hoover insists. "You want to hear the tapes?"

No one does.

"Damn Commies were sending missiles here disguised as dildos," Hoover mutters. "That's the Russkie morality for you."

"Sounds to me," Raymond says, "like *we* were trying to get Castro first. Sounds to me like it was tit for tat."

"That's *tet*," Lyndon says.

The word bursts forth like a silent thunderclap. Lyndon has never mentioned it before. *Tet.* The air is imploding around us, imploding with a suffusion of light. Something is changing, moving. It is Lyndon and I who are changing, moving. The others seem to be receding from us. We are drifting, drifting. Below us, the holes in the ozone layer are clearly visible, each with its billboard alongside: Rise regular; Aqua Net; Lysol spray. We drift past all of them, into a realm of clouds. Purple clouds, and black, and gray. Till we tumble to the cloud of lead.

There is, at first, the tail end of a storm. We huddle together, Lyndon and I, alone in a windy vastness, rather like Lear and his fool; though which of us be king and which be jester I cannot say. We dare not speak lest we cry out in childish fear. Then the wind departs, a veil of vapor rises. And they are there, beside us: the maimed and the naked and the dead. We are not alone in a wasteland, as it had seemed. They are beside us; they are with us; as they have always been with us.

We want to turn; we want to run. Our legs are as leaden as the cloud. It seems for a moment as if we are rooted; as if in single file, one line on each side, they will move toward us, they will file past us, to reveal their wounds; and to revile. But this doesn't happen. Somehow we know, we understand without words, that it is we who must move toward them. We reach down to our thighs, lift our legs with our hands to get them moving; it's as if they've been asleep. We take one heavy step, then another. We are almost at the edge of their being, the edge of their sprawl. I am reminded of the pullback shot in *Gone with the Wind*. The bleeding and the crippled of the Civil War spread wide on the dusty earth for as far as the eye can see. Except that this was *their* civil war, not ours. And there are no nurses dispensing glory; only Lyndon, only me, absorbing guilt. We huddle again, clinging tight, as a great single word seems to roar up from out of their collective mouths: *why*? Except that there is no sound; they are asking nothing, demanding nothing; the word is only an echo in our minds.

Slowly we move among them on leaden legs. The terror of not knowing what to expect is humbling. I fear they will reach out to us, like beggars. The don't. Instead they hide their faces; they turn away. I expect them to flaunt their wounds, to press their festering pus to our eyes. But the opposite occurs; they hide their wounds from us as best they can. It is as if they, not we, are ashamed.

We are like generals inspecting the wounded. We *are* generals inspecting the wounded. They say nothing. They ask nothing. For a moment I am puzzled as to why we are here. Then I understand the obvious. We aren't here for them; we're here for us.

The farther we walk among them, the less heavy our legs become, though not our burdens. There are so many of them, sprawled, silent; I did not know there were so many.

In time, we come upon a clearing. A small group has gathered together, leaving a space. Something is happening in this group. We cross the space; we stand behind the last of them. Above their heads—we are taller than most of them—we see an image: something like an altar of light.

As we watch from afar, one among them mounts a cloud of stairs. It is a young woman, dressed in white, dressed in vapors, dressed in veils. She turns from the altar to face the others. I think I recognize her then: I think it is Kim, the naked girl in the photograph; the one who came and bid us make our visit. There is an essence in the air, a sparkle of golden droplets, that I seem to recognize, that I have known once before. In the last moments with Dag.

And then I understand. The form is different, but this, too, is an ascension. A completion of an earthly turn.

We stand in silence. We watch. One by one her friends move closer. Each in turn embraces her. Their wounds are as nothing in the presence of ascent.

I want to move forward, to embrace her myself. But my motive might be suspect. My legs grow heavy again.

When the last embrace concludes, we grow tense. We prepare to watch the actual ascent. But already the gathering is breaking up; the others are returning to their places. Only the girl is missing. Only she has vanished.

"That's it?" Lyndon whispers. "No . . . ?"

"No what?"

"I don't know. Prayers. Magic. Something."

"I guess that's it," I say.

We turn to resume our journey. Lyndon appears downcast; I myself feel awed, transfixed. I have just seen a miracle.

Again we move among the naked, among the dead. From the left a figure approaches, greets us; she is the first one to do so, the first to speak to us.

"I'm glad you came," she says. "I'm glad you made your visit."

I am puzzled. She looks familiar. "You are . . . ?"

"Kim," she says. "Don't you remember?"

"Yes, of course," I say, "how could I forget? But just now, over there . . . you ascended. We saw it ourselves."

"Not me," Kim says. "I hope to, someday, of course. But not today."

"But . . . we *saw* you," I say.

Kim only smiles, and shakes her head. "Come again," she says, softly.

She turns and walks away. We watch her go.

"Goddamn buggers still all look alike," Lyndon says.

225

In an instant we are back where we had been. Lyndon's lingering prejudice apparently did not sit well. Bobby, Adlai, the reverend, are chatting; they do not seem to know that we've been gone.

They are discussing Marilyn again; she has become the mascot—if not the patron saint—of our crowd. "I don't *know* what happened in there," Bobby is insisting. "Only that the mask was made in the FBI lab. That's all."

I know, of course, but have never said. It's a secret I took to the grave, and beyond. I never told Bobby; he's the last one I wanted to know. And yet, now, with my time here running out, perhaps, I think, it is time to speak.

"I know what happened!" Hoover says. He's horned into the group again, and he says it proudly, almost boastfully.

"I'll bet you do," Bobby says, bitterness still dripping in his voice.

"*Tell them!*" It is a booming command. As if the passing white cloud has gone electric. For that is from where the order emanates. J. Edgar blanches at the sound, the first time he's lost his rosy cheeks. He begins to speak, stutters, begins again: speaking words he's never spoken before.

"We had to do it. Me and Cly— Me and my friend. We had to kill her. It was a matter of national security."

"You!" Bobby says.

"National security?" Dr. King asks. "Killing Marilyn Monroe?"

"She was a sick lady," Hoover says. "Frustrated. Confused. She was having an affair with the president, whom she was growing tired of, and she was in love with the attorney general, whom she couldn't have. We obtained information that she was about to go public with this. She was about to reveal her affair with the president. We made a determination that that could not be allowed to happen. It would have disgraced the president."

"So you killed her for my sake?" I ask, drily.

"Nosir," Hoover concedes. "Not at all. But like it or not,

you were the president. Your disgrace would have been the nation's disgrace. It would have weakened our alliances overseas. It might have led to civil discontent at home. It was in the interest of the United States of America that Miss Monroe be silenced before she dragged your name through the—"

"Semen?"

"Precisely."

"So what did you do . . . precisely?" Bobby asks. He is controlling a rage that Hoover does not even notice; they are discussing the murder of a woman Bobby loved.

"Precisely? Why, we had a couple of masks struck at the lab . . . masks of the concerned spouses, a little private joke there, and Cly— and my friend and I put on a few old things we had in the closet and went on out there and killed her. Just forced some pills down her throat, made it look like suicide. A simple thing, dearie."

"You and . . . your friend," Lyndon asks, "personally put on dresses . . . ?"

"Don't knock it if you haven't tried it, sweets."

Quietly I interrupt. "Why didn't you just have a couple of agents do it, if it was national security at stake?"

"Oh, we could have," J. Edgar says gaily. "But it seemed like such fun. Dress to the nines in vintage threads. Copy *Some Like It Hot*. I mean, some of the agents might not have understood. Besides, if you want the truth, I wanted the pleasure of it. See her die by my very own hand. Sexpot bitch! Sexpot, my ass. That was the real American sexpot, if you ask C— My ass."

J. Edgar is coming unglued. He seems to be unraveling. I feel no pity at all.

"Now," I say, gently, "why don't you tell them the real reason?"

Hoover blanches again. "The real reason?"

"*Tell them!*" booms the passing white cloud.

Hoover stutters again, stammers. He seems incapable of speech. He says nothing.

227

"Very well, I'll tell them," I offer. "It's true Hoover was afraid that Marilyn would go public. She never would have, of course; it was just his own paranoia. But if she did, in his view, it would be his ass in a sling. If the affair became known—mine and Marilyn's—then Hoover's precious secret tapes would be worthless. It would be a front-page scandal: me and Marilyn. Adultery in the White House. Princess Jackie as the wronged woman. A betrayal of the public trust. If that had happened, who would have cared about his twenty-year-old tapes of me and Inga? Or any of the others from my bachelor days. Nobody. Nothing could outdo the president and the sex queen. Hoover would have had no more power to blackmail me. He knew that. And he knew I would know it. And he knew that the first thing I would do would be to boot him out on his ass. End his career. So he decided to terminate Marilyn first."

There is stunned silence when I finish speaking. All the others look at Hoover. Waiting for his denial.

He makes none.

I try to interpret his appearance as abject. It isn't, really. It is merely sullen.

The others are too limp for anger. That this . . . creature . . . before them . . . personally . . . for his own base motives . . . murdered Marilyn Monroe. . . . It was, literally, unspeakable.

He didn't succeed, of course. None of them know that, not even him. I wonder if now is the proper time to tell.

My thought is interrupted by the passing white cloud. The passing cloud's no longer white. It's red. It's red with the reflection of the burning flames below. An effect I have never seen before. The cloud comes closer. The reflected glow seems to be making the cloud itself burn. The tail of a tornado dips down from it. The tornado is real flame, not illusion. As we watch, motionless, transfixed, the point of the serpentine tail dips among us. Instinctively we close our eyes; we shield our faces from the heat. For a moment it is intense, then cold as dry ice, then normal again, as temperate as mist. We open our eyes, hearts alight with fear. All is as before—except that Hoover is gone. J. Edgar is no longer with us.

Raymond is the first to point down below. Hoover is visible in the caldron. He is no longer standing beside the others. He has his own stool. Hoffa, McCarthy, Hoover, Pop. He is clearly one of them now. His commuting days are over.

For a moment I wonder why. For killing Marilyn? That's ancient history. And besides, he did not succeed; though of course he thought he did.

The passing cloud, white again, reads my thoughts. "I ordered him to speak," it says. "He did not speak."

I ponder that. I ponder, too, the cloud's concern with my thoughts. It happens, I have heard, when the end is drawing near.

In the latter part of my administration, the nation became increasingly aware of the issue of civil rights. Or, to call a spade a spade, Negro rights.

"That's *black*," Bobby whispers.

Even so. In those days it was *Negro*. "You were called *Negro*, weren't you, Reverend?"

"In polite company," Martin says.

This is an area I am loathe to discuss; Bobby and I were given a lot of credit for promoting the integration of American life; in fact, we dragged our blue-blood heels as much as possible.

"Amen," says the rev.

The trouble is, the niggers had such terrible timing.

"That's *Nigras*," Lyndon says.

They began the Freedom Rides right during the Vienna summit; we asked them to wait awhile, but they refused. They enrolled James Meredith at the University of Mississippi—where twenty-eight people were shot and two were killed—right at the beginning of the Cuban Dildo Crisis. Rhythm they may have, but timing, no.

"If we waited for white people's time," the reverend says, "we'd still be waiting."

He's correct, of course. In those days even Bobby and I lost no sleep over the Negro plight. And we were educated northerners, hated by the redneck South.

"I lost plenty of sleep over it," Martin notes.

"It's a wonder you had time to dream," Lyndon says.

After the 1962 elections I signed an executive order desegregating federal housing, as I had promised to do in 1960. And in '63 I signed even broader civil rights legislation. But it was Martin who was forcing the issue. I'd just as soon have let sleeping police dogs lie.

"They dynamited my brother's house," the reverend says. "They blew up my headquarters. They bombed a black church in Birmingham and killed four little girls. They assassinated Medgar Evers. They even poisoned a watermelon patch. There are some things you just can't sit by and tolerate."

"Amen," Raymond says.

When push came to shove, I had no choice: the might of the U.S. government had to come down on the side of the blacks. I became a reluctant hero of the civil rights movement— a banner I have carried with greater pride in death than I ever did in life.

"There are worse banners to carry," Bobby says.

"You could have become a reluctant grand dragon," the reverend notes. "Like some who have followed you."

I suppose he means the actor and his court. I choose not to pursue the issue. There were other achievements in which I took more pride. The test-ban treaty with the Russians, for instance. It was the first international agreement to control the testing of underarm deodorants.

"That's aboveground nuclear weapons!" Bobby shouts.

Bobby still takes a dim view of my self-deprecating attempts at humor.

Then there was Vietnam. Vietnam you know about; I shall not discuss Vietnam. Let Kim discuss Vietnam with you—when it's your turn to visit the cloud of lead.

I sent 16,000 troops. Advisers, we called them. As one of my Jewish friends put it, "From such advice you could die."

The Pentagon wanted jets, napalm, defoliants, free-fire zones. I stood firm, I refused their request. And then, little by little, one by one, I gave in: to jets, to napalm, to defoliants, to free-fire zones.

Thus began Lyndon's war.

I had qualms about our being there at all; yet there we were. I hated the mentality of the Pentagon; and yet I succumbed to it, time after time. Once, Daniel Ellsberg, of Pentagon Papers fame, asked Jackie why this was so. "You have to understand," Jackie replied, "my husband is a weak man."

That is an exact quote. I cite it here not to justify Vietnam, however. There is no excuse for Vietnam. I cite it here to justify Marilyn. Judy. Angie. Fiddle. Faddle.

All of them.

"My husband is a weak man. . . ."

With such esteem in the eyes of his wife, what man would do otherwise?

My time is growing short. I must select what to discuss. I do not have the all-encompassing luxury of Sorensen, of Schlesinger. I don't have time to bore you to tears.

I no longer aspire to a Pulitzer for this modest volume; my sexual escapades will have turned the judges red. A humbler aspiration is the Edgar Allan Poe Award for best fact-crime book of the year. For certain revelations concerning the death of Marilyn Monroe.

To wit: Marilyn Monroe is alive and well.

"What?"

"What?"

"What?"

"What?"

"What?"

Bobby, Lyndon, Adlai, Raymond. The Reverend. All of them.

Perhaps even you, dear reader.

The facts are these. Hoover and his friend, wearing Jackie and Ethel masks and dresses, tried to snuff Marilyn, as described earlier, for the reasons previously related. Bobby's late-night visit interrupted them; he saw her apparently lifeless corpse and left her for dead. This, too, you have already heard.

"What do you mean, *apparently* lifeless?" Bobby says.

I can understand his disbelief, even when it's me who's speaking. He did spend twenty years holding her hand here in the afterlife.

He neglected, however, to heed the call of the whippoor-wills, there at the scene. The whippoorwills were in fact two members of the CIA, hiding in the bushes across from Marilyn's cottage, using birdcalls to communicate. As is well known, the CIA had spies in the FBI itself. One of them was loyal to me. Tracking the Jackie and Ethel masks from the FBI lab to the director's office, he did some bugging himself—and picked up the voices of the director and his friend plotting the murder. He came to me with this information. Rather than move against the director, and create a public scandal—

"In which Hoover could make public his own secret tapes," the reverend guesses.

—I decided simply to foil his plan—without his knowing it. It was important for Hoover to believe he had succeeded, or he would simply have tried again. It is not difficult to kill someone so vulnerable as she; like swatting a hummingbird, if one is so inclined. But for Hoover to believe it, of course, the whole country, the whole world, had to believe it. I presented the options to Marilyn as a matter of life or death—which they were. And she agreed to my plan.

When Hoover ordered from the FBI lab enough sleeping pills and barbiturates to kill a dinosaur, my loyal operative substituted harmless placebos. It was these that Hoover and his friend forced down Marilyn's throat that night. Actress that she was, Marilyn played her first big death scene, and played it well. Hoover and his pal believed it; Bobby believed it.

After Bobby left the scene, the whippoorwills in the bushes came out of hiding and entered the cottage. They carried be-tween them a covered stretcher. They took photographs of the "posthumous" Marilyn, which later became part of the official medical report. Then Marilyn rose from the bed, tired from the strain of acting, but otherwise unharmed. The whippoorwills removed from the stretcher the nude body of a Los Angeles prostitute, named, as far as is known, Mary Elizabeth Virgin, who had died of an overdose in a Sunset Boulevard brothel two days earlier. A slightly faded blonde, Miss Virgin had, at times, for the edification of certain customers, pretended, for an extra hundred dollars, that she was Marilyn Monroe. Whether Miss Virgin's opportune death that week was truly accidental, I don't care to speculate on. The CIA has its own mysterious ways.

Lyndon interrupts. "Which CIA are we talking about?"

"What does it matter?" Bobby says, annoyed, fascinated, hardly daring to believe the words of his big brother. "Let him go on."

In any case, the whippoorwills substituted the body of Miss Virgin for the "body" of the very much alive Miss Monroe. They removed all evidence of their intrusion, and whisked Marilyn away with them, to a previously arranged hiding place.

"That's preposterous!" the reverend says. "You're telling us that Marilyn Monroe has actually been alive for the past twenty-six years, and has not been seen by anyone?"

"On the contrary," I say. "She has been seen by, well, almost everyone."

"I don't understand," Bobby says. His face is ashen; his hands are shaking like they used to. "Explain."

"I'm trying to. You're all familiar with the federal witness protection program. Where important government witnesses are given a new identity, a new face, so they can resume their lives without being discovered, without being killed. That was the plan I'd come up with for Marilyn. We had to let everyone believe she was dead; this was the only way to do it without her hiding in a cave for the rest of her life."

"So you gave her a new face, a new name," Lyndon says, jumping the gun, "and she's been living all these years somewhere as an ordinary, homely housewife?"

"Well, not exactly. She still had to make a living. And she

loved acting, she did not want to give that up. She'd always wanted to play serious roles; so she chose a suitable face. After an appropriate period of recovering from the surgery, during which she worked hard at learning other voices, other dialects, Marilyn resumed her acting career. She's made more than a dozen films, displaying the talent which, as a comedienne, she was never given credit for."

"And her new name is?" Raymond asks.

"To throw people off, she chose a name as ridiculous as the name Marilyn Monroe was euphonious. She chose the name—"

"Holy shit!" Bobby says, guessing at last.

"She chose the name *Meryl Streep*."

There is silence as they ponder that, as they try to picture the eyes, the hair, the smile.

"Surgeons did a helluva job," Lyndon says.

The silence becomes more profound as they ponder the implications. That for all these years Marilyn Monroe has been alive . . . awing the film industry with her talent, her versatility. At the biographies that will have to be rewritten, at the myths that will have to be recast. At the awesome capabilities of deception that lie in the hands of the powerful.

"But she was here!" Bobby protests. "I held her hand for twenty years!"

"Mary Elizabeth Virgin," I explain. "Not a bad little actress herself. Which, of course, is why the passing white cloud always winked."

Raymond looks bemused. He hesitates, then speaks. "The one I feel sorry for," he says, "is Joltin' Joe."

"DiMaggio?" Adlai asks. "He was long out of the picture. Why feel sorry for him?"

" 'Cause for the past twenty-six years, he's been paying for a single red rose to be placed every day on the grave of Mary Virgin."

"At the time," I confess, "I felt a little sorry for myself."

234

"Why is that?" Bobby asks, his throat now choked with tears.

"Because with her new face, and her new name, Marilyn's personality seemed to change as well."

"Meaning?" Adlai asks.

Meaning? I should think by now my meaning would be obvious.

I never got to screw Meryl Streep.

Bobby is struggling mightily to sort out his predilections: whether he would prefer to believe, unselfishly, for her sake, that Marilyn is still alive (with the added bonus that Marilyn as Meryl in the end rejected me), or whether he would rather that Marilyn is dead, that the hand he held, the soul he comforted, for twenty years in the afterlife, truly belonged to her, and not to Mary Virgin. Like his conflict in life between passion and fidelity, it is a struggle he seems unable to resolve.

"Jack?" he asks, his confusion evident in his voice.

"What?"

"Way back in one of the early chapters, you were talking about Marilyn—about Marilyn up here! About what a less enchanting place it has been since she left. You speculated about where her soul might reside now—in a rock, I think you said, or in a naked baby, or even in this book. That's what you said, I remember—that the reader might be holding Marilyn in his hand right now. A lovely line, I thought, a very lovely concept, especially for the reader. But now you say she's still alive. Well, which is it? Were you lying then, or are you lying now?"

I nod my head with resignation. I saved her life, but there is no such thing, it seems, as the perfect good deed.

"She's alive," I repeat. "She's alive and well. Back then, in the early chapters, I was not yet ready to confess the deception. Marilyn and I—Meryl and I—had sworn each other to secrecy, forever. Well—how long is forever? The deception was ingrained—and Mary Virgin was such a gentle soul I sometimes almost forgot the truth myself. But now I find, as my hour draws round, that there is a need—a compulsion, almost—to confess. To tell all. To hold back nothing. It is almost as if some *otherness* has invaded my soul, and made me incapable of deception, from this moment onward."

Even as I say the words, I wonder if that is truly possible. It would be such a loss of—me.

Bobby says nothing; he merely absorbs the information. He will cope with this, as he has coped with all that came before. He is a good learner.

"Is it true?" I cry out to the passing white cloud. "Am I, Jack Kennedy—John Fitzgerald Kennedy—no longer capable of lying? Of deception? Of skulduggery? Of lusting in my heart? Is my soul from now on to be, like these pages, an open book? Is this what the old saying means, that some fates are worse than death?"

I cry out for an answer, but the passing white cloud doesn't answer; the passing white cloud merely passes.

Fools have asserted that sex and death are alike. In truth, they are alike only in the lives of nations, which, born without penises, flaunt death-dealing missiles instead. (See Cuban Dildo Crisis.) For human beings, sex is life; death is celibacy. Take it from one who suffers under the burden.

I have dealt at length with sex; now it is time to deal with death; not fake death but real ones, not natural death but violent ones, not the death of the old but the death of the young, not the death of fleas but the death of presidents.

(How's that for style, Sorensen? Read it and weep.)

Not the death of you, but the death of me.

(The death of you will occur, in time. Believe it.)

Will they weep for you the way they wept for me?

We emerged from the plane in Dallas into the glaring bright spotlight of the sun. All that followed would be etched forever with the shadows of high noon. Love Field, they called it, one of the lesser ironies of the day.

237

The crowd at the airport was enthusiastic, as always; airport crowds are hired by central casting. We climbed into the presidential limousine, the bubble top down. Me on the right, Jackie on the left, the John Connallys on the jump seats in front of us. One of the theories that emerged after the assassination was that the principal target had been Connally, who, as Secretary of the Navy, had denied Oswald an honorable discharge. What is it the kids say today? Get real!

The motorcade crossed the airport, moved out onto the highway. Crowds lined both sides, waving, cheering. Son of a bitch, I thought. Dallas loves us.

How many had been paid to be there, I wondered later, to throw the Secret Service off guard?

I was due to speak at a luncheon at the Dallas Trade Mart at 12:30. We were running about five minutes late. The air was moist and hot and the sun so bright that Jackie put her sunglasses on. I told her to take them off, and she did. We moved toward a triple underpass in front of Dealey Plaza. There was a brief, welcome respite from the sun. Then we were out again, climbing a slight incline, passing an unknown building that was about to enter the history books.

I pause. It is all so wearisome.

"And?" Lyndon prompts.

He's like a little boy; he loves to hear the same story, over and over. But he's a brave little boy. The violence doesn't frighten him.

Not anymore.

Does it frighten you, dear reader, anymore?

It would be preachy of me to assert that it should.

"Amen," the reverend says. "Amen."

So now we are here. The moment you have been waiting for. The shots—was it three, or four? The screams. The puffs of smoke. The pieces of flesh and brain splattering through the air. You've all seen the Zapruder film. Some of you can hardly wait.

Alas, I'm afraid you must. In order to make sense of what happened, we must trace the many forces of evil that converged on Dallas that day. And to do that, we must go back, briefly, in time.

Do not worry; we'll get to the blood and gore soon enough.

The date was October 29, 1929. Black Tuesday. The day the stock market crashed, the day the money temples came tumbling down around America. On such a momentous day, little note was taken of a child born prematurely in a small lying-in hospital in Beverly Hills, California. The child, a boy, was born to a pretty but unknown actress named Ginny King. On the birth certificate, the child's father was listed as "unknown." The mother, in her modest but comfortable room, with all the bills prepaid, looked down at her infant son—smaller even than most newborns—and named him Arthur.

Ginny King was happy, eager to love and raise her baby; she would not lack for money—the child's father had assured her of that—as long as she did not bother him; he was a family man, and he did not want trouble.

Two years later, her maternal affection turned to bitterness. The child wasn't growing very well. At first his small size had been attributed to his premature birth; now the doctors informed the young actress that her son was a midget, that he would never reach a height of four feet.

Ginny was horrified. She felt she would be the laughing-stock of Hollywood. She felt God had punished her for her illicit affair.

"I don't *do* that," says the passing white cloud, listening intently.

"Let him continue!" Raymond says, and then turns almost white, remembering who he's talking to.

Ginny went to the bank. She signed papers assuring that her ample trust fund, established by the child's father, would go to the boy if anything happened to her. She wrapped the child in a blanket, pinned his name to it, and late one moonlit night she left him at the door of an orphanage. Then she went to the beach, and, pretending to be a great star of the screen, she walked out into the ocean till she drowned.

"You're breaking my heart, Jack," Lyndon says. "What's this got to do with the good stuff?"

I shall omit the gross depravity of the child's life. Suffice it to say that he grew up in the orphanage, unwanted and unloved. He was mocked by the other children because of his size. He became bitter and hateful, and desperate for revenge. But revenge against whom? The mother who had abandoned him? She was already dead. The father who had conceived him? He didn't know who his father was. The God who had given him this barren life? All he had to do was look around him to know that there was no God.

"A mistake that is often made," the white cloud says.

As a teenager, Arthur King ran away from the orphanage. He lived for a time in the streets. He joined a circus, seeking the adoration of the crowds, but soon grew tired of that. To relieve his boredom he decided to see the world. Drawing on his trust fund, he bought a fancy wardrobe and began to travel: to the Caribbean, to Europe, to Russia, to the Mediterranean, to Chicago, to Detroit, to Miami, to New Orleans. Everywhere he went he had money to spend: on booze to still his loneliness, on women to make him feel big. In many of the places he went, sharp-eyed strangers took note of the free-spending American who harbored so many resentments, who had no purpose in life. They went to their superiors and they discussed an idea: what if we gave this American midget a purpose in life? Something to live for; something, perhaps, to die for.

I don't have time for the details of the recruitment; take my word for it, it was done, and done, and done yet again.

"By whom?" Adlai asks.

By everyone.

As the motorcade inched its way toward Dealey Plaza, Carlos Marcello was in a courtroom in New Orleans, standing trial for extortion. The charges had been brought by the U.S. Justice Department. By my brother Bobby. The jury was out, but Marcello wasn't worried.

240

Marcello looked at his watch; it was 12:28. He turned to a youthful associate. "How come no news yet?" he asked.

"Any minute now," the associate said. "Don't worry. Lee's a good shot. Lee won't miss."

"Fuck Oswald, the poor slob," Marcello said. He looked at his watch again. "You want to get an alligator's tail," he said, "you don't bite off his tail. You bite off his head; then the tail will die."

"I don't get it."

"Nothing to get," Marcello said. "Just some monkey talk."

They were interrupted by the return of the jury. The jury found Carlos Marcello not guilty.

Carlos Marcello smiled. It would be a good day all around.

At the same time, in Havana, Fidel Castro was sitting down to lunch with his good friend Gabriel García Márquez. He seemed anxious, and García Márquez asked him why.

"I'm expecting some news," Castro said, "from America."

"Good news?" García Márquez asked.

"I hope," Castro said. "The death of a dictator."

"That would be a good name for a book," the writer said.

Castro spooned some menudo into his mouth. "Botulism," he muttered. "Depilatories. Poisoned cigars. Deadly pens. Clowns in eagle suits. Tried to turn my midget, did they? I turned their midget back into my midget."

The novelist looked at his friend with fond sadness; perhaps his twenty-hour speech the day before had unduly tired him. Fidel was no longer speaking proper Spanish; he was speaking magic realism.

Castro looked at his watch, impatiently.

"Eat," the writer said, kindly. "Eat."

In Detroit, Jimmy Hoffa was in a barbershop, getting a shave. He screeched when the barber nicked his neck.

"Don't be so touchy, Jimmy," the barber said. "Albert Anastasia got worse."

"Very funny," Hoffa said. "You got a big mouth."

"It's your own fault," the barber said. "You're squirming around like you got ants in your jock. You wanna shave, sit still."

Hoffa grabbed the towel from around his neck, began to wipe off the shaving cream. "Turn on the TV," he barked.

"Since when you like soaps," the barber said.

"I'm expecting a bulletin," Hoffa said.

He leaned back in his chair. "I changed my mind. I do want a shave. I have to look my best for the funeral."

In Russia, it was already night. But the lights were burning late in the Kremlin. In his private office, Chairman Khrushchev unlaced his shoes and spoke to his U.N. ambassador, Andrei Gromyko.

"Any news?"

"Not yet," Gromyko said.

"Not to worry," the chairman said, as if to reassure himself. "The midget won't miss."

"Castro's midget?"

"He's not Castro's midget. He's my midget. Castro thinks he's his midget. He thinks he turned the CIA's midget, who was trying to kill him. He thinks he made him a double midget. But we recruited him the first time he came to Russia. He's been my midget all along."

Gromyko smiled. Khrushchev nearly fell off his chair. He took off his shoe and banged it on his desk.

"Pull my dildos!" the chairman said. "I'll teach that Kennedy to make me pull my dildos! Something there is that doesn't love a putz."

In a secret bathroom in the basement of the Central Intelligence Agency in Langley, Virginia, an aide to the director was seated on a potty next to a leader of the anti-Castro Cubans in Miami.

"Why are we meeting here?" the Cuban asked.

"I always sit here," the CIA man said, "when there's violence afoot. Also, it's bombproof. In case a war starts. In case people really believe the Russians did it."

"You sure the midget won't miss?"

"We've been training him for months," the CIA man said. "The midget won't miss."

"That's what you said every time you sent him to kill Castro. That the midget would do the job. But he never did."

"I told you already," the CIA man explained. "He was a double agent then. We thought he was our agent. But he was really Castro's agent. That's why the plots never worked. It took us quite a while to figure that out. Then we got this note from the CIA at Boondock, explaining the problem. So we turned the midget. We let Castro think he was still his midget who was pretending to be our midget. But now he is our midget pretending to be Castro's midget pretending to be our midget. It's that simple."

"I think I have to shit," the Cuban said.

"Me, too," the CIA man said. "Something must have happened in Dallas."

Lee Harvey Oswald was nervous. Up till now, everything had been going perfectly. He had gotten the job at the Book Depository. Weeks later—just a few days ago—it had been announced that this would be the route—just as they had assured him it would. For weeks he had been practicing with the $12.78 mail-order rifle. It worked just fine. He had taken it from the garage that morning, smuggled it into the building; no one had noticed. He had assembled it a few minutes ago. When he'd seen the motorcade on the highway about half a mile away, he had quietly opened the window, and crouched beside it. Only now, for the first time, he was nervous. What if he missed?

"If you get him," the guy had said, "they'll take care of you for life. But if you miss, they'll kill you."

Lee Harvey Oswald had been very happy to distribute leaflets on behalf of Fidel Castro. But die for him?

His hands began to shake.

Jack Ruby was also nervous as he crouched behind a bush on the grassy knoll beside Dealey Plaza. The crowds were beginning to cheer; the motorcade must be coming into view. And no midget! Where the fuck was the midget? He should have been here minutes ago.

He'd been on the phone for weeks with the boys in Chicago, the boys in New Orleans, the boys in Miami. He was sure he'd gotten it straight. The assassin would be a midget. He'd be crouching behind the white fence on the grassy knoll, with a high-powered rifle, with a telescopic site. He wouldn't miss. The president's head would explode, the crowd would scream in horror, the whole scene would turn to chaos. The midget would drop his rifle into a bush and calmly walk away from the scene, expecting to disappear into the crowd. But they couldn't let that happen; the midget knew too much. As soon as the midget threw away his rifle, he, Jack Ruby, was to step from behind a bush and shoot the midget with his pistol.

It was a foolproof plan, they had said. If he could, Jack should then simply melt away into the crowd, as the midget had planned to do. But if he happened to be seen shooting the midget, if he happened to be caught, then no problem. He, Jack Ruby, would be a national hero. He would have killed the bastard who killed the president!

Either way, he would emerge a rich man. And when the cancer finally got him, then his nieces and his nephews would be rich. They would never forget their Uncle Jack.

Except there was this last-minute hitch: where the fuck was the midget? The midget was nowhere in sight.

Jack Ruby pondered what to do. Usually he did not have to think; they told him what to do, and he obeyed. Thinking wasn't one of his assets. But now he thought fast. What would they want of him?

The answer was obvious. They wanted Kennedy dead. If the midget had chickened out, then he, Jack Ruby, would have to take his place. They would reward him well. They might even give him Mama Marcello's secret recipe for spaghetti sauce. He, Jack Rubenstein. A nice Jewish boy.

Ruby wished he had a rifle, like the midget was supposed to have. But he had never fired a rifle in his life. (Neither, he knew, had Momo, who had evaded the draft during the war, who always let others do his killing.) He stood from behind the bush and moved to the white fence. Nonchalantly he leaned against it, as if he were just one more spectator come to cheer the president, like the thousands he could see lining the road-way below. From the pocket of his jacket he removed his snub-nosed pistol. He gripped it tight.

In the FBI building in Washington, J. Edgar Hoover was seated at his desk when the telephone rang.

"Hello?" he said.

"It's Momo."

"Hi, Mama. How are you feeling today? Look Mama, I'm busy right now. Can I call you back later? After the killing?"

"Not Mama. *Momo.*"

"Oh, you. I told you never to call me here."

"It's important. I just got a call from Dallas. The midget didn't show."

"I know," Hoover said. "I just got the same call myself."

"Well, where the hell is he? He's your midget."

"My midget? He's your midget. He lives in Chicago. He tapes goddamn Cubs games."

"Cut the crap, Hoover," Momo said. "He's your midget pretending to be my midget. Everybody knows that. So if he gets caught you can blame it on the mob."

"That's why you got Ruby there," Hoover said. "To shut him up."

"Of course. But that don't matter now. He didn't show. Does Langley know why?"

"Langley never knows anything. Langley's just sitting there, shitting bricks."

"What do we do now?"

"We pray," Hoover said. "Maybe Oswald will get off a lucky shot."

"Oswald couldn't hit the side of a barbershop."

"Maybe Ruby will get him with the pistol."

"From two hundred feet? You out of your mind? It's all gone. Down the toilet. The fucking Kennedys will hound us forever."

"I told you we should have used the secret stuff," Hoover said.

"We couldn't use the the secret stuff. It would have made him a loose cannon. There was no way to know how he'd react. The son-of-a-bitch midget! The Commies are paying him. Castro is paying him. Anti-Castro is paying him. You're paying him. Langley's paying him. I'm paying him. And Carlos, and Santo. And Hoffa. How the fuck can the bastard not show?"

"It's simple," Hoover said. "He doesn't need the money."

There was silence, defeat, on both ends of the line. Then Hoover's friend, seated on the sofa, spoke. "That's why I showed him the truth. The secret stuff."

"You showed him?" Hoover said. "I told you not to show him."

"Some people can't be bought for money," his friend said. "Believe me, I know. It's passion, not politics, that drives the world. I told Arthur King who he really was. Money, national allegiance, meant nothing to him. It was the only way to nail him down."

"Nail him down?" Hoover shouted, his face redder than anyone had seen it before. "Well, where the hell is this midget! This Arthur King?"

"Relax," his friend said. "There's time."

"Jack." It's Lyndon. "Don't tell me. Don't tell me you're hinting at what I think you're hinting at. Nobody in the world will believe that."

"Don't," Bobby says. "Don't tell him who Arthur King was. That's something you mustn't tell anyone."

"I'm sorry, Bob. It's like I said before. Something has

overtaken me, has entered me, as my hour approaches. It's as if I'm no longer capable of deceit."

"You can just stop talking," Bobby says.

I hadn't thought of that. I turn to the passing white cloud. Bobby turns. Lyndon turns.

"Let us begin," the white cloud says.

"You mean *continia*," Lyndon corrects.

"Let us continia," says the passing white cloud.

Like Lyndon, you, too, must have guessed, dear reader. When my father was playing Movie Mogul in Hollywood in the 1920s, he was not faithful to Gloria Swanson, any more than he was faithful to my mother. He was willing to give the business to any impressionable starlet in sight. So it was with Ginny King; only Ginny gave him the business back by getting large with child. Pop cared little for the feelings of wife or mistress, but even then he was looking down the long road toward the presidency—either his own, or Joe Jr.'s. So when Ginny refused to abort, he endowed her with sufficient funds to ensure her silence forever. Meticulous in all things, he made Ginny sign a blood oath that the child was his—a paper he secreted away against such time as it might be useful to him, should the child prove in some way worthy. This paper the FBI stumbled upon during its investigation of my father prior to his government service; it was this paper, in addition to their shared bigotries, that kept Pop and Hoover buddies for so long.

If Rosemary was the skeleton in the family closet, then Arthur, half-grown and illegitimate, was the festering petri dish.

Arthur grew up ignorant of his paternity, as we have seen, until mid-November of 1963. By that time he was thirty-four years old, three feet eight inches tall, and in the secret employ, as we have also seen, of the Cubans, the CIA, the anti-Castro right wing, the Russians, the FBI, and the mob. Fate had conspired to have all six of those self-serving entities plotting my death simultaneously—and had chosen Arthur King, my own brother, as the rifle-wielding instrument of murder.

"Half brother!" Bobby corrects, in torment.

247

Giving new meaning to the phrase.

As my trip to Dallas neared, Arthur King, premature in all things (including sex) was having a midlife crisis. He had been married briefly—for forty-eight hours—in a brothel in the Casbah, but he did not care to reflect on the caliber of his ex; he had no offspring, no one to love; he was a sextuple agent, but only the word gave him joy. He had subdivided his allegiance so many times that even he no longer knew whom he was really working for, where his true sympathies lay.

It was this internal confusion that Hoover's friend Clyde had sensed; he feared the midget was thinking of backing out. And he decided to gamble: he showed Arthur King the written proof of who his father was. Clyde knew of jealousy, of secret rage; he'd been living in the shadow of the idiot Hoover for thirty years. If Arthur King was having second thoughts about killing the president for money, or for political purposes, Clyde reasoned, he just might do it out of envy. Arthur was short and I was tall; Arthur was hateful and I was charming; Arthur suffered from premature ejaculation and I was a bedroom athlete; Arthur was unknown and I was powerful; Arthur was unappreciated, and I was adored around the world. And we were brothers! If the midget was uncertain about killing me for anyone else, Clyde reasoned, he might gladly kill me for himself.

"But Clyde was wrong!" Raymond asserts, happily.

"Because blood is thicker than politics," Martin says.

"So the midget didn't do it!" Adlai exults.

Except that I am dead..I am here.

"But . . . ," Lyndon begins.

"Let him continia," the white cloud says.

The first to approach the midget about killing me, many months before, had been the Marcello mob. "We want to kill the tail of the alligator," they had said, "and we will do that by killing the head."

These words had been etched in the midget's brain; night after night he had dreamed of the death of alligators. Now, with the new knowledge of who he was—with the knowledge that Pop had denied his existence all these years, and we had as well—his determination to go through with the assassination solidified. Not only would the act kill me, it would destroy Bobby as well. His brother Bobby, too, had fame, had power, and a mess of adoring children. And Bobby wasn't much bigger than he was.

So reasoned Arthur King, the unacknowledged musketeer.

"But he didn't show!" Raymond says.

But he did. He did not appear at the grassy knoll, where they expected him; being a Kennedy, he had brains to spare. He knew how the mob worked; and the FBI, the CIA, the Cubans, the Russians, and the Birchers. He knew that someone would be there to gun him down, to silence him, after the deed was done; at least one hit man would be there, perhaps six. So the midget changed the plan on his own. Instead of going to the knoll, he slipped into the Book Depository. Slowly he climbed to the sixth floor, pausing at each staircase landing to catch his breath. He waddled on stubby legs to the corner room, where he knew that Oswald was perched, rifle in hand.

"New plan," he said to the startled patsy.

"Why?" Oswald asked.

"Shut up and kneel down," the midget said. "If you miss, they'll kill you. But I won't miss."

Lee Harvey Oswald was glad to oblige. He dropped to his knees. Arthur King climbed onto his back.

"Now stand," he ordered. "In the shadow. Near the window."

Oswald did as he was told. Through the open window they could see the motorcade emerging from the underpass, beginning to move slowly up the incline. The midget, perched like a monkey on Oswald's back, raised his rifle and took aim. Through his telescopic sight, my head appeared as large as a cantaloupe.

"A watermelon," Bobby says.

Oswald raised his own mail-order rifle and took aim.

With the cross hairs in place, Arthur King squeezed the trigger. A split second later the bullet tore into my back.

Lee Harvey Oswald fired—and missed.

On the grassy knoll, his snub-nosed pistol resting on the white fence, Jack Ruby fired—and missed.

From his perch on Oswald's back, the midget fired again. The bullet tore into my skull. It blew apart my brain. Fragments of flesh and bone and brain splintered across the car, landed in Jackie's lap, dropped like bits of garbage into the street.

On the curb nearby, a fifteen-year-old boy was holding a movie camera. He kept it running as Jackie, half-crazed, not knowing what she was doing, climbed out onto the back of the car; as a Secret Service man grabbed her hand, vaulted onto the car, shoved her back in; as the motorcade picked up speed and vanished away to Parkland Hospital.

The crowd milled about in noisy frenzy. Abraham Zapruder, who had been stuck about eight people deep and did not have a clear view of the street, approached the boy.

"Thanks for letting me use your camera," the boy said. "I hope it comes out."

"I hope so, too," Mr. Zapruder said. "We'll have you and your folks over to watch it if it does."

Abraham Zapruder took his camera from the boy and walked away. Steven Spielberg watched him go.

There is a long silence when I finish. The others are pondering, examining.

"I guess that explains it all," Adlai says. "The cheap rifle that always seemed suspicious. The three shots in such rapid succession, too rapid for one man. The fourth shot on the Dictabelt tape, from the grassy knoll. And the puff of smoke that dozens of people saw there."

The reverend nods his head, thoughtfully. "That's why Hoover was so quick to announce that Oswald had acted alone. So the trail wouldn't lead back to the FBI. Or the CIA. That's why they both withheld evidence from the Warren Commission."

"Also," Bobby says, "because he knew the mob was involved. And the FBI would look awful if the mob had done it, since they should have uncovered the plot. And since Hoover was still insisting there was no mob."

"It was obvious to me all along that it was some kind of conspiracy," Lyndon says. "But I didn't want to find out. I didn't want it to lead to the Cubans or the Russians. If it did, then the American people would have needed revenge—and what the hell would we have done? Start World War Three? Over Jack? It was better for everyone to leave it at that: that Oswald had acted alone. That's what I told Earl Warren. And he agreed."

The reverend turns to Bobby. "And you?" he asks. "You, and your whole family, accepted, in public at least, that it was only Oswald. You never pressed for a real investigation. Why?"

"Because," Bobby says, "if a probe led to the Mafia, the whole smutty relationship between Jack and Judy Campbell and Momo might come out. As well as the CIA hiring the mob to kill Castro. If the probe led to Cuba, the same things would come out. Jack's reputation would have been destroyed—before his legend could grow."

"Not to mention . . . ," I say.

Bobby frowns.

"Not to mention that I was killed by my own half brother."

"It would have been a smirch on the family escutcheon," Bobby concedes.

"A teensie-weensie smirch," Martin avers.

The rest you know about. How the patsy Oswald, making his getaway, shot and killed J. D. Salinger.

"J. D. Tippit," Lyndon says.

Same difference. How Oswald was captured soon after, while trying to catch a flick, and was taken to the Dallas jail. Where Jack Ruby moseyed in two days later, with the connivance of the Dallas police, and played "You Bet Your Life" on live TV. Oswald the loser, of course.

"And the real killer?" Raymond asks. "Whatever happened to King Arthur?"

The midget dropped out of sight in the commotion, and has never been heard from since.

The Four Days followed. One of those phrases that, seeming innocuous, has entered the language bearing darker implications. Like Safe Sex (of which, to the psyche, there is no such thing). Four days like no others in the nation's history. Four days that belonged to me. (Well, me and the National Football League, which refused to cancel its games; some pastimes transcend history.)

I felt little pain. The first shot produced a spasm of reflexive anger; as when a friend, sneaking up on you from the rear, startles you with a slap on the back. There was an instant of fear, as when lightning crashes close and you inexplicably dread the thunder. Then it came in a single big bang: old worlds colliding, a new one forming. Between the *b* in *bang* and the *g* in *bang* I ejected, like a fighter pilot whose F-16 is going down in the sea. I was no longer a participant, just one more spectator, before my blood splattered Jackie's stockings, before my brain left a trail in the gutter.

So this is how it ends, I remember thinking. I had often wondered how it would end. Each man's life—yes, and woman's too—is a myth of his own creation. God writes only the endings. God deletes.

I look to the passing white cloud for affirmation; the white cloud seems to nod. Only *seems*, however. Even here, He is not specific.

They rushed me to the hospital; they rushed me into surgery. I followed along, a few feet above, watching with only mild interest. I was no longer my problem anymore. I was their problem. I was your problem.

They set my time of death as 1:00 P.M. Central Standard Time. November 22, 1963. A day like all days, filled with those events . . .

Sometimes I've wished that "You Are There" was still on television. I'd like to see how they would do it. "This is Walter Cronkite reporting from Dealey Plaza, where, rumor has it, any moment now the president of the United States will be shot."

The president of the United States.

Me.

At some level, deep down, Pop notwithstanding, it was always a little hard to believe.

At the hospital, the Texas doctors and the Secret Service played tug-of-war with my body. The doctors wanted to perform an autopsy right there, as they were required to do by law. The Secret Service wanted to bring my body to Washington, where autopsy findings could be made to conform to whatever scenario suited the powers that be. The SS won, of course, but not before they almost pulled my head off.

Even as I was being lowered into a coffin, Lyndon was having himself sworn in aboard Air Force One. His baby now. Jackie standing beside him in the splattered pink. On the plane she refused to change clothes; she would emerge looking the same in Washington. "Let them see what they have done."

Little suspecting who *they* was.

Lyndon interrupts, flustered. " 'Having himself sworn in?' Now what's that supposed to mean?"

"That's what you did, isn't it?"

"What was I supposed to do? I was the goddamn VP."

"You did just what you were supposed to do, Lyndon."

"So why are you making an issue of it? As if I did something wrong. As if I did something suspicious. That's how all your buddies felt, I know. As if I had usurped the goddamn throne or something."

"I'm not making an issue of it. I stated a simple fact. You're making an issue of it. Why are you so touchy?"

"I'm not touchy," Lyndon snaps.

Then he adds, woefully, "Unlike Bobby, you were always kind to me, Jack. And it was me who invited you to Dallas. I suppose there's plenty of guilt to go around."

I turn away from Lyndon the Maudlin.

I much prefer Lyndon the Prick.

Warts and all.

253

□ □ □

Images followed, images burned as with a branding iron into the nation's consciousness: the riderless horse, Black Jack, with boots reversed in the stirrups; John-John, three years old that day, saluting his father's coffin. My wife, the bereaved widow, accepting the folded flag at Arlington. And the eternal flame. The flame that will burn forever. (Barring a shortage of propane.)

All of it stage-managed brilliantly by Jackie, who had learned at my side the wondrous power of myth.

Those of you who saw those images, who *lived* those images, will carry them with you to your own quiet graves.

For the children, those too young then or those not born then, I am sorry: you are entering the American movie in the middle: you have missed America's greatest scene.

Nothing to do now but eat your popcorn, and try to enjoy the comedy.

Before I close the book on these events, there is one more vignette I must include. It took place in late summer of 1969. Bobby had already died in Los Angeles, and Teddy at Chappaquiddick. Jackie was newly married to Onassis, the richest man in the world. One fine day, beneath an azure sky, she was sunbathing on a white beach on an island her husband owned off the coast of Greece. It was a private, secluded island and, feeling warm and safe, she dropped the top of her bikini and began to walk about au naturel.

Lyndon, blushing, interrupts. "Cantaloupes?"

"Pomegranates," Raymond says.

"Raymond! I'm ashamed of you. And how do *you* know?"

"Just joining in the banter, boss. I didn't mean nothing by it."

Anyway. Jackie walked along the beach till she came to the wooded half of the island. Feeling adventurous, she continued walking, following a path that led among the trees, till the woods grew almost impenetrable. She was about to turn back when a voice stopped her.

254

"Hey, Jackie, hey, chickie, lookie lookie," it said. "Welcome to Greece, hi Polly, monkey wanna banana?"

Half startled and half amused, Jackie peered up into the trees. Silhouetted against the high noon sun, in the lofty branches, was a family of monkeys. She couldn't imagine who had spoken; there was no one on the island but herself and Ari and Ari's midget servant.

Returning to the beach, she wrapped herself in a robe, stuffed her bikini in the pocket, and walked on up to the house. Onassis was on the terrace, drinking a gin and tonic. She nodded to the mute midget—he had lost his tongue in an accident several years before—and he fixed her a matching drink.

"The most wonderful thing just happened," Jackie said, folding herself into a chair across from her husband. "I went walking in the woods, and I heard voices speaking English. I could have sworn it was the monkeys. I guess I was just hallucinating, but for a moment out there it was fun."

Onassis sipped from his drink. He lifted Jackie's hand and kissed her fingers. "You weren't hallucinating, my dear," he said. "The monkeys do speak English. Teaching them is an old hobby of mine. Didn't I ever tell you that?"

The date today, as I speak, is November 22. The year is 1988.
The time is high noon.

Twenty-five years after the "event."

There is so much more to tell . . . and so little time.

Or put it another way. There is nothing at all to tell . . . and
endless time.

You want a summing up? Some easy answers? You want
to know what I have learned in my twenty-five years in the
hereafter?

I cannot say.

To say would make me sound like Polonius: "To thine own
self be true." I would rather die—again—than sound like Polonius. I would rather go unpublished than sound like Polonius.

I never promised you a self-help book. If that's what you're
looking for, read Ron Hubbard. Or Hugh Prather. Or Seymour
Peck. Read the blasted Bible, if you must.

(The passing white cloud seems not to know whether it
wants to smile or frown.)

A few good laughs. A few good tears. That's all we can

really ask of books. Or of life. It doesn't much matter if you run countries or run tractors, spin thread or spin yarns, pull cotton or pull rank. It's all the same in the end.

But there I go, philosophizing, doing what I didn't intend. I refuse; you have to find out for yourself, in any case. Certain wisdom, however instructive, is not transferable.

Most wisdom, in fact.

Regrets? Do I have any regrets?

Frankly, my dear, it's none of your fucking business.

But obscenities do not become the hour. I shall say no more.

"Jack?"

"Yes, Reverend?"

"Look!"

I turn. I look. I am astonished.

"What the fuck is that?"

Approaching me, stretching out in the distance, as far as the eye can see, is a line of people, a line of souls; an endless line of souls.

"What is it? What do they want?"

"I think," Bobby says, "they're coming to say good-bye."

"I told you no. I said I didn't want any party. Any fuss. Who invited them, goddamnit!"

They look from one to the other.

"I don't think anyone invited them," Adlai says. "It appears to be spontaneous."

For a moment I am mortified. I flinch in distaste. They are not coming to say good-bye at all, I think. They will not be friendly. They are coming to upbraid me. To chastise me. They would rend my clothes, if I had any clothes to rend. You betrayed us, they will say. You fed us platitudes and consorted with actresses. You pledged the high road and took the low. You inspired our children but you slept with whores. With your left hand you held high the torch of liberty; with your right you shook the hands of murderers. You spoke of alliances for peace, but you plotted assassinations. You orated like an

257

angel, but you sold your soul to the devil. There are so many ways they will say it, each according to his, to her, own prejudices. We made you into a hero, they will say, and you took us for fools. You used the public trust to cover a twisted bed of snakes. We thought you were the best of men—and discovered you were the worst of men!

All this they will hurl into my teeth, this endless, endless line of souls. And what shall I tell them in return? Only this: mea culpa; mea culpa.

"Who is this Mia Culpa," Lyndon asks, "and what's *she* got to do with it?"

"Shhhh," Adlai says. "Shhhh."

I am guilty. Not of sin, because I don't believe in sin.

"You don't?" asks the passing white cloud.

"No. I don't."

"Good boy," the white cloud says.

I do not believe in sin, but I am guilty nonetheless. I am guilty of being a man.

"However uncertain you were about your twig," Lyndon says.

I expect to flash with anger; instead, I laugh. Lyndon was never subtle, but he tries. In the end, a sense of humor is our salvation, a sense of perspective, a proper sense of self.

And that I had. That shall be my defense. I kept my sense of humor. I entertained. The Bible doesn't say it, but here's a truth: humor is a saving grace.

"An oversight."

"What?"

"An oversight," the white cloud says. "We'll put it in the next edition."

"If there are any more editions," Adlai says.

"There will be more," the white cloud says. "Believe it."

I look at Adlai. He is not yet Dag. I suspect that he will not be ascending, either.

I wonder what it would feel like, to ascend. I wonder what comes after that.

I still don't know what comes after this.

□ □ □

The head of the line approaches. People. Ordinary people. They do not seem as angry as I had feared.

"Thank you," the first man says.

"Thank you," the woman with him says.

"Thank you," says their child.

"Thank me? Thank me for what?" I ask.

They do not answer; they merely smile in friendship, and move on.

"Thank you," says the next man, and shakes my hand. And the next. And the next. And the next.

All are strangers to me. A few I seem to recognize. When a flicker of uncertainty lights my eyes, they seem to sense it; they state their names as we shake hands.

"Andrew Goodman."

"Michael Schwerner."

"James Chaney."

"Thank *you*," I tell them each. I don't know what more to say; I don't know how to salute their bravery.

"Viola Liuzzo." A flashing smile. "You probably don't remember. It's not important."

I assure her to the contrary. I remember.

The more of them pass, the longer the line becomes. Anonymous handshakes. Anonymous thanks.

A wizened old man pauses, shyly. He looks familiar. "Weren't you the president of France?" I ask.

"Me? de Gaulle? You're still a good kidder, eh, Mr. President."

"Not de Gaulle. One of the ones who came after. I forget his name."

"Yah. People used to tell me that, when his picture was in *The Times*. I looked like him. But it wasn't me. Me, I sold sweatshirts in the Bronx."

Now it is me who is puzzled.

"You spoke of my wife before," the old man says. "Anna. The Jewish lady from the Bronx. The one who died of the cancer."

259

"Yes. Of course."

"I want to thank you for mentioning her. She would have liked that. And for my son, who's still alive. I know he would like to thank you, too. You inspired him, you made him a better person. He's a good boy. He didn't use to visit me enough, but mostly he's a good boy."

"I'm sure he is."

"He's forty-nine now; you want to see a picture?"

I smile.

"But I'm taking up too much of your time," the man says. And moves on.

I cannot count them, this endless line of souls. I don't know why they keep on coming. A tension is building inside me. From far away I hear the sound of bells. Not real bells, exactly, but close.

"I was a fraud!" I scream, at the top of my voice. "You've all just heard my story. I was a fraud!"

They shake their heads from side to side, and keep on coming.

"Thank you."

"Thank you."

"Thank you."

Then it is time.

Now it is time.

They know this, those on the line. They hold back. They will allow me a parting moment with my friends.

12:58 P.M. Central Standard Time.

I turn. Martin and I embrace, without words. Raymond and I embrace. Adlai. Even Lyndon.

And Bobby. Dear Bobby. What more is there to say?

"Virgin?" Bobby says. "Mary Elizabeth Virgin? You're sure?"

"I'm sure," I say.

Bobby nods. "It's okay," he says. "It's okay."

We embrace a second time. I wonder if we shall ever meet again.

260

12:59 P.M.

We stand around, awkwardly. I always hated good-byes.

I have an inspiration. I will get Lyndon and Bobby to embrace each other. As one last favor to me.

I do not do it. That will be up to them. They are no longer my concern.

The light grows brighter. My friends grow dimmer. I reach out, as if I want to hold back, as if I want to stay awhile longer. My friends are fading . . . or is it me who's fading? In the whiteness I see a hand, reaching out to me. Waving. It's Raymond's hand. He wants to say something; he's not sure if I can hear him anymore. He winks, and says it anyway.

"See ya later, alligator."

The tolling of the bell grows louder. All is whiteness now. I no longer see the past. Only the future.

I have . . .

I have a rendezvous . . .

I have a rendezvous with . . .

"Let us begin!" I shout.

(The rest is silence.)

Afterword

The preceding book is a work of the imagination—an attempt to reinvent in comic form one of the primal myths of our time. Like most mythology, it takes germs of truth and transforms them into legend and symbolism.

Most of the characters are real, of course. Their actions and conversations are, for the most part, surreal. As most novelists do, I have employed the fabrications of fiction in search of enlightenment.

It has not been my intent to separate historical fact from historical fiction, nor to pass judgment on anyone.

—ROBERT MAYER
NOVEMBER 1988